SECRET
VIENNA

Michaela Lindinger

Photos
Karl Bach

JONGLEZ PUBLISHING

unusual guide

We have taken great pleasure in drawing up *Secret Vienna* and hope that through its guidance you will, like us, continue to discover unusual, hidden or little-known aspects of the city. Descriptions of certain places are accompanied by thematic sections highlighting historical details or anecdotes as an aid to understanding the city in all its complexity.

Secret Vienna also draws attention to the multitude of details found in places that we may pass every day without noticing. These are an invitation to look more closely at the urban landscape and, more generally, a means of seeing our own city with the curiosity and attention that we often display while travelling elsewhere…

Comments on this guidebook and its contents, as well as information on places we may not have mentioned, are more than welcome and will enrich future editions. Don't hesitate to contact us:

Jonglez publishing,
25 rue du Maréchal Foch,
78000 Versailles, France.
e-mail: info@jonglezpublishing.com

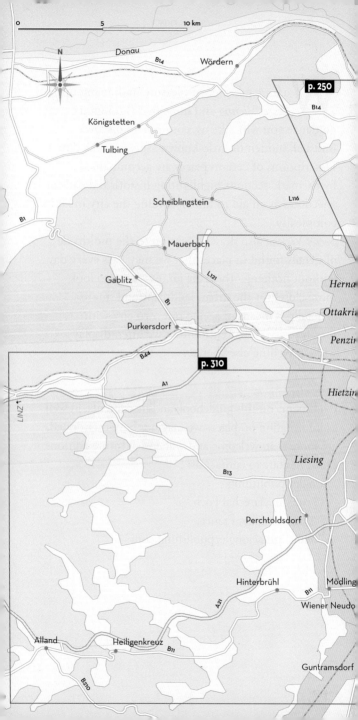

p. 448

Klosterneuburg

Langenzersdorf

S1

B7

A22

B3

Floridsdorf

B7

B8

S1

B8

Döbling

Währing

Brigittenau

p. 122

Franz-Josefs-Bahnhof

Bahnhof Wien Praterstern

Leopoldstadt

Donaustadt

p. 216

Groß-Enzersdorf

Innere Stadt

p. 16

WIEN

p. 62

Westbahnhof

Wieden

Hauptbahnhof

Donau

p. 168

Meidling

Simmering

Favoriten

A4

Schwechat

Flughafen
Wien Schwechat

p. 420

Leopoldsdorf

B10

Biedermannsdorf

Himberg

B16

B15

L154

Ebergassing

A2

p. 364

↓ GRAZ

CONTENTS

City Centre East

City Centre West

Josefstadt, Alsergrund

CONTENTS

Wieden, Margareten, Mariahilf, Neubau

Leopoldstadt, Landstraße

Outside the Centre North

CONTENTS

Outside the Centre West

Outside the Centre South West

CONTENTS

Outside the Centre South

Outside the Centre East

City Centre East

"ORIENTAL" INSCRIPTION ①

Enjoy life!

Griechengasse 7, 1010 Wien
U-Bahn: line U1 / U4, Schwedenplatz station

In a passage to the right of the entrance to No. 7 Griechengasse stands an old water pump, flanked by two wooden panels fixed to the wall and bearing Arabic inscriptions. They represent the meagre booty amassed during the Austro-Turkish wars of the 16th–18th centuries. The words were not deciphered until 2007 by the late Arne A. Ambros, professor of Arabic and Islamic Studies at the University of Vienna:

Embark on an enjoyable life
And relish lasting pleasures.

A barber's sign painted in red, white and blue, like those used mainly in Anglo-Saxon countries, hangs in front of the building. These colours are a reference to the minor surgical operations barbers used to perform with the tools of their trade, before hanging the blood-soaked dressings out on a post to dry.

INSCRIPTION AT THE TOLERANZHAUS

Tribute to the 1781 freedom of worship law

Fleischmarkt 18, 1010 Wien
U-Bahn: line U1 / U4, Schwedenplatz station

At No. 18 Fleischmarkt, look up towards the fourth floor and you'll see a golden medallion in the centre of the façade. This is a relief portrait of the reforming Habsburg Emperor Joseph II. The large letters spread out on both sides mean:

> *Ephemeral is this house, but not the posthumous glory of Joseph II*
> *He gave us tolerance, it gave him immortality!*

These words in homage to the emperor refer to the Toleranz patent (Patent of Toleration) signed in 1781: from 1781 to 1785, the Archduchy of Austria allowed minority faiths to practise their religion more freely. This authorisation was subject to certain conditions and in no case put an end to the supremacy of the Roman Catholic Church, although the Patent of Toleration marked the end of the Counter-Reformation.

The House of Tolerance was built in 1793 and renovated, probably in 1830, by architect Ernest Koch. The late classical design still has Baroque lines.

STEYRERHOF FAÇADE

A single remarkable façade covers several houses

Griechengasse 4, 1010 Wien

The Steyrerhof, now an office and shop, consists of four separate houses built in the early Middle Ages. You can trace Vienna's architectural development in the remarkable heterogeneous façade, repeatedly altered and fitted with windows in staggered rows, which is unusual to say the least.

The names of the various house owners echo down the centuries. In 1466, Jörg and Margarethe Prewer had their initials engraved in the courtyard, itself named after Ulrich Steyr, who owned one of the buildings in the 15th century. In the late 16th century, the courtyard was the scene of a military uprising: demobilised soldiers, feeling cheated because of their poor pay, attacked their officers who were celebrating at the Steyrerhof inn. The riot was put down by force of arms.

The year "1613" clearly visible on the façade shows that some features also date from the Renaissance.

At the end of the 19th century, the buildings were owned by the Steyrermühl printing company, which was responsible for many of the renovations. Most recently, between 1986 and 1991, Austrian architect Harry Glück made further alterations, taking great care to preserve and restore the oldest part of the medieval pediment, which dates from the 13th century.

BERNARDIKAPELLE

Late Baroque sensual splendour

Heiligenkreuzerhof
Schönlaterngasse 5, 1010 Wien
Open during Mass (see website) or for special events (such as "Long Night of the Churches")
https://bernardikapelle.wordpress.com
www.langenachtderkirchen.at

St Bernard's Chapel (1662), one of the most remarkable Baroque buildings in Vienna, is part of the Cistercian Abbey of Heiligenkreuz and is sometimes called the Heiligenkreuz (Holy Cross) chapel.

Dedicated to St Bernard of Clairvaux, who spread the Cistercian Order throughout Europe and personally encouraged the founding of the abbey in the Vienna Woods, it used to be a place of private contemplation for the abbots.

On entering, you are overwhelmed by the profusion of gilded figures by Giovanni Giuliani, teacher of Georg Raphael Donner. The sculptures mainly illustrate the life of Jesus: on the right stands his grandmother Anne, teaching her daughter Mary. On the left, Joseph is shown with his son Jesus. The ancestors and relatives of Jesus are in the foreground: during the Counter-Reformation, Roman Catholic belief in the true

presence of the flesh and blood of Christ was strongly encouraged.

This same intention is to be found in Martino Altomonte's altarpiece: the mother of God appears as *Maria lactans* (nursing Madonna). Although you now have to imagine the stream of milk flowing from her breast in the direction of St Bernard of Clairvaux, it was there for all to see in the Baroque period but later covered up in much less sensual and obviously more pious times.

As St Bernard's Chapel is a popular wedding venue, it's advisable to book well in advance.

BASILISKENHAUS

King of snakes

Schönlaterngasse 7, 1010 Wien
U-Bahn: line U1 / U4, Schwedenplatz station

High on the façade of No. 7 Schönlaterngasse is an intriguing carved basilisk, a legendary creature with a cock's head and a serpent's body. This one also has a crown and a metal tail.

The painting below the sculpture illustrates a legendary incident said to have taken place nearby.

On 26 June 1212, something extraordinary happened at the baker's yard in what is now the Schönlaterngasse: a terrible smell was emanating from the well, at the bottom of which a strange spark was dancing. A particularly daring baker's boy agreed to go down into the pit to check out the mystery. He emerged in a state of shock, explaining that he'd seen a frightful creature with foul eyes and a crown of fire. A knowledgeable physician told him it was a basilisk, hatched from the egg of an old cock incubated by a toad. He added that, as a single glance from this creature was fatal, the solution was to hold up a metal mirror and the basilisk would die of terror before its own reflection.

As no one else dared venture into the depths, the apprentice and the neighbours hurled large stones down the well to crush the beast.

The word basilisk comes from the Greek *basilikos*, literally "kinglet", which is why the creature is often represented with a crown. Blending the attributes of the rooster (bird that heralds sunrise, associated with heaven and the divine) and the serpent (creeping animal, associated with earthly and material temptations), the basilisk symbolises the elevation of earthly temptation (the serpent) to higher principles (the cock, the crown). In this way it became a symbol of lust, one of the seven deadly sins.

Harry Potter fans will have heard of the basilisk: it haunts the plumbing deep under Hogwarts, the young magician's boarding school.

DOMINICAN CRYPT

Empress in a nun's habit

Dominikanerkirche
Postgasse 4, 1010 Wien
Visits by appointment (see website)
http://wien.dominikaner.org/kontakt.html
U-Bahn: line U3, Stubentor station

Several other places besides the imperial crypt below the Capuchin Church, the Stephansdom catacombs, and the "Heart Crypt" in the Augustinian Church, contain the remains of members of the House of Habsburg.

The Dominican crypt is not only the monks' final resting place but also that of Archduchess Claudia Felicitas, second wife of Emperor Leopold I. Their union lasted only three and a half years, the empress having succumbed to tuberculosis in 1676 at the young age of 22.

Claudia, who belonged to the Third Order of St Dominic (Lay Dominicans), aspired to live a spiritual life like them. She wanted to be buried in a nun's habit and, judging by the engravings made of her funeral procession, her wishes were respected. An imposing imperial eagle bearing the monogram "CL" (Claudia and Leopold) watches over her, perched on the altarpiece of her funerary chapel.

A gold and silver urn rests on Claudia Felicitas's tomb. It contains the heart of her second daughter, Maria Josepha, who died in childhood. Anna Maria, her elder child, also lived for only a few months.

Anna de' Medici, Claudia's mother, was laid to rest in the neighbouring tomb later that same year.

The Dominican *Book of the Dead*, begun in 1474, records that the crypt contains the tombs of over 3,000 monks. Among the 20th-century names is Brother Diego Hanns Götz (died 1980). He became one of the best-known postwar preachers. His distinctive performances and theatrical gestures were not appreciated by all believers, but he nevertheless had an impressive fan club, mostly women. They were known as the *Götzen Dienerinnen*: "Maidservants of the Idol".

FRESCO OF A COW PLAYING BACKGAMMON

Mementoes of a love story

Bäckerstrasse 12, 1010 Wien

On the façade of this residence at No. 12 Bäckerstrasse, to the right of the corbel, is a stunning fresco of a bespectacled cow and a fox (or wolf?) playing a board game similar to backgammon.

According to legend, a Viennese judge by the name of Hieronymus Kuh (Kuh = cow), who lived here, regularly played backgammon with one of his acquaintances, a man called Hans Kagelwidt, who was a councillor to Duke Rudolf IV.

Kuh's daughter Trude always welcomed Herr Kagelwidt when he visited her father. One day, Kagelwidt asked for her hand in marriage. She immediately accepted him and asked that the house should be given a special name to commemorate their engagement.

As no suitable name sprang to mind, the girl is said to have suggested that her father and fiancé call it after their notorious games of backgammon. A painter was commissioned to fulfil her wish and this is how the building became "the house where a cow plays backgammon".

The old-fashioned spectacles worn by the cow would indeed have been perfectly suited to an old gentleman. We have to guess at the reason for the second animal. Did the descendants of the young couple perhaps see their ancestor as a wolf or a fox?

It wasn't easy to find your way around the Vienna of the first half of the 16th century. Buildings were just starting to be numbered but, more pertinently, few people could read or write. Paintings or small wooden panels on house frontages nevertheless gave some indication of the occupants or the trade and goods on offer. Thus, a building might bear the name "Where the wolf preaches to the geese" or "Where we quench our thirst". The house at No. 12 Bäckerstrasse was known as "Where the cow plays backgammon".

When the building was renovated in 1978, so was the original fresco. Although very few houses have preserved their Gothic design, here you can clearly distinguish the early Gothic style of the entrance, as well as a small gateway with a typical ogive arch just under the fresco.

ASYLUM RING

Safety in Leo

Stephansdom
Stephansplatz, 1010 Wien
U-Bahn: line U1 / U3, Stephansplatz station

On the left pillar of the Stephansdom north entrance, where the traditional horse-drawn carriages wait for their fares, a metal handgrip attracts curious glances. The handgrip, which dates from the construction of the building, was originally part of a winch.

Later, it came to be known as an *asylring* – a ring offering asylum, referring to an Austrian tradition. In his book *Sprechen Sie Wienerisch?*, Peter Wehle writes under the heading "LEO":

"*Refuge in which one cannot be caught when playing catch. This expression dates back to the Babenberg period, under Leopold VI of Austria, known as the Glorious, which authorised the right to asylum in certain monasteries, in which criminals could not be arrested. (...) there is still a Leopold ring in St Stephen's Cathedral today.*"

When they play catch, Viennese children exclaim "I'm in Leo", touch the object and can't be caught, as they're now in the "safe zone".

Anyone who clutched the metal handgrip was "in Leo" and therefore under the protection of the Church.

STONE OF COLOMAN

The surveyor's blood

Stephansdom, Stephansplatz, 1010 Wien
Behind the door of the souvenir stand
Accessible during cathedral opening hours, usually 7am–10pm

Behind the door of the souvenir stand at the Stephansdom, on the wall, is a dark stone that was worn down and discoloured for centuries by the hands of all the believers who came to touch it.

The legend goes that the blood of the Irish Prince Coloman, executed as a spy, flowed over this stone. He was tortured and hanged in 1012 at Stockerau, near Vienna.

Rudolf IV of Austria, "the Founder" (1339–65), had the stone set into the bishop's door in 1361, as a real cult had grown up around the saint at the time.

Coloman's alleged spying activities are found in his Celtic name: "col" means thin and "men" means stone. Coloman used thin stones (menhirs?) to mark out land or for astronomical and calendrical calculations.

In 1014, his body was transported from Stockerau to Melk, where he was buried in the abbey. A particularly high stone stood for centuries on the rocky outcrop overlooking the Danube, where the Baroque Benedictine Abbey of Melk was built. Was it a marker stone? From a topographical reference point? These questions remain unanswered. The stone itself has disappeared in the meantime. It fell victim to the construction of a bypass for the town of Melk. Coloman still lies in the abbey church.

Originally, the crypt of the Maria Magdalena Church, the floor plan of which can be seen outlined in the paving stones of Stephansplatz, was probably intended as Coloman's last resting place.

MALE AND FEMALE SYMBOLS AT THE CATHEDRAL ENTRANCE

An ancient legacy

Stephansdom
Stephansplatz, 1010 Wien
U-Bahn: line U1 / U3, Stephansplatz station

The main entrance to the Stephansdom is flanked with a pair of double columns, the significance of which is open to interpretation. They have a particular meaning for the initiated.

Surmounting the column on the right (as you face the entrance), a leafy triangle below an astronomical clock decorated with the signs of the zodiac symbolises the female genitals.

The column on the left, beneath another clock – this one with Roman numerals – is topped with an easily recognisable phallus.

These columns, decorated with their rather un-Christian symbolism, date back to the construction of the cathedral in the 13th century, at which time the pagan imagery of the Middle Ages was still common.

So the fertility cult that has been at the centre of religious imagery for centuries still features on the cathedral façade.

Other features of the Stephansdom reflect Celtic and Roman habits and customs. Built over an ancient place of worship, the cathedral is dedicated to St Stephen, patron saint of horses and the prosperity of fields and forests. In fact, the horse fair was held not far from the Celtic town of Vindobona ("White Field", later to become Vienna), where the Boii tribe celebrated their horse and wagon burials at New Year. The Feast of St Stephen is celebrated on 26 December: logically enough as it is the ancient date of the white horse ritual, a celebration of fertility.

The main axis of the cathedral indicates the direction in which the Sun appears on the horizon on 25 and 26 December. 25 December marks the Roman Sol Invictus (Unconquered Sun) celebrations, which lie at the origin of the Christmas festival.

RELIC TREASURY
AT THE STEPHANSDOM

Who will be my Valentine?

Stephansplatz 1, 1010 Wien
Open Monday to Saturday 9am–5pm (cathedral treasury)
www.stephanskirche.at
U-Bahn: line U1 / U3, Stephansplatz station

The patron saint of the relic treasury of St Valentine's Chapel (first floor, above the Chapel of the Cross), isn't the famous Valentine, Bishop of Terni in central Italy, whose memory is celebrated each year on 14 February with flowers and hearts. It's the Bishop of Passau in Bavaria, who died in 475 at Merano, also in Italy.

The collection includes several relics of this other Valentine (ebony shrine and glass vial containing bones), who is also the patron saint of Passau, where he is laid to rest. It used to possess a reliquary containing an arm and a rib from the patron saint of lovers. These artefacts have unfortunately now been lost.

The immense Baroque glass and gold sarcophagus in the centre of the chamber bears a plaque inscribed *Unus S. Valentinus*. But this particular Valentine is not the patron of Passau or of lovers. He is only one saint among many from the catacombs, brought in large numbers from Rome to Central Europe during the 17th and 18th centuries.

In churches and cloisters seeking to boost their status with relics, bones were often reconstituted into skeletons (more or less complete), then suitably attired. Their name was left up to the imagination of the donor.

The contemporary inscription testifies to the difficulty in distinguishing between catacomb relics when purchasing them, as many saints bore the same name.

SYMBOL O5

"Irreplaceable Austria"

Stephansdom
Stephansplatz, 1010 Wien
U-Bahn: line U1 / U3, Stephansplatz station

To the right of the immense main entrance of the Stephansdom, the symbol O5 is engraved in stone. The carving, now classified as a historic monument, is covered with plexiglass. By 1944 the symbol had been chalked on the walls of any number of Austrian cities. Carvings later replaced these chalk markings.

O5 was a codename for Austrian resistance against the Nazi regime. Members were recruited by conservative Catholic forces among the sons of bourgeois and aristocratic families. Patriot and publisher Fritz Molden, who died in 2014, was 20 years old at the time the movement was founded and is one of its best-known members.

The number 5 represents the fifth letter of the alphabet, E. The letters O and E form OE, the ligature represented by the German Ö, the first letter of Österreich (Austria).

Some assert that the letters "AEIOU" also influenced the movement's name – after the motto of Emperor Frederick III (1415–93), *Austria Erit In Orbe Ultima*. This is variously interpreted as: Austria will be the ultimate nation of the world; All land is subject to Austria; or even, as the plaque on the pavement indicates, Austria is irreplaceable.

As Molden's father-in-law was the head of the wartime American intelligence agency OSS (Office of Strategic Services), Allen W. Dulles, special attention was paid to O5 activities, although the communist

and socialist resistance to Austrofascism and Nazism had begun much earlier and suffered many more casualties than O5 ever did.

The myth nevertheless gained momentum – under American influence – to the point that the symbol O5 appears on the canal wall in *The Third Man*.

REMAINS OF THE VIRGIL CHAPEL

An enigmatic site in the heart of the city

Virgilkapelle
Stephansplatz, 1010 Wien
Open Tuesday to Sunday 10am–6pm
24 and 31 December 10am–2pm
Closed 25 December, 1 January and 1 May
U-Bahn: line U1 / U3, Stephansplatz station

In the middle of Stephansplatz (St Stephen's Square), two sets of paving stones (white and ochre) outline the floorplan of two former buildings – the mysterious Vergilius Chapel and the Maria Magdalena Chapel, which was built over it.

As the city centre is generally crowded with tourists, the best plan is to go up to the terrace of Haas-Haus (No. 4 Stephansplatz), which affords a splendid view of the site of the two buildings in the courtyard below.

Although the Maria Magdalena Chapel, built in the 14th century, was completely destroyed in 1781, the Vergilius Chapel still exists (currently closed for renovations).

The chapel, 12 metres below ground, is the largest Gothic structure still standing in Vienna. Built around 1200, this rectangular *capella subterranea* (about 10 by 6 metres) is a mystery: there is no documentation to explain its subterranean construction.

The vault is not the original and the walls once rose 1.5 metres above the present ground level. The building therefore stood 13 to 14 metres high, a considerable size for the Middle Ages. The construction is oriented in a manner that is almost certainly based on astronomical calculations.

The chapel walls, 1.5 metres thick, are embellished with six niches, each containing a Byzantine cross like that of the Templars. Further on, a representation of a "magical face" has been preserved.

This intriguing windowless and doorless building was probably accessed by a rope ladder and a trapdoor leading to the raised section on Stephansplatz, the nerve centre of Vienna.

From 1300 onwards, the chapel was the burial site of wealthy Viennese families.

It is dedicated to the Irish churchman and early astronomer Fergal (*c.* 700–84, later Vergilius of Salzburg). This king's son, nicknamed "the geometer", was denounced to the pope by the English missionary Boniface on 1 May 748 for his recognition of ancient pagan beliefs. The success of his evangelisation was based on his great tolerance and his capacity to integrate religion with long-established practices.

The Virgilius Chapel, which had fallen into oblivion after the destruction of the church, was rediscovered in 1972 during the construction of Stephansplatz underground station. Some people find that a powerful force emanates from this place, even greater than that from the Stephansdom.

TREASURES OF THE TEUTONIC KNIGHTS

Vipers' tongues

Singerstrass 7, Stiege I, 1010 Wien
Open Tuesday, Thursday and Saturday 10am–noon, Wednesday and Friday
3pm–5pm, closed Mondays and public holidays
Guided tours by appointment
www.deutscher-orden.at/site/lang/en
U-Bahn: line U1 / U3, Stephansplatz station

The second floor of the Deutschordenshaus, the Order of Teutonic Knights' headquarters near the Stephansdom, houses one of the oldest collections of art objects in the city – a treasure trove on a European scale.

The Teutonic Order was originally a religious and military chivalric organisation that contributed to the subjection of Eastern Prussia in the Middle Ages. When the Order was dissolved by Napoleon around 1805, the seat of the Grand Master was transferred to Vienna.

The Schatzkammer (Treasure Room), contains pieces inventoried for the first time under Grand Master Archduke Maximilian III of Austria. They testify to the Habsburgs' passion for art, whether Gothic, Renaissance or 19th century.

The exhibition gives pride of place to fine chalices, glassware, exquisite clocks, vessels made from coconut shells decorated with coral animal figures, and artlessly hand-crafted trinkets. Portraits of several Grand Masters, altarpieces and ancient documents complete this remarkable collection.

The death mask is that of Archduke Eugene of Austria-Teschen (1863–1954) the last secular Grand Master of the Teutonic Knights. The heraldic symbol of the fleur-de-lis on the Teutonic Order's coat of arms has also been inscribed in literature to the Priory of Sion, a mysterious and controversial fraternal organisation.

The centrepiece of the museum is a very special 15th-century artefact: a salt-cellar tree made from red coral and hung with sharks' teeth. In medieval times these were thought to be the fossilised tongues of vipers – or more specifically dragons – because such magical powers were attributed to them as the ability to detect poison in food and drink.

The headquarters of the Teutonic Order has since 1667 incorporated its church as well as its treasury. Members of the Golden Fleece – including Roman Catholic priests of noble descent, reigning princes and kings – gather there on 30 November each year.

WÖCKHERL ORGAN

The oldest organ in Vienna, concealed behind a painting

Franziskanerkirche
Franziskanerplatz 4, 1010 Wien
Open every Friday 3pm–3.40pm from April to September (excluding public holidays)
http://wien.franziskaner.at/
U-Bahn: line U1 / U3, Stephansplatz station; Tram: 2, Weihburggasse stop

From April to September, guided tours on Friday afternoon let you discover Wöckherl's exceptional organ and hear its unique tone. The organ has been preserved in its original state and offers contemporary listeners an incomparable experience, straight from the 17th century.

It was in 1642 that the Franciscan Church acquired Wöckherl's organ, which owes its name to the manufacturer, Johann Wöckherl or Weckerl (1594–1660). This was a sign of hope during the tumultuous times of the Thirty Years' War, which wreaked havoc until 1648.

In the 18th century the organ was eclipsed by a more modern instrument installed in the gallery and it was concealed behind Andrea Pozzo's sumptuous high altar, erected directly in front. The almost walled-up organ has escaped any renovations or conversions, and the religious paintings on its double doors are intact.

Another feature of Wöckherl's organ, still hidden from view and accessible only from the convent, is that it can be played with the doors either open or closed.

To prolong the tour experience, a 14-track CD is available.

RELICS OF ST HILARIA

Former prostitute and patron saint of unhappy lovers

Franziskanerkirche
Franziskanerplatz 4, 1010 Wien
Open daily 9am–noon and 2.30pm–4.30pm
http://wien.franziskaner.at/
U-Bahn: line U1 / U3, Stephansplatz station; Tram: 2, Weihburggasse stop

To the left of the altar in the Franciscan Church, the wax statue lying in a glass coffin represents St Hilaria, a little-known saint whose extraordinary life's journey led her from a brothel in the Bavarian city of Augsburg to this Viennese church. Her remains were embalmed in wax in 1720.

The martyrdom of Hilaria dates back to the year 304, during the reign of Emperor Diocletian. Hilaria and her daughter Afra, who has also been canonised, made their living from prostitution in Augsburg, known as Augusta Vindelicum under the Roman Empire. According to legend, an itinerant bishop presented himself at this brothel one evening, thinking it was an ordinary tavern. Jesus Christ appeared to him as he ordered his meal in the presence of Hilaria and Afra. After this incident, the two women converted to Christianity and were baptised. They abandoned their trade and founded the first Christian community in Augsburg.

However, their conversion provoked the anger of a group of men, who had Afra executed. During the funeral ceremony, Hilaria and the other Christians were arrested and condemned to be burned at the stake. Hilaria's remains could be "identified" because she clung to her daughter's coffin. Afra still lies in the Basilica of St Ulrich and St Afra at Augsburg. She was elevated to the rank of patron saint of the city and is invoked whenever there is a fire, while her mother protects unhappy lovers and repentant sinners. The relics of St Hilaria were brought to Vienna around 1720.

Towards the front of the Franciscan Church a small door to the left, behind a prayer stool, leads to the tomb of Father Petrus Pavlicek, who founded the Crusade of Reparation of the Holy Rosary in 1947.
In 1936 the visions of the mystic and stigmatic farm girl Therese Neumann ("Resl von Konnersreuth" – the Wonder – or Fake – of Konnersreuth) encouraged him to become a priest. His beatification has been in progress since 2000.

FRANZISKANERKIRCHE CRYPT

A deadly task

Franziskanerplatz 4, 1010 Wien
Open 2 November (see website)
http://wien.franziskaner.at/
U-Bahn: line U1 / U3, Stephansplatz station; Tram: 2, Weihburggasse stop

The Franciscan Church crypt, the oldest in Vienna, is open once a year on All Souls' Day. It is said to date back to 1370.

The first chamber contains the funerary urns of monks, impeccably arranged one beside the other, while the lower chamber houses long rows of tombs. This place used to be popularly known as the "Crypt of Horror" because a clutter of broken and crushed coffins, bones, and even mummified pieces of corpses lay scattered around.

This chaos was the result of successive wars: the French under Napoleon, like the Soviet liberators in 1945, realised that this was not the last resting place of poor Franciscan monks. They knew very well that the splendid Baroque coffins actually contained the remains of wealthy noble families, descendants of the houses of Gonzaga, Hoyos and Trautmannsdorf.

Around 1930, a young monk decided to put an end to the chaos that prevailed in this burial place and create some order there. But sadly he contracted a lethal infection from contact with the corpses and died in 1932 at the age of 22.

It was not until 1990 that Brother Elias Unegg began working on the task that had been left unfinished for almost 60 years. He stored some of the mummified bodies in a ventilation shaft and then had the tombs restored before replacing their contents. In 1998, a Mass was celebrated on All Souls' Day in the newly presentable crypt.

During the open day, you'll see a well that probably dates back to Roman times, tableware from the Middle Ages and, on some tombs, well-preserved leather shoes that were found during the clean-up.

There is also the tombstone of an abbess who belonged to the Convent of the Penitents before the building became the property of the Franciscan Order.

All the tombs in the crypt are now sealed. Only a few skulls have been left above the metal coffins of children, while the body of someone who was buried alive, arms raised to lift the lid, has disappeared.

KAISERBRÜNDL HERRENSAUNA ⑱

One of the most beautiful saunas in the world

Weihburggasse 18–20, 1010 Wien
Open Monday to Sunday 2pm–midnight
www.kaiserbruendl.at
U-Bahn: line U1 / U3, Stephansplatz station; Tram: 2, Weihburggasse stop

K aiserbründl Men's Sauna, in the heart of the city centre, is probably one of the most beautiful in the world: sauna, bio-sauna, steam bath, massage rooms, solarium and restaurant, over three floors. Relaxation and pleasure in an exceptional setting.

Stefan Riedl, the owner, has decorated the place with scenes from Greek mythology and also designed a Roman grotto with nymphaeum.

Although the Vienna Tourist Board homepage states that prostitution is strictly forbidden in gay saunas, this has not always been the case.

In the 19th century, the homosexual jet set frequented the Centralbad (Central Baths), the predecessor of the Kaiserbründl. Philipp Graf Eulenburg, German ambassador to Vienna, was allegedly relieved of a tidy sum by a "lifeguard" in exchange for his silence. The diplomat apparently said there'd been "just a problem with a lady". A rather unlikely explanation, because ladies didn't really use the Central Baths ...

Archduke Louis Victor had his face slapped here, an incident thought to have led to his being banished to Salzburg.

Women are only allowed into the sauna at special events open to all.

The Kaiserbründl is often used as a film set (*Kommissar Rex*, a police-dog procedural; *Comedian Harmonists*, the story of a German male sextet).

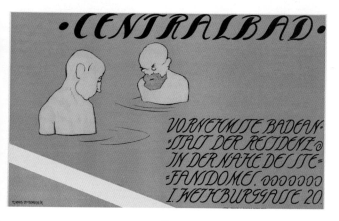

GRAND LODGE OF AUSTRIA DOOR ⑲

The "Magnum Opus" of a Freemason

Rauhensteingasse 3, 1010 Wien
U-Bahn: line U1 / U3, Stephansplatz station

Above the entrance to the Grand Lodge of Austria, a "rough stone" (*rauhe Stein*) hangs from a metal hook. The street is named after this stone, the symbol of the apprentice Freemason who, initiated as a "dressed stone", will one day contribute to the construction of the temple and the creation of a better world.

The Vienna Lodge represents all 33 of the Masonic degrees of initiation. The wooden door is decorated with an elaborate pattern made up of a cross and several squares to form an intricate octagon over a Sun motif – an ancient symbol of fertility and growth. Technically, the cross holds the two leaves of the door closed. Symbolically, the vertical bar represents a plumb line, the horizontal bar the base of a triangle – the tools of the builders of medieval cathedrals, from whom the Freemasons draw their traditions.

The other geometrical figures on the door are the square and compass, the two best-known Masonic tools. Interlocking squares formed part of the construction secrets of cathedral builders. This technique dates

back to Eastern architecture and was probably brought to France by the Templars, regarded by many Masonic lodges as their spiritual predecessors.

The three doorknobs correspond to the signs, words and handshake that allow Freemasons to recognise one another.

The "Magnum Opus" (Great Work) of a Freemason can assume very different forms according to the personal knowledge and preferences of the initiate: for example, it could be a musical, intellectual or craft pursuit, or the setting up of a charity.

SALA TERRENA, WINTER PALACE ⑳ OF PRINCE EUGENE

Grotesques

Himmelpfortgasse 8, 1010 Wien
Open during temporary exhibitions
www.belvedere.at/de/schloss-und-museum/winterpalais

For many years, the street name Himmelpfortgasse had unpleasant connotations for the Viennese, as it had been the address of the Austrian Ministry of Finance since 1848. But the Winter Palace, designed by legendary architect Johann Fischer von Erlach, has also been a museum since 2013, when Prince Eugene's Baroque apartments were completely renovated and opened to the public. Over the previous few decades, tax officials may still have been smoking on the premises, but they could no longer see the grotesque-style paintings on the vaulted ceiling of the *Sala Terrena* (ground-floor hall). It had been covered with plaster and the room fitted with metal shelves for storing documents.

Most visitors to the Winter Palace immediately go up the grand staircase to the first floor to visit the magnificent suites, missing the access to the *Sala Terrena*, to the right just inside the entrance.

In his day, Prince Eugene was probably Europe's richest citizen. His love of grotesque decorative art, very fashionable in early 18th-century Vienna, can be seen in almost all the rooms: the surfaces are covered with playful creatures that frolic among vine shoots and exuberant ornamentation. The master painter of these curious mythological figures is none other than Jonas Drentwett, from Augsburg (Germany), who was also responsible for the decoration of the Hall of Grotesques in Eugene's summer residence, the Lower Belvedere.

When the renovations were under way on the first floor, Drentwett's paintings on the floor below were masked by a false ceiling, so Eugene's aesthetic taste has been preserved intact. Among the Cupids are a lion, Pegasus the winged horse, and Hercules – an omnipresent figure in the Winter Palace. The old dog, often derided for his homosexual tendencies, identified with Hercules. There are many mementoes of his victorious military campaigns that led to the name Eugene of Savoy going down in history. Medallions painted in grisaille (shades of grey that create the illusion of sculpture) represent allegories such as "War", "Victory" and "History". The historical motifs, in particular, contain important details, for the paintings bear the names of decisive victories from the Spanish War of Succession (1701–14): Carpi 1701, Blenheim (Höchstädt) 1704, Turin 1706, Malplaquet 1709. This suggests that the *Sala Terrena* frescoes date from the first extension of the Winter Palace, between 1708 and 1711. Unfortunately, historical sources reveal no more about this room.

The restoration took five years and was completed in 2012. There is an inscription on the ceiling by a mason called Franz Wimmer, noting that he had covered over this space on 19 September 1904.

The Winter Palace is now an exhibition venue for the Belvedere Palace Museum.

PALAIS SAVOYEN-CARIGNAN COURTYARD

The Messerschmidt women

Johannesgasse 15, 1010 Wien
Inner courtyard: sometimes accessible on request

Princess Maria Theresia Antonia von Liechtenstein, widowed soon after her marriage to a nephew of Prince Eugen von Savoyen (Eugene of Savoy), had a convent built in 1770 for "noble ladies" in the grounds of Savoyen-Carignan palace in Johannesgasse. The convent, Savoysches Damenstift, was in fact more of a charity as the women were allowed to move around freely, travel, and even marry.

The palace façade is adorned with an impressive Maria Immaculata lead sculpture dating from 1768. This is one of the major works of Franz Xaver Messerschmidt, otherwise known for his "character heads" – busts meant to represent the full range of human expressions, like today's emoji.

The picturesque courtyard features a mural, dating from 1900 rather than the Baroque period, representing the government supposedly responsible for the well-being of the people.

A sundial overlooks the scene. In collaboration with Johann Martin Fischer, Messerschmidt also designed a beautiful wall-mounted fountain in a style reminiscent of master sculptor Georg Raphael Donner: *Witwe-von-Sarepta-Brunnen* (Fountain of Sarepta's Widow). In the niche is a statue of a woman emptying a pitcher, which serves as a waterspout. The lions that flank the fountain are also by Messerschmidt and Fischer. In 1987 the fountain was replaced with a copy by Alfred Zöttl – the original is at Liechtenstein Garden Palace. According to the inscription, the woman is not the widow of Zarephath (Sarepta) but a poor woman who, as described in the Old Testament, received pitchers of oil from the prophet Elijah. The bas-relief above the inscription shows the prophet writing in the desert.

The property still belongs to the Liechtenstein family but is now rented out.

LITERATURMUSEUM

In Franz Grillparzer's office

Johannesgasse 6, 1010 Wien
Open Tuesday to Sunday 10am–6pm, Thursday 10am–9pm
www.onb.ac.at/literaturmuseum.htm
U-Bahn: line U1 / U3, Stephansplatz station

The National Library's Literature Museum, opened in 2015, occupies the premises of the former imperial court archives, built between 1843 and 1846 and classified as a historic monument. The great Austrian dramatist Franz Grillparzer served as director of the archives until 1856. His office, conserved in its original state, is part of the permanent exhibition, which also includes a wide variety of manuscripts, books and letters as well as audio and cinematographic documentation.

The museum extends over 750 square metres on two floors and the collection ranges chronologically from Enlightenment writers to contemporary authors such as Gerhard Roth and Elfriede Jelinek,

winner of the 2004 Nobel Prize for Literature.

A visit explains much about individual authors' circumstances as well as the contemporary literary scene, as major works are placed in their historical context. Finally, a room devoted to writers' personal effects displays Heimito von Doderer's dressing gown, travel writer and explorer Ida Pfeiffer's protective mask, and the revolver used by novelist and poet Ferdinand von Saar to commit suicide.

The decision to set up the Literature Museum in Austria's oldest archives has attracted much criticism. Moving the imperial documents stirred the same emotions as the illegal destruction of a monument. The special aura of this building, with its endless rows of files, has disappeared, although the smell of wax and paper and the creaking of the timber floor are still omnipresent. The documents have gone to the National Archives in the city's 3rd district (Landstrasse).

RELIC OF ST ANNE'S HAND

A wedding gift from Portugal?

Annakirche
Annagasse 3B, 1010 Wien
Access: once a year on 26 July (St Anne's Day)

Annakirche (St Anne's Church) is one of Vienna's Baroque treasures. Construction began in 1320 but it acquired its present architectural style only in the 17th century. Around a hundred years later, in 1743, one of the most precious relics in Vienna was stored there: the right hand of St Anne, the maternal grandmother of Jesus, which can be seen once a year on the saint's feast day, 26 July.

The relic is thought to have been a particularly generous gift from Maria Anna of Austria, daughter of Holy Roman Emperor Leopold I. She had herself received it as a gift from the House of Braganza on her marriage to King John of Portugal.

Another legend is that Rudolfo Dane, a Roman Catholic Armenian born in Istanbul who was a messenger and interpreter at the imperial court, carried an extraordinary artefact with him as part of a delivery of goods to Emperor Leopold I in 1678. It was said to be St Anne's hand, bought in Istanbul's famous relics market. The long-awaited heir to the throne was born shortly after this incident and the women of the court came to venerate the relic. It is still credited with the power of overcoming sterility.

In fact, the relic kept in St Anne's Church is probably part of the saint's shoulder rather than her hand. But the most important factor is obviously the symbolism itself: the right hand takes the oath and represents justice. And the hands of criminals used to be cut off. In the rituals of magic, the hand also plays an essential role, while hands clasped in prayer repel Evil, and the laying on of hands can heal.

Anne is not mentioned in the canonical Gospels and very little is known about her or her husband, Joachim. She only gained popularity in Central Europe at the time of the Crusades. It is said that Chartres Cathedral could not have been completed in all its glory without the generosity of the pilgrims attracted by the presence of the head of St Anne within its walls.

For a long time, a second "right hand of St Anne" existed at Oberthalheim in Upper Austria. This was finally declared to be a fake by the Apostolic Nuncio.

REMAINS
OF THE BOULEVARD THEATER

The classiest old theatre in the city centre

Annagasse 3, 1010 Wien
Open daily during store or restaurant hours

When the young owner of the sportswear store at No. 3 Annagasse decided in 2008 to rent and convert the premises, then occupied by a discotheque,* he uncovered vestiges of the Boulevard Theater, which the Viennese believed had been demolished a long time ago.

Nowadays, between displays of trainers and hoodies, you can admire what remains of the most chic boulevard theatre in the city centre, one level below the street. The tropical jungle wallcovering design, *Brazil*, was created by local craftsman Otto Prutscher. The fabric, which had largely been removed or torn, has been carefully restored under the aegis of the Federal Office of Historic Monuments.

In 1893, the famous architectural studio Fellner & Helmer (Ferdinand Fellner and Hermann Helmer) was commissioned to build this 1,000-square-metre hall on the model of the Parisian *Bal Tabarin* cabaret. Specialists in theatre design, they dotted the empire with spectacular monuments as far as the Galician border.

Around 1910, a false ceiling was added to divide up the premises for theatre performances and cabaret numbers. As illusionists were very popular at the time, a basement was needed to make the artists "disappear".

Now there's a fast-food restaurant on the ground floor, featuring the original stucco ceiling and a poster-sized photo of the magnificent auditorium at the entrance.

Legendary actor Hans Moser launched his career at the Boulevard Theater in 1911, and cabaret star Fritz Grünbaum was also hugely popular. Later, clarinettist Fatty George ran Austria's first jazz club there.

The beginnings of entertainment in this street go back even further in the 19th century. As early as the Vormärz period (before the 1848 Revolution, which saw the rise of middle class cultural interests), Annagasse housed a kind of theme park called *Neue Elysium*, which offered a virtual world tour. The lavish attraction took visitors on a train journey to discover pantomime in an Ottoman seraglio, an Egyptian magic room and a Chinese emperor's palace.

---

*The 1980s disco was called "Montevideo" in tribute to a track by Austro-pop legend Hansi Lang (1955–2008).

City Centre West

SKELETON IN THE ROCHE BOBOIS STORE ①

A Roman skeleton in a furniture store

Roche Bobois
Wipplingerstrasse 27, 1010 Wien
Open Monday to Friday 9am–6pm, Saturday 9am–5pm
Tram: 1, Börse stop

At the back of the Roche Bobois store in Wipplingerstrasse, a flight of steps leads to the basement, which has been converted into a furniture showroom.

Remarkably, an opening has been made in the basement to reveal a well-preserved Roman skeleton, stretched out 3 metres below ground. The corpse was buried in late antiquity (4th or 5th century) in the cemetery at this site. The remains of a Roman wall can also be seen.

The history of the area around Renngasse and Wipplingerstrasse has been well documented since the archaeological excavations of the late 20th century. The settlement of central Vienna dates back to the Roman era and the legionnaire camp of Vindobona.

The site of the Roche Bobois store was once next to the Roman camp, which started at Limesstrasse. The remains of workshops were discovered during the excavations – a round kiln, copper and iron slag. The clay soil was used to make ceramic objects. A clay excavation pit down to 9 metres below today's road level has also been identified. Pits of this type have been detected as far as the Freyung. When these pits were exhausted, they were filled in with fragments of pottery, which explains the wealth of finds in the store basement. Some of the more valuable remains are displayed in a glass case in the stairwell.

In the 4th century AD, when Teutonic invasions were frequent and times were uncertain, the workshops were moved behind the walls of the Roman camp. The former excavation grounds became a cemetery.

In the 16th century this was the site of the imperial arsenal, an impressive collection of weapons taken as booty during the 1848 revolution. The heavily damaged buildings were redesigned in the 1870s by Heinrich von Ferstel, an Austrian architect who played a vital role in building late 19th-century Vienna. One of these residential and commercial buildings now houses the Roche Bobois store.

The skeleton lying in the basement has a large hole in its skull, although the Roman didn't die from this wound, which is of much more recent origin – damage from an excavator grab!

HOTEL ORIENT

Historic "love hotel" with great charm

Tiefer Graben 30, 1010 Wien
A three-hour stay costs between €70 and €100
Full night available only at weekends
http://www.hotel-orient.at/

Hotel Orient, a kind of historic "love hotel" (the building dates from the 1870s and the lift was only installed after the Second World War), is an amazing place where rooms can be taken for three hours, or for the whole night ...

Although Franz Joseph himself is thought to have set up surreptitious meetings here, the portrait of his mistress Katharina Schratt displayed in the bar belongs to the realms of fantasy. Discretion is still top priority today.

Each room has its own ambience: Imperial or Baroque, Art Nouveau or exotic, and each is named accordingly. Married couples often opt for *Engerl & Bengerl* (the name of a game), but you might prefer *1001 Nights*, *Amethyst* or the *Kaiser Suite*, a bathroom with a domed roof, a starry sky or even a see-through shower.

Here you don't choose a room from a brochure. The concierge sums up the clients and with great tact suggests a suitable room. You can't book in advance at the Hotel Orient, not even if you're a regular guest. Three hours will cost you between €70 and €100 and a full night is only available at weekends.

In the past, rooms on the lower floors were reserved for "professionals" and their clients. Today, most customers are legitimate (or illegitimate) couples. The employees are all related or linked to the owner: friends and family only, everything very "discreet". Generally, the busiest times are Christmas and spring. "Hormones ...", muses the owner.

A tavern at the hotel's present site, then close to the water, became an unloading point for goods from the Orient in the days when a tributary of the Danube still ran through the Tiefer Graben ("Deep Ditch"). Ships loaded with goods destined for the city centre used to dock there.

Additional proof that the set-up is really out of the ordinary – you're even allowed to smoke ...

HOFBAUER RELIQUARY

The Apostle of Vienna

Church of Maria am Gestade
Salvatorgasse 12, 1010 Wien
Museum open Sunday 2pm–5pm
www.redemptoristen.com

Born Johannes Hofbauer in 1751, in the Znojmo district of South Moravia (now in the Czech Republic), this patron saint of the City of Vienna served his apprenticeship as a baker's boy – he also represents the Guild of Bakers and Confectioners.

St Klemens Maria Hofbauer (St Clement) is venerated at the church of the Redemptorists (Congregation of the Most Holy Redeemer), Maria am Gestade (Mary at the Shore), one of the most attractive and little-known churches in Vienna.

A side chapel to the right of the nave shelters his glass reliquary. As it has been covered with a strikingly modern tombstone, the contents of the shrine can only be glimpsed.

Hofbauer joined the Redemptorist Order in Rome before settling in Vienna, where he became confessor to the Ursuline nuns and attended to their spiritual welfare. Both they and the lay people who came to the Ursulinenkirche greatly appreciated the help that Hofbauer gave to the sick and needy. The secret police on the other hand were well aware of his influence on the pope and politicians, and consequently on the deliberations of the Congress of Vienna. His sermons during the age of anticlerical Enlightenment attracted the attention of Austrian statesman Metternich's spies and earned him the nickname "Apostle of Vienna". His discussion groups – attended by such intellectuals as Prussian writer and critic Joseph von Eichendorff, Austrian Orientalist and historian Joseph von Hammer-Purgstall, and German poet and novelist Clemens Brentano – further added to Hofbauer's reputation as an influential preacher.

The former sacristy on the left was converted into a museum in 2014. It contains some of the saint's personal effects, such as a confessional from the Ursulines chapel and the coffin used to transport his body to Vienna, as well as documentation on the Redemptorists. Hofbauer introduced this Order to Vienna, where in 1820 it was officially authorised and he was assigned to the Church of Maria am Gestade, which had been closed down by Joseph II. But the preacher who was to set up the first Redemptorist foundation in Austria died in the spring of the same year, so never saw this plan through. He was interred in the cemetery of Maria Enzersdorf, Lower Austria. In 1862, his remains were exhumed and transferred to Maria am Gestade. The empty tomb can still be seen at his original burial site. He was canonised by the Roman Catholic Church in 1909.

On 15 March, the anniversary of the saint's death, *Klemens-Weckerln* (white breadrolls in human shape) are blessed and distributed to the people.

BILLERBECK DEPARTMENT STORE ④ RUINS

Bombs over Vienna

Fischerstiege 9 (inner courtyard), 1010 Wien
Officially closed to the public but worth a try ...

The last ruins attributable to the Second World War still to be seen in Vienna are near the Salzgries restaurant. Around the corner of the new buildings, you can still see in an inner courtyard the blackened walls of the old Billerbeck department store, hit by a bomb and then completely burned out. This four-storey ruin has remained more or less as it was in 1945 although the front wing was rebuilt in 1947 and it was roofed over at the beginning of the 21st century.

Originally, the building was an apartment block. The store was designed in 1887 by Arnold Lotz. A residence by the same architect, a specialist in the late historicist style, has survived just a stone's throw away: Marc-Aurel-Hof at No. 6 Marc-Aurel-Strasse.

DOKUMENTATIONSARCHIV DES ÖSTERREICHISCHEN WIDERSTANDES (DÖW)

⑤

Memory, research and recognition

Wipplinger Strasse 6–8, Altes Rathaus, Innenhof, 1010 Wien
Open Monday, Tuesday, Wednesday and Friday 9am–5pm, Thursday 9am–
7pm, also by appointment
www.doew.at
Tram: 1, Salztorbrücke stop

The Documentation Centre of Austrian Resistance, founded in 1963 and supported by the Federal Republic and the City of Vienna, is a non-partisan association of former resistance fighters against the Nazi regime. Its members were tasked with studying Austrian resistance, persecution and exile, Nazi power and postwar justice, and right-wing extremism.

A permanent exhibition analyses the history of the 20th century. The antecedents of National Socialism, resistance and persecution are highlighted. Extensive research has been carried out on National Socialism after 1945 and on past and present extremist tendencies. The DÖW exhibition is the only one in the whole of Austria to tackle this issue in such a comprehensive way. Nazi medical policies and resistance from within concentration camps are among the many other topics covered in detail, using original source material, correspondence, brochures and databases from the Austrian resistance archives.

KORNHÄUSELTURM

An eccentric architect's studio apartment

Fleischmarkt 1B / Seitenstettengasse 2, 1010 Wien
U-Bahn: line U1 / U4, Schwedenplatz station

Josef Kornhäusel was one of the leading architects of the 19th century. Among his most important works are the oldest theatre in Vienna (Theater in der Josefstadt), the Husarentempel (temple) in Mödling, the fantastic Lednice Castle in the Czech Republic and many classic Viennese apartments. This prolific architect also designed Seitenstettengasse synagogue, next to his Kornhäuselturm (tower).

The vast dimensions of the tower, which stands nine storeys high, came as a surprise at the time of its construction. It was also completely surrounded by other buildings and had no entrance on the street. To reach his studio apartment in the tower, the eccentric Kornhäusel had to cross the drawbridge from the fifth floor of the neighbouring building. He died in this studio in October 1860.

The Austrian writer Adalbert Stifter also lived in the tower between 1842 and 1848. He witnessed a total eclipse of the Sun from the panoramic terrace in the summer of 1842 and described this experience in a work entitled *Aus dem alten Wien* (Tales of Old Vienna).

In 1910, the demolition of several adjoining houses opened up access to the tower. It was renovated in the 1970s by Stefan Passini, a contemporary architect. Today, a plaque affixed to the façade by the Vienna Tourist Office recalls the building's almost unknown history.

The first skyscraper in Vienna, reserved for singletons

If today you have trouble envisaging the building at Nos. 6–8 Herrengasse as a skyscraper, in the 1930s it towered majestically over the city.

Until 1913, one of the Liechtenstein royal family's many palaces stood on this site. After the First World War the plot stood vacant for almost 20 years, until a new building was commissioned directly from architects Theiss & Jaksch, without being put out to tender. Initially, 105 of the 225 housing units were designated "single apartments", mainly due to the economic crisis. The press seized on this, calling the building "the skyscraper enemy of matrimony" to which was soon added an aura of "indecency". The apartments had no kitchens: tenants had to eat in the roof terrace restaurant. But this idea did not catch on and minimalist kitchenettes were later installed. The building, labelled the *Hochhäuserl* (Little Big House) by some architects, was inaugurated in the presence of the Austrian president of the time, Wilhelm Miklas. This was far from being a social housing programme. Rents were high and the building was occupied, not by blue-collar families or impoverished single workers, but by artists, intellectuals and a number of stage and screen actors attracted by the proximity of the main theatres and the open, cosmopolitan atmosphere of the city centre. Curd Jürgens (usually billed as Curt Jurgens), Paula Wessely and Oskar Werner, as well as literary phenomenon Daniel Kehlmann, were among the residents, who called themselves the *Hochhäuslern*. Actor Christoph Waltz, widely known for his work with Quentin

Tarantino, even announced that if he ever managed to get an apartment here, he would return to Vienna.

In the 1938 novel by Annemarie Selinko, *Morgen wird alles besser* (*Tomorrow is Always Better*), a young female graduate rents a bachelor pad in the Herrengasse building for 80 schillings.

The Panoramaraum, part of the former restaurant on the 14th floor, can be booked for events and functions. The fantastic terracing over 50 square metres affords superb views across the city.

NEIDHART FRESCOES

The oldest non-religious frescoes in Vienna

Tuchlauben 19, 1010 Wien
Open Tuesday to Sunday and public holidays 10am–1pm and 2pm–6pm

Neidhart's remarkable frescoes were (re)discovered by chance in the late 1970s, in a beautiful house in Tuchlauben, concealed behind a thick layer of plaster. These are Vienna's oldest secular frescoes, dating from 1407. Despite the loss of some of the paintings in the 18th century, the frescoes give an unrivalled glimpse of everyday life in the late Middle Ages.

Contrary to popular belief, the chastity belt was virtually unknown at the time. These erotic drawings were made to reflect the chants of the minstrel Neidhart "von Reuenthal" (1180–1240), one of the most famous German-speaking lyric poets, himself represented in the wall paintings. It's a safe bet that the village of Reuenthal only exists in his imagination. He would have been a major attraction today. His rather bawdy songs, passed down the generations, have been immensely successful for over 400 years. Walther von der Vogelweide, another great medieval lyric poet, envied Neidhart his success and described him as a "croaking frog".

The sardonic minstrel openly attacked the morals of the time, just as the crude manners of the peasants in the frescoes undermine any idea of chivalry – a man gropes a woman's breast and a girl's mirror is spirited away, a sign that she is about to lose her innocence. The fable of the violet is Neidhart's best-known story by far: he discovers the first violet of summer and runs to inform the duke, but on their return they find only a pile of excrement under a hat. The boorish insolence of the peasants would have to be severely punished.

Such depictions of peasant joys and sorrows throughout the seasons recall the extremely detailed works of Flemish Old Master, Pieter Bruegel the Elder.

The tomb said to be Neidhart's, south wall of the Stephansdom (St Stephen's Cathedral)

Nobody knows who actually lies in this medieval tomb, which has recently been renovated. In any case, the remains of two men were discovered here. One of them may be Neidhart, but remember that Neidhart of Reuenthal had many imitators, and they all used his name ...

TURKISH HORSEMAN STATUE

Memories of a band of Turks who drowned here?

Heidenschuss 3 / corner of Strauchgasse, 1010 Wien
U-Bahn: line U3, Herrengasse station

The alley that connects the Freyung and the adjacent square Am Hof is now known as Heidenschuss ("where the heathen was shot"). Its actual connection with heathens – in other words, the Turks – is not clear. The name of the alley comes from a sign with the slogan "where the heathen shoots" (or "shits", some say). However, as this slogan was already mentioned in 1365, it has no connection with the first Ottoman Siege of Vienna in 1529.

The present statue of the "Turkish horseman" has nothing to do with either the first or the second (1683) siege of the city: it dates from the construction of the new palace of the Italian Prince of Montenuovo in the 19th century.

According to legend it was the bakers of Heidenschuss who saved their city from the first Turkish invasion. Josef Schulz, a journeyman working in the bakehouse, is said to have called on neighbours for help when he realised that the invaders were gathering just beyond the cellar walls. Together they filled the basement with water and the Turks drowned even as they succeeding in demolishing the walls.

The Turkish version of the story, however, is rather different: a seasoned traveller from the 1683 delegation of Kara Mustafa Pasha, having already visited Vienna in 1665, described in his travel journal the courage of a Turkish horseman abandoned by his fellow warriors,

who fought to the death. He further disclosed that the corpses of the brave rider and his horse were preserved and displayed in Heidenschuss – the rider once more astride his horse in full armour, weapon in hand, under the brick archway of this house. Emperor Ferdinand I, impressed by the soldier's nerve, is said to have named the square Tcherkesse (Circassian) in his honour.

A variation on this story adds that Ferdinand had the valiant soldier's assassin walled up in the structure of the house.

YELLOW FOG INSTALLATION

Olafur Eliasson's play of light

"Verbund"-Hauptgebäude, Am Hof 6a, 1010 Wien
U-Bahn: line U3, Herrengasse station

In central Vienna, passers-by are sometimes stopped in their tracks by plumes of yellow smoke that seem to rise from the ground. But very quickly another veil of smoke creeps up the 48-metre façade of the Austrian electricity company offices.

Since 2008, this phenomenon has taken place every day at nightfall for about an hour: *Yellow Fog* is an open-air art installation by Olafur Eliasson, who chose the colour for good visibility in the dark. For this well-established Icelandic-Danish artist (born 1967), the yellow veil that lends the scene a new identity symbolises the passage between day and night, light and darkness. Space, buildings and space fade. Then the golden fog escapes towards the city centre.

The lighting is supplied by 32 fluorescent tubes under a grid build into the sidewalk.

The artist worked for three years to obtain the 40 authorisations required for his installation in the urban landscape. At the first attempt, the police arrived, fearing a fire. Luckily the Firefighters Museum is just next door ...

> *Yellow Fog* has also appeared on the façade of the Jewish Museum in New York City since 1998.

FEUERWEHRMUSEUM

Fire!

Zentralfeuerwache
Am Hof 7, 1010 Wien
Open Sunday and public holidays 9am–noon, by appointment during the week
www.wien.gv.at/menschen/sicherheit/feuerwehr/museum/
U-Bahn: line U3, Herrengasse station

This building, which now belongs to the Vienna Fire Service, is worth a visit. The mansion, also known as Merkleinsches Haus (named after its patron Christoph von Merklein), was designed by Baroque architect Johann Lukas von Hildebrandt. As the bas-relief on the façade shows, it was the scene of a dramatic event in 1683: Mayor Johann Andreas Liebenberg was killed two days before the victory over the army of Ottoman grand vizier Kara Mustafa Pasha during the second Siege of Vienna. The ravages caused by the Turks, as well as the high incidence of fires in the city, led to the establishment of the world's oldest professional fire service in 1686.

The Firefighters Museum, on the first floor of the building, is also relatively old: it dates back to 1901, when Vienna Fire Station took first place at the Berlin International Firefighters Exhibition. As the registration fees were high, it was agreed that the exhibition material should later be made use of in Vienna. And so the museum was opened.

The eight exhibition halls highlight the tragic fires that the service has been called out to over the years. Time and again, whole districts of the city have been reduced to ashes, notably in the Ringtheater fire in 1881, the burning of the Justizpalast (Palace of Justice or courthouse) in the 1927 riots, and the destruction of the Rotunda, centrepiece of the 1873 Vienna International Exhibition, in 1937.

The fleet of historic fire-fighting vehicles is not on display in the museum but in the main fire station at Floridsdorf (21st district). There are horse-drawn vehicles, the first water tanker from 1903, and other trucks from the 1970s and 80s. One of the oldest restored vehicles is known as Froschkönig (The Frog King). Phone for an appointment (+43 1 531 9951207).

"NINE CHOIRS OF ANGELS" CRYPT ⑪

The true face of Ignatius of Loyola

Kirche "Zu den neun Chören der Engel" (Kirche am Hof)
Schulhof 1, 1010 Wien
Visits by appointment (see website)
www.jesuitenwien1.at
U-Bahn: line U3, Herrengasse station

You need to be quite fit to enter the crypt of the Nine Choirs of Angels Church – a trapdoor in the sacristy vestibule opens onto a very steep staircase that leads to the crypt itself and to only partially explored passages.

As Enea Silvio Piccolomini, the future Pope Pius II, once declared: "Vienna is as big under ground as above ground."

The *Pietà* displayed in the crypt unexpectedly depicts three figures rather than the usual two. The founder of the Jesuit Order, Ignatius of Loyola, is shown kneeling beside Mary, who has her arms around her Son's body. The features of St Ignatius' face have been reproduced from his mortuary mask, so are authentic.

An 18th-century columbarium, also in the crypt, houses the remains of Jesuit brothers wrapped in simple shrouds as a sign of their vow of poverty.

Andrea Pozzo, Baroque painter, architect and sculptor from Trento (Italy), was a Jesuit lay brother. He died in Vienna in 1709 and is probably laid to rest in this crypt. His bones, however, have never been found.

A priest named Anton Khabes, confessor to Maria Theresa, was interred here too.

STANISLAUSKAPELLE

The young patron of the last sacraments

Zur Goldenen Schlange (Stanislaushaus)
Eckhaus Steindlgasse 6 / Kurrentgasse 2, 1010 Wien
Open 13–20 November 9am–noon and 3pm–6pm or by appointment (see website)
www.jesuitenwien1.at/index.php?id=282
U-Bahn: line U3, Herrengasse station

Every year from 13 to 20 November, during the Festival of St Stanislaus, you can visit the charming chapel built around 1583 on the site where Stanislaus Kostka lived during his stay in Vienna.

It contains scenes from the saint's life as well as an 1840 altarpiece by the Austrian Jesuit painter Franz Stecher, showing the young Stanislaus in the presence of St Barbara. The tower in the painting, one of St Barbara's attributes (she was imprisoned in a tower), is none other than that of the former Jesuit seminary on Freinberg hill in Linz (now the Collegium Aloisianum).

Stanislaus Kostka, who died in Rome in 1568 aged 18, is undoubtedly one of the youngest saints. He is none the less a patron saint of Poland, student youth, the dying, and Jesuit novices.

Born into a noble Polish family, Stanislaus was sent to the Jesuit College of Vienna to continue his studies at the age of 14. Around this time, he decided to enter the Society of Jesus against his parents' wishes. In 1566, while staying at the Zur Goldenen Schlange (The Golden Serpent), he fell gravely ill. But the proprietor, a fervent Protestant, adamantly refused to allow a priest to cross the threshold of his house to administer the last rites. Two visions then appeared to the young man, wracked by disease: St Barbara, who came to give him the Eucharist; and the Virgin Mary, who instructed him to join the Jesuit Order.

As soon as he was strong enough, Stanislaus decided to flee. He exchanged his clothes for those of a beggar and set off on foot in the direction of the Eternal City. He became a Jesuit novice and died

before his parents could force him to return home. He is buried in Rome, at the Church of St Andrew in the Quirinal (see *Secret Rome* in this series of guides).

The Counter-Reformation or Catholic Revival favoured the Jesuits and hastened the beatification of the young Polish student in 1605. Numerous miracles have been attributed to him and the Catholic Habsburg Emperor Karl VI took part in the High Masses and processions in Vienna following his canonisation in 1726.

There are other chapels dedicated to Stanislaus Kostka in Vienna, notably in the Jesuitenkirche (Jesuit Church), also known as the Universitätskirche (University Church), with a depiction of him being received into the Jesuit Order; and Annakirche (St Anne's Church), which features the *Death of St Stanislaus*.

CAFÉ GUTRUF

Helmut Qualtinger's favourite diner

Milchgasse 1, 1010 Wien
Open Monday to Saturday 8.30am–midnight
U-Bahn: line U1 / U3, Stephansplatz station

About 60 years ago, Café Gutruf was an inescapable part of the Viennese art scene. Its famous back room was a meeting place for theatre personalities, singers, politicians and even the police chief, Josef Holaubek. The establishment is cramped and its furniture hasn't changed since the 1960s or 70s.

The café is at the heart of many topical tales, such as the one about cartoonist Erich Sokol, who was spending the evening at the Gutruf when the young painter Christian Ludwig Attersee came in, flanked by two ladies, and took a seat next to the illustrator. Sokol addressed him in these terms: "Tell me, aren't you the one who paints outside the frame?" Women were officially banned from the café, with the exception of journalist Eva Deissen and actresses Erni Mangold and Louise Martini. These two were friends of writer and actor Helmut Qualtinger, a faithful habitué since the 1950s.

At that time, the Gutruf was run by Hannes Hoffmann, an operetta singer who was considered the model for Helmut Qualtinger and Carl Merz's play, *Der Herr Karl* (Mr Karl). This controversial monologue attempted to depict the typical behaviour of the average citizen between 1918 and 1950. Mr Karl has this to say about the years before 1934:

Later I went to demonstrate for the "Blacks". For the Austrofascists.
The Heimwehr. I received five schillings.
Then I went over to the Nazis. Again, I received five schillings.
In the end, Austria has always been apolitical.

This typically "Viennese" character recites his tirade during working hours in the warehouse of a grocery store. In its early days (around 1906), the Gutruf was indeed a shop selling drinks and fine produce.

Qualtinger lived in the Heiligenkreuzerhof neighbourhood near the café, where there is a commemorative plaque to the man whose formidable incarnation of "Mr Karl" is engraved in people's memories.

ST APOLLONIA'S TOOTH

(14)

A cure for toothache

Peterskirche crypt
Petersplatz, 1010 Wien
Open every year around 9 February
www.peterskirche.at/st-peter/

Every year around 9 February, Viennese Catholic dentists celebrate Mass on the anniversary of their patron saint's death. As the saying associated with her feast day goes: *Ist's an Apollonia feucht, der Winter spät entfleucht* (If it's raining on St Apollonia, there's still a long winter to go).

At this time of year, a relic of St Apollonia is displayed in the crypt of St Peter's Church. It only takes a little imagination to recognise a tooth covered with white lace.

Apollonia of Alexandria was martyred in the 3rd century. During a local uprising against the Christians, pagans are said to have knocked out this harmless elderly woman's teeth before leading her to the stake. Nothing else is known about her life.

In some parts of Central Europe, Apollonia is one of the 14 Auxiliary Saints – no wonder, given the terrible pain that broken teeth could inflict until the modern age.

The saint is generally represented with the palm frond of martyrdom and a set of pincers gripping a tooth.

SAINTS IN PETERSKIRCHE CATACOMBS

Boneyard

Petersplatz, 1010 Wien
Accessible during church opening hours
www.peterskirche.at/st-peter

They rest in their Baroque gilded glass reliquary shrines, draped in richly embroidered robes of pseudo-antique style to indicate their origins.

Since early modern times, vast quantities of saintly remains and personal effects have been imported to Austria from Rome. These relics are said to be of "Christian martyrs" who were buried in the catacombs of ancient Rome when Christians were being persecuted.

During the Counter-Reformation and the Baroque period (16th–17th centuries) the Church was in urgent need of relics – not barely presentable bones or shreds of clothing, but exhibits worthy of the name and that would attract worshippers. As there was no lack of old bones in the ancient tombs in and around Rome, looters could easily satisfy the growing demand.

Traditionally, bones from unknown bodies were arranged to form complete skeletons, and any missing parts were carved from wood and added to the model. In 1860, after over 1,000 years of flourishing trade, the sale of these relics was officially banned by the Roman Catholic Church.

The Archbishop of Vienna, Sigismund Graf von Kollonitz, was appointed Cardinal of Rome in 1727. A distant relation had made sure that this promising young man had a good Jesuit education in Bohemia. He is said to have bought two saints from the Roman catacombs and donated their bones to the Jesuit church in Vienna, to mark its dedication to St Peter in 1733.

Today, to the right and left of the main altar of St Peter's, the draped skeletons bear two typical saints' names found throughout Central Europe: Benedict and Donat. They were identified as known saints and prepared accordingly.

Donat rests beneath a portrait of the Opus Dei founder, Josemaría Escrivá, and Benedict below St Michael's altar on the right. A second Donatus (or Bonatus) can be seen in Vienna's Rochuskirche. St Benedict also crops up regularly, the best known example being Benedict of Nursia, buried at the monastery of Monte Cassino.

Sigismund von Kollonitz himself lies in the Stephansdom crypt.

Kara Mustafa's skull

Sigismund had perhaps learned from his uncle Leopold Graf von Kollonitz, also a cardinal, how to add value to a skull. In 1683, he'd made sure that the skull of the Ottoman commander-in-chief,

grand vizier (chief minister) Kara Mustafa Pasha, was authenticated. The Jesuits had reconsecrated the mosque near Mustafa's place of execution in Belgrade, and dispatched his skull to Vienna. At the same time, the cardinal delivered a certificate of authenticity supplied by the municipal armoury. The skull now lies in Vienna's Central Cemetery.

GRABEN PUBLIC TOILETS

The world's most beautiful WCs?

Graben, 1010 Wien
Admission: 50 cents

Most Viennese pass by at least once a week without even noticing these magnificent Art Nouveau public toilets. Unsignposted, they are located right in the middle of the Graben, or more exactly in a former cellar *under* the pedestrianised street.

These facilities, built in 1905, are thought to have been designed by the renowned architect Adolf Loos, although no one has ever proved

this. On the other hand, artists such as writer Karl Kraus and composer Gustav Mahler were known to frequent them. To mask any odour, the former Berlin court officer Wilhelm Beetz had invented an "oil urinal" system, which is no longer in use today.

Modern urinals are now ensconced in the historic setting, all dark wood and subdued lighting, and always clean and shining. Each stall has a washbasin and mirror. A visit costs 50 cents.

At a time when WCs were rare in private homes, the treatment of human waste was somewhat different from what we know today. "Bucketmen" and "bucketwomen" shrouded in long cloaks that concealed wooden pails paced the streets to offer a little privacy to passers-by, who could relieve themselves in exchange for a few coins. The waste was collected throughout the city, stored in barrels and sent to the farmers of the Marchfeld plain to the north-east, where it was used as fertiliser. Meanwhile cholera and typhus were regularly wreaking havoc in Vienna.

Other noteworthy WCs in Vienna

Opera Toilet at Karlsplatz station (with *Blue Danube* background music)
WC built by Wilhelm Beetz on the other side of Richard-Wagner-Platz in Ottakring (16th district)
WC at Stöberplatz (16th district)
Wilhelm Beetz's underground WC (Amerlingstrasse in the 6th district)
WC at the Jazz Museum in the 22nd district

NAIL TREE

A holy tree

Stock-im-Eisen-Platz 3, 1010 Wien

Since 1891, a nail tree protected by metal bands and a glass case has stood at the corner of the Palais Equitable. This is Europe's oldest surviving example of a so-called "nail tree" Before the Christian era they were very widespread in the region.

According to a written account from 1533, the *Stock im Eisen* (staff in iron) stood at the intersection of these streets (today Rotenturmstrasse / Kärntner Strasse and Singerstrasse / Graben), where there was a fountain. This is the oldest mention of the former monument supposed to mark the mythical central point, the "navel", of the city.

The initials HB and the year 1575 on the metal band probably refer to Hans Buettinger, the former owner of the estate on which the tree once grew. Nails continued to be driven into it right up until the 19th century.

The story goes that one day an apprentice locksmith designed an intricate padlock in order to close a metal band encircling a tree trunk. Nobody could open it. When the journeyman returned, desirous of becoming a master locksmith, he produced a key to open the magic lock. As this skill inevitably required diabolic intervention, he sold his life and soul to the devil and became a rich master locksmith. Since then, every locksmith who comes to Vienna is supposed to hammer a nail into the trunk with the legendary lock.

Driving nails into trees was in fact a common practice in fertility rituals and in the prevention or cure of certain diseases. The first nails were driven into the *Stock im Eisen* while it was still alive.

Before the Babenberg era (10th–12th centuries), the tree stood outside the city limits, perhaps to mark a boundary. The lock is now just a hollow box and the trunk is upside down: the "branches" are actually roots. The old tree was probably set up this way in order to illustrate the powerlessness of mythological gods and the beginning of the Christian era.

Palais Equitable

Between 1887 and 1891, the New York life insurance company Equitable commissioned architect Andreas Streit to build the most impressive mansion in the city.

The building will always retain its "palace" title although no noble family has ever occupied it. The American eagle on the roof indicates the nationality of the sponsors.

The bronze sculpture at the entrance representing the history of the nail tree is by Rudolf Weyr; the bas-reliefs are by Viktor Tilgner and Johann Schindler. The vestibule and corridor are faced with tiles and majolica.

The building is open to the public from 9am to 6pm on weekdays.

The imperial suppliers company of Wilhelm Beck & Söhne had their offices in the Palais, which was a tourist site before 1918. They manufactured men's uniforms and accessories.

PETER ALTENBERG'S PORTRAIT

"If he isn't in the coffeehouse, he's on his way"

Loos Bar
Kärntner Durchgang 10, 1010 Wien
Open Thursday to Saturday noon to 5pm, Sunday to Wednesday noon to 4pm

The American Bar (also known as the Loos Bar after its designer Adolf Loos) in the city centre is very popular but tiny, so always crowded. It's not easy to spot the painting hanging on the right behind the tables.

It depicts Peter Altenberg, a man who claimed to be overwhelmed by all these bars capitalising on his name, whether or not he'd set foot in their premises. His contemporaries said of him: "If he isn't in the coffeehouse, he's on his way."

Vienna honours Altenberg in countless ways: a statue in the Café Central, this canvas in the American Bar, and even a café named after him, the Café Engländer. (Before adopting the pseudonym Peter Altenberg, which he considered more conducive to his future career as a writer, he was Richard Engländer.) He was to become the most celebrated Viennese of his day.

In 1909, Expressionist painter Gustav Jagerspacher made an almost caricatural image of Altenberg, with his favourite checked coat, rather over-large, and his bald head, bushy eyebrows and characteristic moustache. The skeletal fingers gripping his broad-brimmed hat are also striking.

Adolf Loos, like Peter Altenberg, particularly appreciated all that was British or American. Together they spent entire nights skimming the bars and cabarets. One night, around 4am, they wound up in the studio of leading portrait photographer Trude Fleischmann. There and then she took an emblematic shot of the two of them: Adolf Loos, distinguished in his tweed coat, and Peter Altenberg, bleary-eyed in his casual gear.

Altenberg was supposed to be a witness at the wedding of his friend Loos and his fiancée Lina in Lednice (Czech Republic). But he never arrived. He was infatuated with the daughter of a coffeehouse-owner

called Caroline Obertimpfler, and claimed that he hadn't woken up in time. Years later, when Altenberg wanted to convert to Catholicism, Loos became his sponsor.

Adolf Loos and Peter Altenberg, the infernal *fin-de-siècle* duo, are still united today: an enormous wooden cross designed by Loos stands on the writer's tomb while the brilliant architect is buried nearby, in the same aisle of the Central Cemetery.

PETER ALTENBERG'S OFFICE

Peter Altenberg spent his last years here, when not in a psychiatric hospital

Hotel Graben
Dorotheergasse 3, 1010 Wien
www.kremslehnerhotels.at/de/hotel-graben-wien/

Known for its Art Nouveau façade, Hotel Graben, under the name of Einkehrgasthof zum Goldenen Jägerhorn (Inn of the Golden Horn), opened its doors to travellers around the end of the 18th century. Only later did writers adopt it. First Franz Grillparzer and his entourage, soon followed by Franz Kafka and Max Brod. But only one of them officially chose the hotel as his permanent address: Peter Altenberg.

His room bill was settled by friends, mainly by noted journalist and writer Karl Kraus. From 1913 to 1919, Altenberg spent his last years in room 51, when not incarcerated in a psychiatric hospital. He was already the hotel's most iconic guest. His office is still there today, yet he used to write lying in bed, surrounded by his collection of photographs of pretty underage girls and some other oddments now housed in Wien Museum. Visitors dropped in by day and by night, but their host was often unwell. In which case he hung a sign on the door of his hotel room: "I'm not in for anyone today. Without exception. Peter Altenberg".

The hotel, renovated in 2014, has belonged to the Kremslehner family since 1927. At the entrance, a plaque installed by the Austrian Society of Literature commemorates Altenberg and other writers.

Peter Altenberg's funerary cross: a forgotten work by Adolf Loos

Adolf Loos is well known to Austrians for his hatred of ornamentation, for his love of little girls and for the asteroid named after him. But not many people know that this world-renowned architect and designer was responsible for the gigantic funerary cross of his best friend. The carved wooden cross looms high above the walls of the Central Cemetery at the grave of Richard Engländer (later known as Peter Altenberg as far as the Russian border for his talents as a writer, journalist and provocateur). Homeless, he died in 1919 in his room at Hotel Graben. His second-best friend, Karl Kraus, wrote him a funeral oration in rhyme. In harmony with his erratic but eventful life, Altenberg's grave bears the simple epitaph: "He loved and he saw."

The designer of the cross rests in a plot close to him, in group 0, row 1, no. 105. But whereas Peter Altenberg still has his *Ehrengrab* (Memorial Grave) that of Adolf Loos has been removed because of his conviction for paedophilia in 1928.

DEMEL MUSEUM

Whipped cream, please

Kohlmarkt 14, 1010 Wien
Open Friday 10am–noon, admission: €4
www.demel.at/frames/index_wien_museum.htm

Although Demel Konditorei, the pastry and confectionery shop, is known worldwide, the museum of the same name (open only on Friday mornings) is rather less so. It offers a fascinating journey through the history of this Viennese institution.

Marzipan objects, ornate rooms and a glass-fronted bakery giving a glimpse of the pastry cooks at work are among the attractions of this museum dedicated to sugar.

Demel's former owner, Federico Berzeviczy-Pallavicini, the husband of heiress Klára Demel, was responsible for the legendary shopfront dating from the 1950s. He called his fairy-tale window-dressing "Street Theatre", using precious and stylish materials for religious festivals, changing seasons and visiting heads of state. He also wanted passers-by who couldn't afford to venture into the expensive shop to enjoy the spectacle. He had a scale model of the shop built for his office, in order to test the decors, in the manner of a theatre director.

The shop window is still under the watchful eye of Mr Berzeviczy-Pallavicini: the most successful exhibits are then added to the museum collection, where every visitor is given a sample of confectionery.

The building was also a meeting place for the Austrian elite in the 1970s: the Club 45 "Red Lodge" had premises above the café. Leopold Gratz, former secretary of the Social Democratic Party of Austria (SPÖ), formed a group of high-ranking officials, including the Kreisky IV government's finance minister Hannes Androsch and Demel owner Udo Proksch, as well as media personalities, business leaders and bankers. Club 45 had no fewer than 200 members, also said to be Freemasons. The "Lucona affair", named for a freighter sunk in an insurance scam that involved several leading politicians, saw the demise of this men's club, which closed down in 1992.

The "Demelinerinnen"

The women who serve the bewildering array of coffees and cakes wear a black uniform, with white collar and apron, inspired by a nun's habit. The reason for this attire is that, in the 19th century, the owner wanted to show that the poor reputation generally associated with waitresses in no way applied to his staff. The Demelinerinnen looked like members of the Order of Penitents – former prostitutes who lived in a convent but worked outside, still wearing nun's clothing.

ESPERANTO MUSEUM

Do you speak Klingon?

Palais Mollard-Clary
Herrengasse 9, 1010 Wien
Open Tuesday to Sunday 10am–6pm, Thursday 10am–9pm
www.onb.ac.at/esperantomuseum.htm
U-Bahn: line U3, Herrengasse station

The internationally recognised Esperanto Museum deals not only with the origin and history of Esperanto but also with other "constructed languages", around 500 of which are featured. Sound recordings help visitors to familiarise themselves with the mysterious "Lingua Ignota" of the 12th-century German mystic Hildegard von Bingen; or to learn Klingon, the fictional language of the aliens in the *Star Trek* TV series.

The Esperanto Association, founded in 1927 by railway inspector Hugo Steiner, set up the museum in the Austrian National Library in Vienna.

During the National Socialist occupation of the Third Reich, Esperanto was banned. The museum's holdings were supposed to be

transported to Berlin to be burned as "unpopular books" but as they were the property of the National Library, this fate was mercifully avoided.

This huge collection is of inestimable value to linguists. It includes 35,000 books and 2,500 magazine titles, as well as handwritten documents, photos and posters.

The recently refurbished Esperanto Museum, once part of the Hofburg Palace collection, has occupied the Baroque palace of Mollard-Clary since 2005.

Esperanto: a language invented to promote peace

In 1887, Polish physician Ludwik Lejzer Zamenhof, under the pseudonym Doktoro Esperanto ("Doctor Hopeful", who later gave his name to the language), published his first project for an international language. Based on regular grammar and phonetic orthography, where all words are spelled as pronounced, Esperanto is easy to learn and use. Not being the official language of any state, its objective is to solve communication problems between people with different mother tongues. Today, the number of Esperanto speakers is estimated at 2 million people in 120 countries.

Bertha von Suttner and Alfred Hermann Fried, notable pacifists who were awarded the Nobel Peace Prize in 1905 and 1911 respectively, were both committed to this "neutral" language.

TOMB OF PIETRO METASTASIO

"My life was like a dream"

Michaelerkirche crypt
Habsburgergasse 12, 1010 Wien
Guided tours only
www.michaelerkirche.at/content/fuehrungen/0

Contrary to the popular belief among Vienna's Italian community, the poet Pietro Metastasio is not buried in the Minoritenkirche, the church of the Order of Friars Minor (Franciscans) belonging to this community. However, his funerary monument, attributed to Canova's pupil Vincenzo Luccardi of Udine, has stood there since 1855. Metastasio died in 1782 after a long illness, and was actually buried in the Michaelerkirche (Church of St Michael) after a high-ranking funeral. His embalmed body now rests here, in his parish crypt, which can only be visited during guided tours. He is the best-known figure in this vast necropolis. His self-penned epitaph proclaims: "My life was like a dream."

During the renovation of tombs scarred by the depredations of insects, Metastasio's Baroque untreated wood and pewter coffin was restored. Meanwhile, the poet's body lay in a tomb on loan from the City of Vienna. His original coffin was then reinstalled at the front of the vault and can be seen below engravings by Austrian painter Herwig Zens, depicting some of the mummies from St Michael's crypt.

Pietro Metastasio's funerary monument in the Minoritenkirche

This church is also where Vienna's Italian community worship, which is why Metastasio's cenotaph was erected there in 1855. Pope Pius VI stands at the centre of the monument, blessing the dying poet, while alongside are the composers Antonio Salieri, Wolfgang Amadeus Mozart and Joseph Haydn, all three members of the Masonic Lodge of Vienna.

Pietro Antonio Domenico Bonaventura Trapassi, Metastasio's real name, was the son of a Roman grocer. From an early age he began to recite impromptu verses, which led to his discovery and adoption by an Italian jurist in 1709. This erudite man gave the boy the patronymic "Metastasio", which means "transformation". In 1729 he became a poet at the Vienna court of Charles VI and moved into the Grosses Michaelerhaus, near St Michael's Church in the city centre. Joseph Haydn also lived there, in one of the garrets. Metastasio was one of the most eminent figures of the 18th century. His proximity to the imperial court and his longevity – he died at the age of 84 – made him a symbol of his time. For several decades he was librettist for Mozart and Glück, among others, and he became friendly with Farinelli, the celebrated Italian castrato.

"DEATH OF EMPEROR FERDINAND III" WAX SCULPTURE

A spectacular work of art

Treasury, Hofburg, Schweizerhof, 1010 Wien
Open daily except Tuesday, 9am–5.30pm
U-Bahn: line U3, Herrengasse station

Habsburg Emperor Ferdinand III died on 2 April 1657 in Vienna. In keeping with the Baroque tradition of depicting death, the court's wax sculptor Daniel Neuberger represented the sovereign surrounded by nine dancing skeletons. The scene could have come straight out of a Tim Burton movie: in a spectacular setting, the skeletons act as musicians while the deceased rests in a sort of shimmering crypt, sumptuously attired in his black armour and imperial cloak, his crown as halo.

As allegories of the ephemeral nature of life, the skeletons carry out various tasks: one extinguishes torches, another blows soap bubbles, a third leans on an hourglass. A particularly convincing Grim Reaper staggers under the weight of the Habsburgs' imperial insignia such as crown, sceptre, orb and sword.

In reference to eternal life, the inscription *VIVIT* (he lives) appears above the corpse.

Neuberger's great artistry is illustrated not only in the very detailed characterisation of the skeletons but also in the highly realistic portrait of the emperor.

Saxon Ambassador Johann Sebastian Müller saw this fantastic work in the artist's studio in 1660 and described it as follows: "Ferdinand III, more true to life than nature, resting dead with numerous figures signifying mortality, a very scrupulous waxwork."

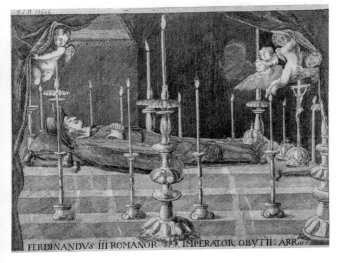

FERDINANDVS III ROMANOR IMPERATOR OBYT II ARR

JESUS'S FEET IN THE MINORITEN-KIRCHE *LAST SUPPER*

The complete Last Supper

Minoritenplatz 2A, 1010 Wien
Accessible during church opening hours
www.minoritenkirche-wien.info/
U-Bahn: line U3, Herrengasse station

One of the world's best-known paintings, Leonardo da Vinci's *Last Supper* in the refectory of the Dominican Convent of Santa Maria delle Grazie in Milan (Italy), is no longer quite complete. At some point, a door has been added in the wall below, just at the point where Jesus's feet would be visible under the table.

To see the entire work, there's only one solution: visit the Minoritenkirche in Vienna, which has a remarkable copy with the same dimensions as the original.

Including the frame, the work measures 4.47 by 9.18 metres and weighs 20 tonnes. It is a mosaic in 12 sections, each made from 10,000 pieces.

French Emperor Napoleon Bonaparte is said to have given orders for the Milan mural to be dismantled and transferred to Paris in 1805. That plan failed, so he commissioned a copy from the artist Giacomo Raffaelli, a native of Rome. The monumental artwork wasn't finished until 1814, by which time Napoleon was in exile. His father-in-law, Holy Roman Emperor Franz II, inherited it. Finding it too large for the Belvedere where he would have liked to display it, Franz offered it to the Italian community of the Minimes.

It was placed on an end wall exactly like the Milanese original, illuminated by the windows to the left so that the group of Apostles is lit from the front, centred on the head of Jesus.

According to respected art historians, the colours of the Vienna copy are also very close to those of the 15th-century *Last Supper*.

STADTPALAIS LIECHTENSTEIN

A Viennese hall of mirrors

Bankgasse 9, 1010 Wien
Individual or group guided tours on request (see website)
www.palaisliechtenstein.com/de/stadtpalais.html
U-Bahn: line U3, Herrengasse station; Tram: 1 /71, Rathausplatz / Burgtheater
stop

"There's nothing like it in the world," said Viennese architect Manfred Wehdorn at the reopening of the Liechtenstein City Palace after its renovation in 2013.

Wehdorn had led the restoration work on this architectural gem, which had been terribly damaged after a plane crashed into the roof in 1945. Superficially rebuilt after the war, it was in danger of falling into complete ruin before the decision to restore it was finally taken in 2008.

The palace was built as a town residence for the influential Liechtenstein royal family in 1691 and converted in 1847, when it acquired its neo-Rococo style. The renovation essentially concerns this period. Below the Baroque stucco ceilings are magnificent interiors decorated with over a kilo of gold leaf. To reproduce the various richly coloured silk hangings, a loom with more than 20,000 warp threads was required.

Now the technical skills from before the Vormärz period could be used once again: the doors of the grand ballroom were raised, while others (decorated in white and gold on one side and with a mirror on the other) pivot. In a few moments, the room can be transformed into a sublime mirrored gallery to compete with Versailles. Original furniture as well as grandiose chandeliers with drifting cherubs complete the effect.

The palace tour (by appointment only) allows you to discover the princely universe as well as an excellent collection of paintings from the classical and Biedermeier periods, uncommon in Vienna. Masterpieces by Friedrich von Amerling, Friedrich Gauermann and Ferdinand Georg Waldmüller complete the show. Social critic Josef Danhauser's moralising painting *Die Testamentseröffnung* (Reading the Will) is also among the works on display.

The palace has recently acquired *A Nubian* (1875/76), a fine oil painting by Hans Makart. A full-length portrait of Caroline von Liechtenstein (1768–1831) as Iris, messenger of the gods, perfectly illustrates the classical style. It was painted by Élisabeth Vigée Le Brun, none other than the famous portraitist at the court of Marie-Antoinette.

Some of the rooms can be hired for functions.

PLASTER STATUES IN THE HOFBURG CELLAR

Mozart in the wine cellar

Hofburg, Leopoldinischer Trakt, 1010 Wien
Open only on special occasions such as Heritage Day, or by appointment
www.hofburg-wien.at/sitemap/kontakt.html
www.tagdesdenkmals.at

The Leopold Wing of the Hofburg imperial palace complex owes its name to Emperor Leopold I, who had it built between 1660 and 1666. After suffering severe damage in a fire in 1668, it was refurbished in its present form during the reign of Maria Theresa. This wing is built over three floors of vaulted cellars, where the court wine, champagne, spirits and liqueurs were stored. The first basement contains a wine vat with a capacity of 70,000 litres. Its contents were not intended for the emperor, who drank only what was stored in the third basement – the coolest. The immense vat was constantly filled from above, and the tepid mixture was destined for the thirsty court servants.

Since the 1950s, the wine cellar has housed an unusual museum with a remarkable collection of plaster models, providentially discovered while the palace boiler was being repaired. The statues, friezes and architectural details, once piled up unceremoniously, have now been restored. There are around 500 models of sovereigns, poets, musicians and intellectuals, as well as original details from the Ringstrasse buildings, including the Burgtheater. At the time these grand buildings were going up it was customary to show a client plaster models before commissioning a work: when approved, it could then be carved in stone or cast in bronze.

Some works by artists such as Rudolf Weyr, Caspar von Zumbusch and Stefan Schwartz did not find favour with the emperor, so were relegated to the cellar. These include a monument to the glory of Maria

Theresa, two groups for fountains designed for the Hofburg, Franz Joseph and Sisi, a bust of Goethe and a statue of Mozart that was originally intended for a Japanese town.

As found in other crypts, a sign around the neck of some of the plaster figures bears the name of their famous creator, while other figures, wrapped in plastic film, cast strange shadows on the walls.

The two other basements in the Leopold Wing now stand empty. There has been no wine in the cellars since 1918, when the last remaining barrels were sold at auction in aid of disabled war veterans.

"LANCE OF LONGINUS"

The lance that pierced the side of Jesus on the Cross?

Treasury, Hofburg, Schweizerhof, 1010 Wien
Open daily (except Tuesday), 9am–5.30pm
U-Bahn: line U3, Herrengasse station

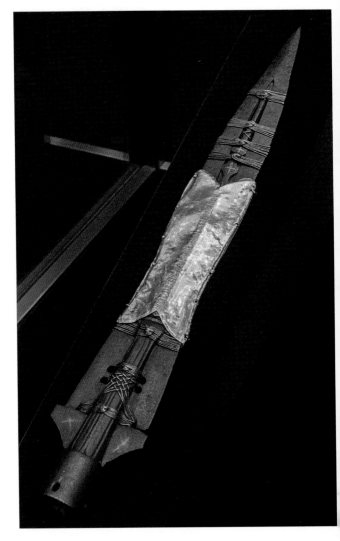

Displayed as a secular object in the Hofburg Treasury, the Lance of Longinus, sometimes also called the Holy Lance or Holy Spear, is linked to one of the greatest secrets of European history.

The words *lancea* and *clavus domini* ("lance" and "nail of the Lord") on the thin sheet of gold enclosing the blade have long suggested that this was the spear with which the Roman legionary Longinus pierced the right side of Jesus on the Cross (a medieval inventory referred to the artefact as the "Spear of God"). But, in fact, this 50.7-centimetre weapon was probably made north of the Alps during the first half of the 8th century.

What is not known is *when* a metal nail, allegedly from the Cross, was driven into the steel lance. This must have happened before AD 926, for at that time the artefact, including the nail, was already in the possession of Emperor Henry I of Germany, founder of the Saxon dynasty. The Ottonians (Saxon kings of Germany, named after Otto I the Great) took this so-called miraculous relic with them on their military conquests.

In the 10th century the lance broke, weakened by the addition of the nail. Otto III had it repaired, Holy Roman Emperor Henry IV had its case covered with silver and Karl IV had it covered with gold in the 14th century. Fortunately, the sovereigns didn't fail to leave an official record of their pious actions, so they are now well documented.

Probably in the Middle Ages, part of the nail disappeared: the groove on the lance is one-third longer than the existing nail.

As part of the crown jewels, the Holy Lance was preserved in Nuremberg from the Middle Ages. In 1796, it had to be sheltered from the advancing French troops and was brought first to Regensburg (Ratisbon) in south-east Germany, then to Vienna in 1800. At the end of the Germanic Holy Roman Empire in 1806, the insignia remained in Vienna until the annexation of Austria in 1938.

It is said that when Adolf Hitler had the lance taken to Nuremberg, along with other artefacts, it was the only piece that mattered to him. Whether the medieval relic had a special significance for him or for Heinrich Himmler, the SS Reichsführer, is controversial. What is certain, however, is that the lance and the other pieces were brought back to Vienna by the Allies in 1946. Archaeological analyses have confirmed their authenticity.

For more on the history of holy relics, see the following double-page spread.

Several other places traditionally harbour "the true Lance of Longinus": Etchmiadzin in Armenia, St Peter's in Rome, etc.

The cult of Christian relics

Although rather neglected these days, with their devoted following

greatly diminished in numbers, saints' relics had extraordinary success from the Middle Ages onwards. Their presence today in numerous churches across Europe is a reminder of those exceptional times.

The cult of Christian relics goes back to the beginning of Christianity, to the deaths of the early martyrs and the creation of the first saints. The function of these relics was threefold: they bore witness to the example of a righteous and virtuous life to be copied or followed; they possessed a spiritual energy and power that could even work miracles (it was believed that the miraculous powers of the saints themselves was retained by their relics); and over time, with the rise of the contested practice of granting indulgences, relics bestowed indulgences on those who possessed them.

As demand dictated supply, it was not long before unscrupulous parties were competing to invent their own relics, aided in their task by the Church which, for political reasons, canonised a great number of undeserving individuals (see opposite). Over-production went to absurd extremes: if one accepted the authenticity of all their relics, Mary Magdalene would have had six bodies, and St Biagio a hundred arms.

These excesses, of course, raised suspicions and the popularity of relics gradually waned, although many people still believe that the true relic of a saint possesses spiritual power. How else can one explain the numerous pilgrimages in the footsteps of Father Pio throughout Italy? There are around 50,000 relics scattered around Europe, from some 5,000 saints.

Note that most of the world's other religions also worship relics, or used to do so.

21,441 relics for 39,924,120 years of indulgences!

The greatest collector of relics was Frederick III of Saxony (1463-1525), who procured 21,441 of them in all, 42 of which were fully preserved bodies of saints. Based on this unique collection, he calculated that he had amassed a grand total of 39,924,120 years and 220 days of indulgences! However, under the influence of Luther, who opposed indulgences, he abandoned the cult of relics in 1523.

When saints are not so holy: Saint George, Saint Christopher, and Saint Philomena struck from the list...

From the Middle Ages onwards, the pursuit of relics continued, as did their falsification. Not only relics were fabricated, however. Sometimes, even the saints themselves were a fabrication. Recently – an event that passed almost without comment – the Church purged Saint George, Saint Christopher and Saint Philomena from its calendar, the very existence of all three now being in doubt.

The totally abusive canonisation of certain real personalities also took place, allowing the objects connected with them to feed the market for saintly relics.

For diplomatic reasons linked to the Counter-Reformation of the 16th century, canonisation was often based on political rather than religious or moral criteria. As a result of this *Realpolitik*, many rulers of the time were thus sanctified in a bid to ensure their subjects' allegiance to the Roman Catholic Church, then under pressure from the Protestant movement. Saint Stanislas of Poland, Saint Casimir of Lithuania, Saint Brigitte of Sweden, Saint Stephen of Hungary, Saint Margaret of Scotland, Saint Elizabeth of Portugal, Saint Wenceslas of Bohemia ... The list is long, indeed.

Relics of the feathers of the Archangel Michael, the breath of Jesus, and even the starlight that guided the three Wise Men!

Leaving no stone unturned in their efforts to make money at the expense of the most naive believers, relic merchants showed unparalleled imagination in their quest for sacred paraphernalia and invented some fascinating objects, such as the horns of Moses or the feathers of the Archangel Michael, recorded as having been on sale at Mont-Saint-Michel in 1784.

The most highly prized relics were of course those of Christ. Unfortunately for relic hunters, as Christ had ascended to Heaven, his body was by definition no longer on Earth. Imagination again came to the rescue in the form of the quite extraordinary relic of the breath of Jesus (!) which was preserved in Wittenberg cathedral, Germany, in a glass phial.

The remains of Christ's foreskin, recuperated after his circumcision seven days after birth, and of his umbilical cord (!) were preserved at Latran, Rome while bread from the Last Supper was kept at Gaming, Austria. Certain medieval texts lost to us today even spoke of the relic of the rays of the star that guided the Wise Men, also preserved at Latran.

HABSBURG HEARTS AND TONGUES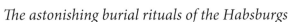

The astonishing burial rituals of the Habsburgs

Loretokapelle
Augustinerkirche, Augustinerstrasse 3, 1010 Wien
Guided tours only (see website)
http://augustinerkirche.augustiner.at/

The Loreto Chapel in the Church of the Augustinian Friars dates from the time of Empress Eleonora Gonzaga (Ferdinand II's second wife) who, in 1624, had this private court chapel built to the dimensions of the original shrine of our Lady of Loreto in Italy. You can book a visit to the chapel, which was refurbished in 1802 with the addition of a heavy wrought-iron door to the right of the main altar. A small window reveals the "Heart Crypt" containing 54 silver urns that preserve the hearts of Habsburg rulers, arranged in wall niches, in chronological order of death. The only golden vase is that of Emperor Matthias. The great urn on the right contains the hearts of Maria Theresa and her husband, Franz I of Austria. Another urn bears the colours of France: it contains the heart of Napoleon's son, the Duke of Reichstadt, which the Nazis "forgot" in 1940 when his remains were transferred to Paris.

The last embalming of a heart took place in 1878, on the death of Archduke Franz Karl Joseph, father of Franz Joseph.

For a long while, the Habsburg burial ritual was carried out in three stages. First, the intestines were removed at autopsy. Then the heart and tongue were placed in a silver chalice and preserved in the Loreto Chapel. Finally, the embalmed entrails, and sometimes also the eyes and brain, were displayed in the Stephansdom crypt, where the metal urns can still be seen today. The body was then filled with beeswax, deposited in its coffin and finally lowered into the Kaisergruft (imperial crypt) of the Capuchin Church.

The origin of this complex ceremonial is unclear, but it seems to be closer to that of ancient Egypt. Richard the Lionheart (1157–99) and Frederick Barbarossa (1122–90) had had their organs buried in different

places. The Habsburg ritual was established by Ferdinand III (1608–57), who decreed that the hearts and tongues of family members would be buried in the Augustinian Church. However, the hearts of the last emperor and his wife, Charles I and Zita, lie in the ancient mausoleum of the imperial family at Muri Abbey in Switzerland, near Habsburg Castle. The heart of Otto de Habsburg, who died in 2011, was transferred to the Hungarian cloister of Pannonhalma, where he had been brought up by the monks.

Emperor Franz Joseph (died 1916) refused to be subjected to a rite that he considered outdated. His body, embalmed and entire, rests in the imperial crypt.

CENOTAPH OF ARCHDUCHESS MARIA CHRISTINA

A pyramid for Mimi

Augustinerkirche
Augustinerstrasse 3, 1010 Wien
Open daily 7am–6pm

The Augustinerkirche (Church of the Augustinian Friars) used to be the Habsburgs' parish church. On the right of the nave is a pyramidal cenotaph ("empty tomb") in memory of Archduchess Maria Christina, who died in 1798 at the age of 56. Like almost all members of the Habsburg family, the favourite daughter of Maria Theresa and Franz 1 (Francis Stephen of Lorraine) was buried in the imperial crypt of the Kapuzinerkirche (Capuchin Church).

This 5-metre high cenotaph of Carrara marble is the work of Italian neoclassical sculptor Antonio Canova. It was commissioned by Prince Albert of Saxony, Duke of Teschen, the widower of "Mimi", as Maria Christina was affectionately known to her family. Albert had indeed had the rare privilege of concluding a love match with the emperor's daughter. Only Mimi obtained this privilege from Maria Theresa – her brothers and sisters had to settle for political unions favourable to the dynasty or were consigned to a monastery.

The terror of death usually present in the Baroque style has no place here. On the contrary, classical light and beauty predominate.

The inscription *UXORI OPTIMAE ALBERTUS* ("Albert to the best of wives") is seen above the entrance.

Virtue, dressed in flowing Greek-style robes, is crossing the threshold of the pyramid, symbol of death, a funerary urn in her hand. She is flanked by two young girls carrying torches. The procession continues with Charity, supporting a blind old man by the arm. A lion, representing power, lies to the right of the entrance. On the pediment of the pyramid, two spirits display a portrait of the shrine's owner, encircled by an *ouroboros* (symbol of resurrection and divine illumination, see following double page).

Although Antonio Canova originally intended the pyramid design for the tomb of Titian in Venice, in the absence of a firm order the artist welcomed Prince Albert's desire to erect a monument to his wife. Canova's pupils later used a similar design for the sculptor's own tomb in Venice. A medallion encircled by an *ouroboros* also surmounts the entrance to his sepulchre in the famous Frari basilica (see *Secret Venice* in this series of guides).

GEORGSKAPELLE, AUGUSTINERKIRCHE

Heirs of the Knights Templar

Augustinerstrasse 3, 1010 Wien
Open during Easter and Christmas markets held in the chapel
Market dates: http://augustinerkirche.augustiner.at/events-calendar/

St George's Chapel, which used to be totally independent of the Church of the Augustinian Friars and accessible only by a corridor from the Hofburg, can now be entered by the right nave of the church. It was once a meeting place for members of the Order of Knights of St George.

The Order, founded by Duke Otto IV, "the Merry", was in a way the heir to the Knights Templar in Austria, banned in 1312. The chapel was consecrated in 1341.

The chapel is unusual in having two naves and two apses. The aristocratic brotherhood known as the Societas Templois gathered here and administered the abundant possessions of the Templars.

A discreet plaque on the floor recalls the life of Gerard van Swieten (died 1772), a Freemason who was Maria Theresa's personal physician and decided to be buried here. For some, this plaque is a reminder of the close link between the Templars, their successors the Knights of St George, and the 18th-century Freemasons.

St George's was used as a funerary chapel as early as the 16th century. The empty tomb in the centre was designed by Franz Anton Zauner for Leopold II, one of the 18th-century reformist rulers known as the "enlightened despots". In the end, he was buried in the imperial crypt of the Capuchin Church.

Josefstadt, Alsergrund

LEHERB'S *KONTINENTE* MOSAIC ①

"Experts bow before it. Nobody thought such a thing was possible."

Former Wirtschaftsuniversität Wien
Augasse 2–6, 1090 Wien
Open Monday to Friday 10am–4pm
U-Bahn: line U4, Spittelau station; Tram: D / 33, Liechtenwerder Platz stop

Born Helmut Leherbauer in Vienna, "Maître Leherb" (1933–97) was a leading representative of the Vienna School of Fantastic Realism, an artistic movement close to Surrealism.

His faience (glazed ceramic mosaic) entitled *Kontinente (The Continents)* is the greatest work of its kind produced in Europe during the 20th century. He created it in Faenza, the Italian city where this technique was developed. However, working with ceramic dust seriously damaged his health and he finally succumbed. He had also spent a year on a windswept scaffold and was suffering from an incurable kidney disease.

Leherb's major work, made up of more than 3,500 ceramic tiles forming 8 x 8 metre frescoes, decorates the six walls of what was the Vienna University of Economics atrium between 1982 and 2013. The inhabitants of all four continents, as well as their flora and fauna and all kinds of human activity, are represented.

The North and South Poles are also depicted in shades of steel blue. American materialism is embodied in a bottle of Coca-Cola, Marilyn Monroe and a skyscraper forest, while a broken telephone symbolises the linguistic diversity of Africa. The master's reaction during the presentation of his monumental work in 1982? "Experts bow before it. Nobody thought such a thing was possible."

MARINE LIFE FROM WERKSTATT BLASCHKA

The glass menagerie

Zoological Collection of the University of Vienna, Department of Theoretical Biology
Biozentrum, Althanstrasse 14, 1090 Wien
Visits by appointment
Tel: +43 (0)1 4277 567 07
Email: hans.leo.nemeschkal@univie.ac.at

Jellyfish, corals, microscopic protozoa, octopus ... the spectacular and little-known Blaschka collection of the University of Vienna contains 146 anatomically precise glass models of marine species. This is the second-largest collection of such models in the world, after that of Harvard University (United States). It came about through a purchase by the former director of the University of Vienna's Institute of Zoology and Comparative Anatomy, Carl Claus (1835–99).

These remarkable glass pieces were created between 1863 and 1890 by Leopold Blaschka and his son Rudolf from Bohemia – both glass-blowers, artists and naturalists.

Although Leopold began his career by making glass eyes for taxidermists, he turned out to have a very good business sense, selling his glass creations by catalogue and presenting them as "ornaments for elegant interiors" and "marine aquariums". A customer once asked him to make a glass sea anemone, as they were so ephemeral.

There were scarcely any conservation methods for fragile marine life at that time, so models from the Blaschka workshop were soon prized by schools and universities for demonstration and study purposes. They were sent around the world.

In just 17 years, the two artists made thousands of pieces. However, because of their great fragility, only a few have survived. Blaschka models were particularly prized in Britain and America for their aesthetic qualities. Today, the Harvard collection attracts almost 200,000 visitors a year.

SCHUBERT'S ORGAN

Schubert's neighbourhood

Lichtental parish church
Marktgasse 40, 1090 Wien
Open during services and by appointment
www.schubertkirche.at

On the staircase at the Schubertkirche (Schubert Church) rectory, the composer's original organ console stands behind a glass partition.

Franz Schubert (1797–1828) lived at Lichtental, in the picturesque 9th district. Baptised in the parish church in 1797, the year of its centenary, he went on to compose and conduct a celebration Mass at only 17 years of age. Some of his compositions were performed in the district church, while other more modest efforts were intended for his parish.

The suburb of Lichtental had grown up about a century earlier. As there was then no place of worship, Masses were celebrated in the local brewery. The design of the present church is attributed to Lucas von Hildebrandt and Andrea Pozzo, the main work having been inaugurated with a High Mass in 1714.

However, it was not until 1730 that the 14 Auxiliary Saints could be consecrated. Veneration of these "Holy Helpers" of Roman Catholicism had been especially widespread in southern Germany since the 14th century, particularly for their intercession during epidemics and contagious diseases. Around 1713–14 Lichtental suffered its last epidemic of plague, causing the death of thousands of people.

The large altarpiece that can still be seen today was designed by Franz Anton Zoller in 1776 for a church that had already been enlarged because the 1730 construction could no longer accommodate the growing population. The Holy Trinity representing Mary and St Anne

figures above the Auxiliary Saints.

The North Tower remained unfinished for a long time. It was finally completed in 1827, at the same time as the classical façade.

Originally, parishioners were buried in Währing Cemetery (now Schubertpark). Because of the plague, they were given a separate burial site in 1713 between Nussdorfer Strasse, Nussgasse, Vereinsstiege and Rufgasse, which is no longer there.

The Schubert Society regularly organises concerts and guided tours of the church tower.

DEPARTMENT FÜR PHARMAKOGNOSIE MUSEUM

Mumia vera aegyptica

Universität Wien
Althanstrasse 14, 1090 Wien
Guided tours by appointment: Email liselotte.krenn@univie.ac.at
Tram: D / 1 / 33, Althanstrasse stop

Visits to the Department of Pharmacognosy at the University of Vienna must be booked. The museum collections include over 18,000 medicinal drugs of animal and plant origin as well as 2,000 pharmaceutical objects. Most of the items were transferred in 1977 from the former imperial pharmacy, including acquisitions from the Far East and South America brought home between 1857 and 1859 on the imperial frigate *Novara* by Franz Joseph's younger brother Maximilian, rear admiral in the Austrian navy and future Emperor of Mexico.

The collections also include glass bottles, medical bags and transport crates marked with the Maltese cross, which were used to treat wounded soldiers during the First World War.

There are several showcases containing mummified heads and other body parts. They were collected in the late 19th century by Czech explorer Emil Holub during his four journeys to various parts of Africa.

He donated them to the Apothecary Employees' Association, founded in 1889, of which he was an honorary member. One head of a mummy is particularly distinctive in that its wide-open mouth is filled with a sticky material. The outside of the skull is covered with black bitumen, which was lavishly applied (mainly during the Ptolemaic period) for better conservation of the bodies.

"Mummy powder" and fragments of corpses to prepare medicines ...

It would be very unusual to have a pharmaceutical museum without mummies: apothecaries were using mummy powder and fragments of corpses to prepare medicines, ointments or potions as early as the late 14th century. The high demand for *mumia vera* (true mummy) in the late Middle Ages – not in the 19th century, as is sometimes believed – led to the trafficking of countless forgeries. Until the early 20th century, mummies were imported into Europe, whole or in fragments, for medicinal purposes. Incidentally, the word "mummy" comes from the Arabic *mumiyah*, which means bitumen.

TOMB OF SABBATAI SCHEFTEL ⑤

The miraculous rabbi

Jüdischer Friedhof, Seegasse 9–11, 1090 Wien
Open Monday to Friday 7am–3pm (access via Haus Rossau retirement home)

Scheftel, the descendant of an eminent Viennese family, was also known as Sabbatai Horowitz. He died on 9 April 1660. His grave in the Jewish Cemetery on Seegasse is No. 106, easy to find towards the back of the cemetery. The heaps of gravel on the tomb testify to the number of visitors who place their supplications in a tin box in front of the grave.

Rabbi Scheftel lived in Prague and then Poznań (Poland) before settling in Vienna around 1655, where he ran a Talmudic school and wrote several mystical treatises. Because of his status as an enlightened scholar, some revered him as a miracle worker. Believers still come today to bow before his grave in this 500-year-old Jewish Cemetery. The epitaph on his headstone reads: "I had searched below the roses, and here before me is a vine, whose buds and leaves invite a cure."

Under the Third Reich, members of the Jewish community moved a number of headstones to the Central Cemetery to protect them from desecration. In 1981, 250 of these were returned to the Seegasse site and reinstated.

Two of the tombs are those of major historical figures: banker Samuel Oppenheimer (died 1703), one of the chief financiers of the Habsburgs; and Chief Rabbi Samson Wertheimer (died 1724), who also supported the imperial family. Wertheimer's house in Eisenstadt is now the Austrian Jewish Museum.

A fish that converted

Among all the other tombstone art is an eye-catching fish sculpture. According to Jewish folklore, a fish buried here adopted their religion at the very moment it was killed.

PEREGRINI-KAPELLE

Saint of the Green Party

Servitengasse 9, 1090 Wien
Visits by appointment and around 1 May
www.rossau.at/peregrin

A few years ago, St Peregrine was shown on the Vienna Greens' website as the forerunner of the ecological movement, proof of his immutable popularity down the centuries. He is the most revered saint of the Servites (Order of the Servants of Mary).

His celebrity is longstanding – in the 18th century, Servite priests were already distributing *Peregrinikipferl* (Peregrine's croissants) to poor children.

The monk Peregrinus Pellegrino Latiosus, to give him his full name, lived in the 14th century. His name means "pilgrim", but also "walker". That's why Peregrine is the patron saint of cripples, who of course may not be able to get around on foot – to the dismay of the Greens.

The Church of the Servites of Vienna, in which Italian nobleman Ottavio Piccolomini is also buried (on the left under the Pietà), was completed in 1670. The Peregrine Chapel was added in 1727, in tribute

to the many miracles attributed to the saint. A life-size wooden sculpture depicts him in his sixties as he was healed from cancer of the leg. As he prayed before a fresco of the Crucifixion, he seemed to see Jesus descend from the cross to touch his leg. He lived another 20 years and died in 1345. His body rests in a glass coffin in his native village of Forlì in northern Italy. On 1 May, the saint's feast day, a fragment of bone is displayed in a monstrance (sacred vessel for transporting the host or relics) in the Peregrine Chapel. The chapel was completely restored in 2014.

Peregrine's croissants are still around. Sold at the end of April and beginning of May in the church square, they are greatly appreciated for their healing qualities.

GARTENPALAIS LIECHTENSTEIN ⑦

The largest Baroque-style secular hall in Vienna

Fürstengasse 1, 1090 Wien
Garden open daily 7am–8.30pm
Palace open during guided tours and for special events
www.palaisliechtenstein.com/de/gartenpalais.html
Tram: D / 1, Bauernfeldplatz stop

In 1687, Prince Johann Adam Andreas I von Liechtenstein bought a plot of land in Rossau (then outside the city walls) and by 1700 had had a "Garden Palace" built in the middle of it. Wanting his house to resemble an Italian palazzo – a palatial urban villa in the Roman style – he commissioned the work from architect Domenico Martinelli of Lucca.

Nowadays, although the Baroque garden is open to the public every day, the magnificent palace can only be visited during pre-booked guided tours or special events.

The frescoes on the ground floor and in the monumental stairwells are by Johann Michael Rottmayr from Salzburg. *The Admittance of Military Genius to Olympus* (east stairway) and *Battle of the Gods and the Giants* (west stairway) were uncovered during recent renovation work and have been painstakingly restored. The gigantic Hercules Hall ceiling fresco of *The Admittance of Hercules to Olympus* was painted by the 17th-century Baroque master painter and architect Andrea Pozzo while at the height of his creative powers.

The beautiful Italian-style stucco sculptures in the palace and garden, all executed by Venice-born Giovanni Giuliani, merit a long stroll around the park.

The guided tour also takes in some remarkable Rubens paintings, as well as major works by Van Dyck, Lucas Cranach, Raphael and Rembrandt. There is also a large collection of bronzes and porcelain objects. Last but not least, a unique 18th-century French ceremonial coach stands in the *Sala Terrena* on the ground floor.

The first floor houses Messerschmidt's original statue of Sarepta's widow, a copy of which has been at Savoysches Damenstift since 1987.

The centrepiece of the palace is undoubtedly the "Badminton Cabinet", one of the most expensive pieces of furniture in the world. This ebony and bronze cabinet was completed by Florentine craftsmen in 1732. The *pietra dura* inlaid mosaics depicting birds and flowers are of lapis lazuli, jasper, amethyst and quartz. The first owner of this unique masterpiece was an Englishman, Henry Somerset, 3rd Duke of Beaufort, who named it after his country seat of Badminton House.

In the latter half of the 20th century, the palace premises were used as a second exhibition building by the Museum of the Twentieth Century (later the 20s House). Its works are now on display in the Modern Art building of MuseumsQuartier Wien cultural centre. During the Nazi era, the whole collection was transferred to Vaduz, capital of Liechtenstein. The Liechtenstein museum returned to its original site in 2004, but since 2012 the owners have concentrated on hiring out this exceptional venue. Gala dinners, conferences, concerts and weddings are regularly held there.

ST JOHANNES NEPOMUK KAPPELLE ⑧

Otto Wagner's work in miniature

Währinger Gürtel, U-Bahn Bogen 115–116, near Volksoper, 1090 Wien
Open for Mass and special events
www.johanneskapelle.at/termine.asp
U-Bahn: line U6, Währinger Strasse-Volksoper station

Many Viennese are unaware of the existence of a chapel designed by the great Otto Wagner, surrounded as it is by the swirling traffic on the Vienna Gürtel (Beltway or ring road).

One of the Linienwall chapels built at the city gates for travellers and dedicated to St John of Nepomuk (which dates back to 1740, as noted on the marble plaque in the sacristy) had to be removed during the construction of the metropolitan railway in 1893. A replacement chapel, designed by Wagner on the plan of a Greek cross, was built between 1895 and 1897. The funds came from an association headed by Princess Fanny Liechtenstein, which is why her family's coat of arms is emblazoned on the high altar above the figure of John of Nepomuk. The altarpieces are in neo-Renaissance style.

This chapel with its characteristic dome, inaugurated on 19 November 1897, was Wagner's second religious building – some 25 years earlier, he had designed the Budapest synagogue.

The building was completely renovated in 2000 and acquired a new organ the following year – the previous one had been out of order since 1986. Concerts and lectures are now regularly held there.

The chapel is thought to be the model for the Kirche am Steinhof (also known as the Church of St Leopold), built 10 years later on the outskirts of Vienna.

The hill on which this world-famous Art Nouveau monument stands has been sarcastically dubbed the "Lemoniberg" (Lemon Mountain) because of its dome shaped like half a lemon.

WILHELM EXNER HALL

⑨

A rare Secessionist-style hall

Michelbeuern fashion school - Severingasse 9, 1090 Wien
Visits by appointment
www.hlmw9.at/de/quiclinks/kontakt.html
Tram: 5 / 38 / 40 / 41, Spitalgasse stop

Wilhelm Exner Hall, open to the public only by appointment, is a Secessionist-style meeting room located in Vienna's Michelbeuern fashion school. Despite appearances, the designer was not Josef Hoffmann but one of his fellow architects, Heinrich Kathrein (albeit with Hoffmann's support), who worked on the project from 1911 to 1913.

As many of Hoffmann's buildings have since been converted or demolished, this now-restored hall has a unique value today.

Kathrein's interior design style used typical Hoffmann devices such as breaking up surfaces into even pieces and the diamond as a decorative motif. The black-etched painted wood with white joints blends harmoniously into the overall design, as do the carefully selected upholstery fabrics and lighting fixtures.

The building that houses Wilhelm Exner Hall is a former machine shop built for the Sigl'schen locomotive factory in 1866. The workshop later produced light bulbs, before becoming a bureau for the development of small enterprises managed by Exner. Since 1979, it has been a fashion school.

Railway engineer Wilhelm Exner (1840–1931), after whom the hall is named, was little known even in Vienna. Nevertheless, he was one of the great figures from the *Gründerzeit* (Founders' era, 1850–1914). He set up the Museum of Technology and Industry (the present WUK, or Werkstätten- und Kulturhaus),

forerunner of the Technical Museum, which was very dear to his heart. He provided the template for the modern vocational school in Austria and was one of the founders of the Chamber of Labour. In his time he was also a driving force behind the 140-year-old TÜV Austria (Technischer Überwachungs-Verein / Technical Inspection Association), successor to the 1872 Mutual Steam Boiler Inspection and Insurance Society. Last but not least, he was one of the promoters of Türkenschanz Park, and welcomed the emperor in person when it opened in 1888.

Wilhelm-Exner-Gasse starts at the corner of the WUK building, also in the 9th district. The street was named in Exner's honour in 1930, on the occasion of his 90th birthday.

ARNE-CARLSSON-PARK BUNKER ⑩

Shelter for mothers and children

Junction of Spitalgasse / Währinger Strasse, 1090 Wien
Guided tours by appointment
Tel: 0676 611 92 32 / 0699 196 70 332
www.befreiungsmuseumwien.at
Tram: 5 / 38 / 40 / 41, Spitalgasse stop

Camouflaged under heavy graffiti in bright colours, the air-raid shelter in Arne-Carlsson-Park has almost been forgotten. Yet during a guided tour lasting about an hour, the old units, airlocks and multiple inscriptions still reveal the oppressive atmosphere of the place.

Viennese residents who lived through the war and who knew this bunker well explore their memories at sessions reserved for children and adolescents. A woman born in 1941 shows the doll she hugged to herself in the shelter, trembling at the sound of the planes.

A new permanent exhibition ("April 1945 to Liberation") opened in 2015 in the "In Memorial Bunker", run by the Alsergrund District Museum. Emphasis is on the final days before Vienna was liberated from National Socialism. Photographs, films and period objects illustrate those April days experienced in very different ways by the people of the time. The history of Austria since 1918, focusing on the years of Austrofascism (authoritarian rule established in the 1934 Constitution) and Nazism (after Hitler's annexation of Austria in 1938), is briefly covered.

This shelter, built in 1940–41, had to be completely self-sufficient, so there was an emergency generator. Originally designed to accommodate 300 people in 40 small rooms, the shelter actually took in as many as 500 at a time. The areas for women with children were eventually dropped to accommodate more people. Some Vienna residents still hold a birth certificate stating that they were "born in the bunker" – which had a first-aid room because of its proximity to Vienna General Hospital. By the end of the war, only women and children still had the right to use the shelter.

In recent years, students from local schools have decorated "spaces for reflection" dedicated to Anne Frank and Erich Fried.

The park is named after Arne Carlsson, the director of a Swedish organisation responsible for providing food to the Viennese population after 1945..

The condition of the shelter led to its closure in 2008, but the district president decided to upgrade it to commemorate the atrocities of National Socialism and the Second World War. It is now run by local historians.

HEIMITO VON DODERER'S STUDY

Poetry on the drawing board

Alsergrund Bezirksmuseum (ALSEUM)
Währinger Strasse 43, 1090 Wien
Open Wednesday 11am–1pm and 3pm–5pm, Sunday (except during school holidays) 10am–noon
Tram: 38 / 40 / 41, Sensengasse stop
http://www.bezirksmuseum.at/de/bezirksmuseum_9/veranstaltungen/

In a writer's study, you'd expect to find a desk, chair, shelves, wastebasket, but probably not drawing boards such as those in the workplace of Austrian novelist Heimito von Doderer (1896–1966).

Von Doderer stood them in various places around the room, their presence helping him to organise his ideas. In creating his literary work, he took Beethoven and Schubert's compositional technique as a model. He himself played the cello.

Von Doderer was also quite "sporty". As a child, he took archery lessons, using straw bales. He hand-carved the bows now on display in Alsergrund District Museum. While he was staying in the mountains at Prein an der Rax, Lower Austria, he assiduously practised his archery. Under his full name, Franz Carl Heimito Ritter von Doderer

wrote the major part of his most celebrated work, *Die Strudlhofstiege oder Melzer und die Tiefe des Jahre* (*The Strudlhof Stairs or Melzer and the Depth of the Years*, 1951) in Riegelhof, the family's summer residence. The house features in the novel as "Stangeler'sche Villa". A 72-page newspaper in which the author reported his sports performances is also on display. Von Doderer saw sport as a metaphor for his work: just as the arrow seeks its target, the author is constantly searching for the right words to express himself.

A historian by vocation, Von Doderer spent most of his life in Vienna's 9th district, at No. 50–52 Währinger Strasse. The now famous author died at the age of 70 at Vienna's Rudolfinerhaus Hospital, suffering from late-diagnosed colon cancer.

Fritz Wotruba, considered one of Austria's most prominent 20th-century sculptors, came here to create Von Doderer's funerary mask, which is also displayed in the study. Heimito von Doderer rests in a tomb of honour at Grinzing Cemetery.

Four years after Von Doderer's death, his widow, Maria "Mienzi" Doderer, donated the room and her husband's collection of personal effects to the Alsergrund District Museum, which subsequently arranged the commemorative hall. The couple's daily life was rather unusual: even after their marriage, Mienzi continued to live in her native Bavarian village, while her husband lived in an apartment in Alsergrund. Moreover he had a mistress, the writer Dorothea Zeemann, who was much younger than him (died 1993).

A short walk from the District Museum takes you to the Strudlhofstiege (Strudlhof Stairs), a site of both architectural and literary significance in the neighbourhood where key events in Von Doderer's novel take place.

A sign reminds walkers:

Many things lead us to sadness
While beautiful things are ephemeral.

In the footsteps of the novel Die Strudlhofstiege

Heimito von Doderer spent the last 10 years of his life at No. 50 Währinger Strasse, almost opposite the District Museum. Strudlhofgasse leads to Boltzmanngasse: No. 16 housed the Consular Academy before the Embassy of the United States. Strudlhofstiege, which lent its name to the novel, leads to Liechtensteinstrasse and then via Fürstengasse to Porzellangasse, with at Nos. 44–46 the "Miserowsky twins", No. 48 Melzer's restaurant and No. 51 the General Directorate of the Austrian Tobacco Board. Porzellangasse ends at Julius-Tandler-Platz (formerly Althanplatz), the homes of Mary K. (and the site of her accident), of Siebenschein and of Von Doderer himself. Crossing the parish of Liechtental with its Church of the 14 Auxiliary Saints, you reach a house named "Zum blauen Einhorn" ("Blue Unicorn") at the junction of Lichtentaler Gasse and Liechtensteinstrasse.

At the Alserbachstrasse / Boltzmanngasse junction stood the Zur Flucht nach Ägypten (Escape to Egypt) restaurant and the patisserie was at No. 6. A few steps take you back to the museum.

ZAHNMUSEUM

Rather like a carpenter giving lectures today

Bernhard Gottlieb University Clinic of Dentistry
Josephinum
Währinger Strasse 25a (to the right in the courtyard), 1090 Wien
Open Wednesday and Friday 10am–1pm or by appointment
www.zahnmuseum.at

Dentists as we know them today have only existed since the early 19th century. Previously, people with dental problems were sent to men "with enough strength to pull teeth", as we learn during the tour of Vienna Dental Museum. In other words, barbers, hairdressers and assorted charlatans.

How did the ancient Egyptians treat a broken tooth? What techniques were used by medieval barbers? The museum is buzzing with tales about how to replace a tooth and ingenious ways of relieving pain. There are cauterising irons for root-canal work, examples of early drills and wax casts of rotten teeth, not to mention a splendid 19th-century dentist's chair.

The exhibition also commemorates Georg Carabelli (1787–1842), an eminent Hungarian who pioneered dental surgery in Vienna with "courses for new dentists" at the university. "Rather like a carpenter giving lectures today", explains the guide, himself a dentist. Moriz Heider, one of Carabelli's pupils, set up the Austrian Association of Dentists, which provided full medical training. The centrepiece of the museum is a picture of Heider's investiture. The dental surgeon poses, elegantly dressed in suit and tie, surrounded by pedal-operated drills.

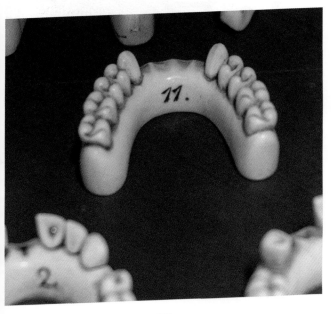

JOSEPHINUM ANATOMICAL MODELS

Chill out

Medical University of Vienna
Währinger Strasse 25, 1090 Wien
Open Wednesday 4pm–6pm, Friday and Saturday 10am–6pm
Special collection of gynaecological interest can only be visited by appointment
in the context of guided tours
www.josephinum.ac.at
Tram: 37 / 38 / 40, Sensengasse stop

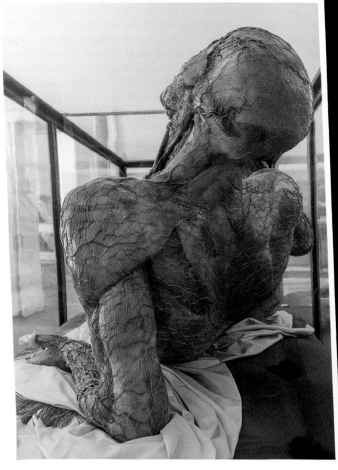

This remarkable collection of 18th-century anatomical wax models from the Medical University of Vienna is housed in six rooms on the first floor of the Josephinum, three of which can be visited during regular opening hours and the others on request.

The models, originally the property of the Academy of Medicine and Surgery founded by Emperor Joseph II, were designed as educational tools as well as public information material. The emperor's health reforms, which focused on more practical training for medical students, were meeting resistance from academics. Inspired by anatomical models that his brother, the future emperor Leopold II, had commissioned in Florence, Joseph hastened to order 1,200 pieces of wax. They left Florence for Vienna on the backs of donkeys, and crossed Europe between 1784 and 1788.

The wax models are now displayed in their original cases made from rosewood and Venetian glass, a treasure trove of medical history on a worldwide scale. Around 1780, about 200 corpses were dissected to create three-dimensional images of human organs and blood vessels. Anatomists, specialists in wax moulding and designers began by modelling the various parts of the body in an inexpensive material. Plaster moulds made from these models were then filled with wax from Ukrainian wild bees, which was resistant to extremes of temperature. A mixture of animal fat and resin was then applied to stabilise the preparation and give the appropriate colours.

Most models in the Josephinum are hollow, and two centuries in a display case mean that they are somewhat fragile. There are sixteen complete bodies, of which the best known is the blonde "Anatomical Venus", complete with lipstick, a double row of pearls and removable organs.

For several centuries, these anatomical tools have played an essential role in the dissemination of medical knowledge and research on the human body. The wax figures are a good example of the close links between medicine, art and science.

Until the 19th century, the fields of anatomy and general medicine had to cope with the very brief shelf life of human tissue. Leonardo da Vinci was the first to model in wax.

The collections of the Endoscopy Museum and the History of Anaesthesia can also be visited on request.

"GUIDO HOLZKNECHT DOOR"

Entrance for clandestine pregnancies

Altes AKH – former Vienna General Hospital
Alser Strasse 2–4, 1090 Wien
Access by Courtyard 7 (Rotenhausgasse)
Tram: 43 / 44, Lange Gasse stop; 38 / 40 / 41, Schwarzspanierstrasse stop

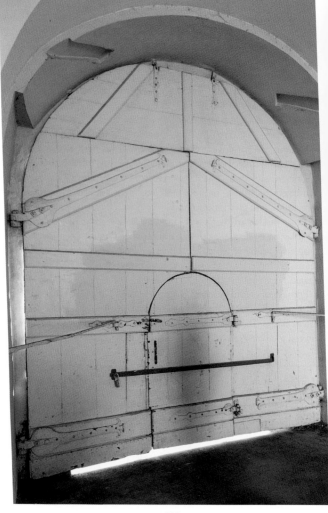

The "Guido Holzknecht door", the back door to the maternity unit of the former General Hospital (Altes AKH – Allgemeines Krankenhaus – today a university campus), is a reminder of the services offered by radiologist Guido Holzknecht (1872–1931), who installed a "baby box" where you could discreetly give up your baby.

In 1784, Emperor Joseph II had the workhouse converted into a general hospital modelled on the Hôtel Dieu hospital in Paris. The east wing housed the obstetric service that also admitted unmarried pregnant women, who could leave their newborn children there. An estimated 700,000 women used this service before the institution was closed in 1908. The babies were then placed in a foster home run by the hospital.

But none of this came cheap. In keeping with the spirit of the Enlightenment, those women who couldn't afford to pay for their care were used in the teaching of gynaecology students.

Wealthy women, on the other hand, enjoyed complete anonymity. They could arrive at the maternity unit with their features concealed by a mask so that they were unrecognisable. They took the "pregnant women's door", always carefully locked and monitored by a porter, who only opened up if someone rang the bell and asked to enter.

What is a foundlings' wheel?

As early as 787, a Milanese priest named Dateo is said to have placed a shell outside his church to collect abandoned babies.

From 1188, the first initiatives to save such infants were organized at Chanoines hospice in Marseille (France), before Pope Innocent III (1160–1216, pontiff from 1198 until his death) institutionalized the practice.

So the doors of convents were equipped with a sort of rotating cradle which made it possible for parents to leave their infant anonymously and without exposing it to the elements. The infant was left in the outside section of the cradle, and then the parent rang a bell so that the nuns could activate the mechanism and bring the child inside.

Abandoned during the 19th century, the system had to be readopted after some twenty years at various places in Europe due to the sharp upturn in the number of infants abandoned.

You can see historic foundling wheels at the Vatican, Pisa and Florence (see the *Secret Tuscany* guide from the same publisher), in Bayonne and in Barcelona (see the *Secret Barcelona* guide).

VIKTOR FRANKL MUSEUM

The museum of the meaning of life, so that visitors can explore their true potential

Mariannengasse 1, 1090 Wien
Open Monday and Friday 1pm–6pm, Saturday 11am–6pm, every first Friday of the month 1pm–8pm
Tram: 43 / 44, Lange Gasse stop

„Nicht im Dass, im Wie des Leidens liegt der Sinn des Leidens."

"The meaning of suffering is not that we suffer but how."

Viktor E. Frankl

Neurologist and psychiatrist Viktor E. Frankl lived at No. 1 Mariannengasse until his death in 1997 at the age of 92. In 2015, on the occasion of the 110th anniversary of his birth, a museum dedicated to the founder of logotherapy and existential analysis opened its doors in his former offices. Over nearly 100 square metres, the museum explores the human quest for meaning: according to Frankl, man is a spiritual being capable of defying all adversities once a sense of purpose is found in life.

Although the museum documents Frankl's life and ideas, its main objective is to provide visitors with more information about their own opportunities and potential.

"Man should not demand something from life; rather, he has a duty to answer the questions that life poses," Frankl explained. As human beings, we discover the meaning of life through "living", "suffering" and "creating". These three fundamental clues to meaning are explored in the main room of the museum, which also has a multimedia library.

In his youth, Frankl was imprisoned in various concentration camps because he was Jewish. His parents, brother and first wife were murdered by the Nazis. He moved into the Mariannengasse apartment when he was freed.

Next to the museum, the Viktor Frankl Zentrum organises courses, seminars, workshops and lectures on Frankl's healing methods and vision. His teachings are used internationally and are constantly being developed.

GRAFFITI IN THE TRINITARIAN CRYPT

Refuge with the Grim Reaper

Minoritenkirche - Alser Strasse 17, 1080 Wien
Open on All Souls' Day (2 November) and certain other occasions
Tel: +43 (0)1 4059 142
http://www.cordeliers.ch/kloster/osterreich/wien/

The Trinitarian crypt of the Minorities Church, open once a year on All Souls' Day, is definitely worth a visit. It was used as a refuge in wartime, and also occasionally taken over by the military. The soldiers left evidence of their passage in the graffiti on the walls, notably a life-size Napoleonic soldier with fur cap and bayonet.

One of the pillars in the crypt has a figure of Death brandishing a scythe. The winged hourglass above his head symbolises the passing of time and the constant approach of the last moment. The image dates from about 1800.

In 1689, a few years after the second Turkish siege, Trinitarian monks acquired land in the Alser district to build the church and the monastery. Following the suppression of their Order by Joseph II in 1783, the buildings were handed over to the Italian community and became the property of the Minor friars (Franciscan monks).

The crypt is roughly the same size as the church nave above. Trinitarian monks as well as various benefactors of their Order were interred in wall niches. In 1809, French soldiers stationed in the basement of the church destroyed the coffins and stole anything of value. Since 1973 the front part of the crypt has again been used for Franciscan burials.

The funeral of Ludwig van Beethoven, who died at his home in the nearby Schwarzspanierstrasse, took place in this church on 27 November 1827. His house has unfortunately not survived.

An inscription on the wall of the Trinitarian crypt (dating from 1 February 1945) goes something like this:
Since the planes up there are droning
We've come to love this crypt!
While the ack-ack guns and bombs are roaring
We'll lie low here, safe from death!
The anti-aircraft security regulations from the Second World War are still displayed, a reminder that Vienna was the target of bombing campaigns towards the end of the conflict. As in the great Turkish sieges, people took refuge in the crypts and subterranean streets of the city.

LORENZ GEDENKSTÄTTE

The bloodless surgeon

Rathausstrasse 21, 1010 Wien
Visits by appointment, contact Wolfgang Riemer
Tel: 0699 1198 8553; Email: wolfgang.riemer@chello.at
Tram: 43, Landesgerichtsstrasse stop

The Adolf and Albert Lorenz Memorial Museum, on the second floor of No. 21 Rathausstrasse, is as important for orthopaedics as No. 19 Berggasse (now the Sigmund Freud Museum) is for psychoanalysis. From 1903 onwards, it was here that Dr Adolf Lorenz (1854–1946) had his practice before leaving it to his son Albert (1885–1970), also an orthopaedic surgeon. Adolf Lorenz is considered to be the founder of modern orthopaedics.

Until 1993 Albert's widow Helga provided remedial gymnastics in the original surgery. She then placed the premises at the disposal of the Adolf Lorenz Association, which planned to convert them into a museum in tribute to the father of orthopaedics.

Today, a bust by Viktor Tilgner stands proudly in the entrance, next to Dr Lorenz's coat. His glasses lie on the desk, next to his pens and his patient records from around the world, as if the professor had just left the room. A cupboard contains reference books that belonged to Lorenz, father and son – Albert worked in the practice from 1924 onwards. The office even has a signed photo of Josephine Baker.

Adolf Lorenz's hands were the favourite subject of American press photographers to illustrate features about Austria's "bloodless surgeon". Yet his hands almost cost him his career – he developed a severe allergic reaction to carbolic acid and could no longer scrub up or touch surgical instruments. In his own words, his fingers swelled up like

boiled sausages. So the young surgeon specialised in joint function and "dry" surgery, then little developed, which aimed to straighten bone deformities without resorting to invasive surgery. His "Doctor Plaster" nickname was no handicap in his career – he developed and gained recognition for the Lorenz method of treating congenital dislocation of the hip.

The remedial gym, filled with equipment designed by the professor himself to treat orthopaedic conditions, is the highlight of the visit. An early fitness centre …

Adolf Lorenz spent several months a year in the United States, a very lucrative posting that allowed him to build the sumptuous Villa Lorenz in Altenberg, which until 2013 housed the Konrad Lorenz Institute for Evolution and Cognition Research.

Adolf Lorenz missed out on the Nobel Prize for Medicine 1923 by a single vote. His second son, the renowned ethologist (animal behaviourist) Konrad Lorenz, did however become a Nobel Laureate in 1973.

THE IRON MAN

18

"Nails Against War"

Felderstrasse 6–8, Arcades, 1010 Wien
Bus: 38A, Cobenzl Parkplatz stop / 39A, Sievering stop

Beneath the arcades in front of Felder House (named after liberal politician and former mayor Cajetan Felder, 1814–94) is an astonishing "Iron Man", a rare example of the many installed during the First World War.

From March 1915 onwards, in exchange for a donation to war widows and orphans, the Viennese could drive a nail into a wooden knight carved by Josef Müllner under the exhortation *Kriegsnägelaktion* (Nails Against War). Generous donors could even opt to receive gold points in order to raise the stakes. Propaganda was of course behind this enterprise: the patriotism of good citizens was rewarded with postcards, pins or certificates. To publicise this patriotic gesture, the first nails were planted by archdukes and ambassadors of the states allied with Austria-Hungary. In the end, some 500,000 nails were embedded in the statue.

The iron man that originally stood on Schwartzenbergplatz was moved to its present location near the City Hall in 1934, when the outer door of the castle was converted into a monument to First World War dead. More nails were added on this occasion, not to the statue itself but to its new base.

There you can read a quotation from Ottokar Kernstock, a German patriotic poet turned National Socialist, which translates as:

The Iron Man of Vienna recalls the time
When love and compassion reigned
As inexhaustible as the sufferings of war.

WIENBIBLIOTHEK IM RATHAUS
MUSIC COLLECTION

19

Music in an apartment by Adolf Loos

Bartensteingasse 9/5, 1010 Wien
Open Monday to Friday 9am–1pm

"The dining room was graced with a magnificent fireplace, trimmed with lavish mahogany wood panels, decorated with stucco friezes and a massive sideboard. Among the staterooms, there was a music room and a smoking room with a fireplace." Such was a description of the apartment designed and decorated by Adolf Loos and occupied since 1907 by leading Jewish industrialist Friedrich Boskovits and his family at Frankgasse in the 9th district.

Following the marriage of their daughter Alice to the son and heir of Swiss entrepreneur H.O. Wessner, Friedrich Boskovits and his wife Charlotte felt that their apartment was too small. So they decided to have all Loos' designs transferred to their new, much more spacious accommodation on Bartensteingasse, a few steps from the City Hall.

From July to September 1927, costly renovations were undertaken in order to replicate the original decor. The furniture, tapestries, chandeliers and carpets were all moved at great expense, as evidenced

by the removers' invoices that were kept and can be seen during the visit.

The Boskovits-Wessner family lived until the mid-1980s in this little architectural gem, which is still there today.

The private apartment was bought and renovated in 1991 by the City of Vienna, which installed the internationally renowned music collection of Vienna City Library (also known as the National Library at that time).

In addition to original scores by famous names such as Franz Schubert, Joseph Lanner, Richard Strauss, Hugo Wolf and Ernst Krenek, the exhibition includes documentation on the history of the apartment and its former owners, as well as on the life, work and writings of Adolf Loos.

The highlight of the tour, however, is the richly appointed dining room. The functions and concerts that are regularly held in the house bring the smoking room and salon back to life.

ISIS FOUNTAIN

Egypt at the heart of Josefstadt

Albertplatz, 1080 Wien

The cast-iron statue of the ancient Egyptian goddess Isis in Albertplatz does not actually come from Egypt, but from the Salm'schen foundry near Brno (Czech Republic) – it was installed in 1834 in the presence of Emperor Franz I.

The fountain was connected to the Albertine water pipe (hence the name Albertplatz) that brought water from Hütteldorf in the west of the city to supply the central Breitenfeld neighbourhood. Nevertheless, a single well failed to satisfy the demand for water, despite the intercession of the goddess of rebirth and healer of the sick. The crowds that gathered at the Isis fountain were such that long queues formed daily in the square. When the output of the source later diminished, the

fountain was connected to the Emperor Ferdinand Aqueduct (built in 1836).

At that time, all things Egyptian were highly fashionable in Europe, thanks to the Napoleonic campaigns. Emperor Ferdinand's third wife even had a room entirely furnished in the Egyptian style (some pieces are now part of the Imperial Furniture Collection at the Hofmobiliendepot).

Until 1912, the Isis fountain stood in the centre of the square, but it had to give way to the new tramline and is now on the north-east side. It suffered bomb damage in the Second World War and was restored in 1961.

The statue was modelled on an ancient Egyptian statue, part of the imperial collection now owned by the Kunsthistorisches Museum (Art History Museum) (see photo).

WIENER SCHUHMUSEUM

Foot service

Florianigasse 66, 1080 Wien
Open second Tuesday of the month or by appointment
http://schuhmuseum.at/

The Viennese Shoe Museum, opened in 2002 at the heart of the former multipurpose hall of the shoemakers' guild, has various curiosities illustrating the history of shoemaking. Besides shoes, the museum has a collection of traditional tools as well as a 19th-century sewing machine and a sole-pressing machine.

Among the highlights of the collection are Emperor Franz Joseph's riding boots and some shoes belonging to his wife Sisi. From the boots of soccer legends and clowns to the favourite shoes of former mayor Helmut Zilk, all types of footwear are represented, ranging from 19th-century ski boots to contemporary hi-tech models.

Footwear dating back to the Stone Age is also on display, and you'll discover when and why right and left shoes appeared. You may be surprised to hear that this refinement emerged fairly recently, around 1850. In antiquity, both the Greeks and the Romans had different shoes for the right and left feet, but this tradition had been lost during the 17th century. For nearly 200 years, pairs of shoes were cut in identical fashion and just adapted to the shape of the foot while being worn.

The museum has a particular focus on the internationally known Viennese shoe manufacturers Rudolf Scheer & Söhne and Materna Schuhe.

> A shoemakers' ball takes place every spring in Vienna. The most unusual footwear is awarded a prize and then displayed in the museum.

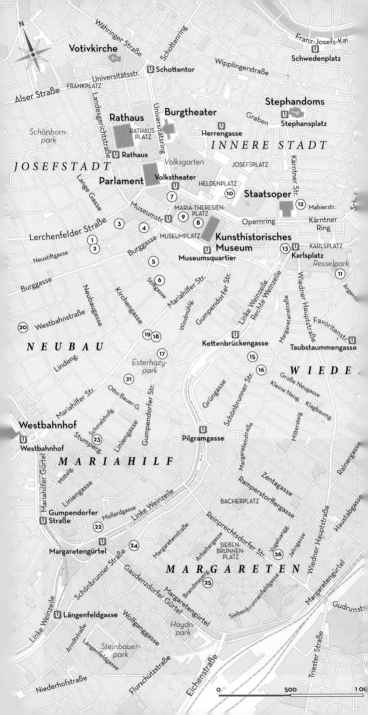

Wieden, Margareten, Mariahilf, Neubau

SITE OF KARA MUSTAFA'S COMMAND POST

Another Turkish horseman...

Street corner, Neustiftgasse / Kellermanngasse, 1070 Wien
Bus: 13A / 48A, Kellermanngasse stop

At the Neustiftgasse and Kellermanngasse junction, a gilded stone effigy of a Turkish horseman is protected by a metal grille. The inscription below claims that this is the site of the encampment of Ottoman grand vizier Kara Mustafa Pasha.

It is said that during the 1683 Siege of Vienna, Kara Mustafa had a sumptuous canvas fortress erected on this spot.

The encampment was actually further to the west at Schmelz, near the 15th-district military parade ground, in other words at a respectable distance from the fighting. The Turkish headquarters, directly under the command of the grand vizier, was however in the 7th district on the left bank of Ottakring Creek. According to Turkish sources, Kara Mustafa often rested there and had set up his command post on the tower of St Ulrich's Church, near the battlefield.

> A 1955 mosaic by Walter Behrens, depicting an Ottoman tent, can be seen above the entrance to an apartment block at No. 43 Neustiftgasse.

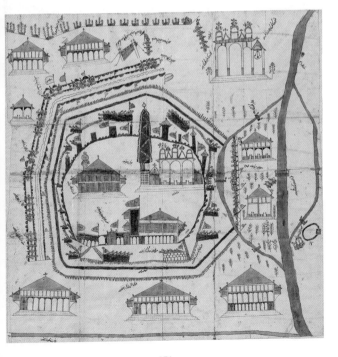

FORGOTTEN HISTORY OF THE AUGUSTIN FOUNTAIN

Black Death and brown plague

Augustinplatz, 1070 Wien

The name Augustinplatz has only been official since 2009, although this little square with its pretty fountain had long been known as Augustinplatzl without having any sign to that effect. Josef Humplik's legendary sandstone effigy of Augustin, a drunken piper and ballad singer at the time of the great plague of 1679, was erected in 1952 to replace a bronze dating from 1908, which like many other artworks had been melted down during the Second World War. Once the earlier statue had been dismantled, someone is said to have climbed onto the pedestal and declared: "I escaped the Black Death, but the brown plague has done for me."

During the plague, two mass graves were dug in the neighbourhood between St Ulrich's Church and Neustiftgasse, outside the town walls. It was customary at the time to cover the trenches with lime so that more victims could be added later.

One night the piper Augustin fell into a drunken stupor in the street. The plague workers, taking him for dead, threw him onto the cart laden with corpses on its way to the burial pit. The next day Augustin was shouting and skirling his bagpipes until some good souls finally heard him and pulled him out. Some contemporary sources also mention an "Augustin" thought to have emerged from a limestone tomb.

Abraham a Sancta Clara, a German preacher with a great reputation in Austria, also used this story of the street-singer in his proselytising, calling him a "well-stocked wine cellar" as a way of dissuading people from drinking.

In addition to Augustinplatz's legendary namesake, the square is also a nod to singer Liana Augustin, who came fifth when she represented Austria in the 1958 Eurovision Song Contest.

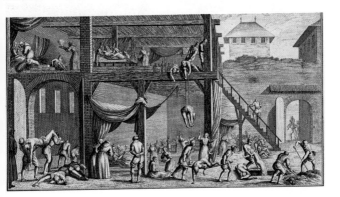

MEKHITARIST MONASTERY'S MUMMY

The monks' mummy and heritage library ...

Mechitaristengasse 4, 1070 Wien
Visits by appointment: Father Vahan Hovagimian
Email: vahanhov58@hotmail.com
http://mechitaristen.org/

Book a visit to the museum of the Mekhitarist Congregation in Vienna to see an imposing Egyptian sarcophagus whose contents have not yet been scientifically studied. It is thought to contain the mummy of a religious singer presented to the monastery in the 19th century by an Egyptian diplomat.

The Catholic Mekhitarists have occupied this building (a former Capuchin monastery in the 7th district) for over 200 years, since Emperor Franz I granted shelter to a group of Armenian monks in 1811. The monks still produce their famous aromatic herb liqueur there, *Mechitharine Kloster Likor*.

After you've seen the sarcophagus, don't miss the magnificent library. With its collection of some 150,000 books and 28,000 manuscripts, this is the fourth-largest Armenian collection in the world. When Mekhitar of Sebaste founded the Congregation in 1701, one of his aims was to preserve the Armenian culture and language. To date, only young men of Armenian descent can join the Order.

The monastery church, dedicated to Maria Schutz, was constructed to Josef Kornhäusel's plans between 1871 and 1874 in Early Renaissance style. Notable Viennese architect and urban planner Camillo Sitte, who designed the interior, was in charge of the project.

SETZER-TSCHIEDEL STUDIO

A society photographer

Museumstrasse 5, 1070 Wien
Visits by appointment: www.tschiedel.at

The top floor of No. 5 Museumstrasse is a treasure trove of the history of Austrian photography: an authentic studio from the early days of the art, preserved in its original condition. This light-filled attic studio, opened in 1909 by Franz Xaver Setzer (1886–1939) on his graduation from the Institute of Graphic Design, soon became *the* place to have your picture taken.

Theatre and cinema greats often presented themselves in stage costume and particularly appreciated the neutral background, which was seen as very modern at the time. The visual memory of Viennese society is gathered here: opera divas Maria Jeritza, Jarmila Novotná and Lotte Lehmann, tenor Leo Slezak and composers Richard Strauss, Maurice Ravel and Arnold Schönberg were among Setzer's models, as were notable literary figures such as Arthur Schnitzler, Felix Salten and Richard Beer-Hofmann.

The studio was ideally located just behind the Volkstheater and, as mentioned in one of its first promotional brochures, boasted an elevator and an intercom system.

Setzer married star opera singer Marie Gutheil-Schoder, which further enhanced his notoriety and social status. He went regularly to the Salzburg Festival to take pictures and win new contracts. Theatre director Max Reinhardt was full of praise for his skills. In 1920, young photographer Marie Karoline Tschiedel began working for the Setzer studio. She directed it from 1935, renaming it Setzer-Tschiedel in May 1939.

Before she died in 1980, Tschiedel left the workshop to her nephew Walter Tschiedel, who used it as an office. He made no changes, so

everything has remained as it was in the glamour days. Contemporary cameras, archives, plaques and negatives, as well as customer records, have all been kept. The studio now belongs to Walter Tschiedel's son.

This historic location can be booked for events, exhibitions or conferences.

INSCRIPTION AT WITWE BOLTE RESTAURANT

An emperor was chucked out of here

Gutenberggase 13, 1070 Wien
Open daily, 11.30am–11.45pm
U-Bahn: line U2, Volkstheater station; Tram: 49, Stiftgasse stop

Witwe Bolte restaurant is located in a beautiful Baroque house at Spittelberg in central Vienna. Inside, the inscription on the pediment of one of the doors translates as: "Emperor Joseph was shown the door here in 1778".

The slogan was originally on the outer façade, but during the latest renovations it was reinstalled indoors, to protect it from the weather.

During the time of Maria Theresa and her son Joseph II, Spittelberg was a suburb of many narrow, gloomy alleys, livened up by the presence of countless taverns. Prostitutes from all over the realm waited for their customers in these hostelries. One of the best-known madams, Rote Warbel (Red Warbel), ran her business at No. 13 Gutenberggasse.

Joseph II loved to travel around his empire incognito in order to keep abreast of the lives and concerns of his subjects. Thus he ventured one day into the red-light district of Spittelberg to see for himself the alleged rampant immorality there. He is thought to have availed himself of a lady's favours and then refused to pay the asking price, which got him thrown out by the door you can still see today.

When he became ruler on his mother's death in 1780, Joseph tried to suppress prostitution in Vienna. His advisers suggested that he should open brothels, as was customary in Paris and Berlin. The great reformer was heard to murmur disdainfully: "In that case I'd have to roof over the whole of Vienna."

STIFTSKASERNE TOWER

A discreet blockhouse

Stiftgasse 2–2A, 1070 Wien
Exterior always accessible
To visit contact administrative building: +43 (0) 50201 / 1033006

The Stiftskaserne, although 40-metres-high and sunk more than 5 metres into the ground, blends imperceptibly into a background of commercial buildings and apartment blocks, not to mention a church. Built in the years 1943–44 to counter bombing raids over the city, this is the last of the anti-aircraft flak towers still used by the Austrian Army.

Today officially designated the "Stiftgasse administrative building", the Stiftskaserne was built exclusively as a military base in the 18th century, during the reign of Maria Theresa. The tower now houses a service that organises the deployment of Austrian troops abroad. In a crisis, it can also be used as a control centre.

The tower also houses the Landesverteidigungsakademie (National Defence Academy) for the training of men and women officers: the elite of the Austrian armed forces. The passing-out ceremonies take place in the *Sala Terrena*, a Baroque hall with a stuccoed and medallioned ceiling. The church within the compound has a remarkable organ. A plant nursery was established in the so-called sappers' wing. An inscription at the entrance notes that here the children of poor and noble officers were prepared for higher education at the Military Academy. The editorial staff of the military review *Truppendienst* now use this wing.

Esterházypark is home to the second (command) tower associated with that of the Stiftskaserne (combat). It has become an aquarium and vivarium, the Haus des Meeres, complete with climbing wall.

Vienna's wartime flak towers

During the Second World War, three pairs of flak or combat towers and a huge blockhouse were built in Vienna as part of the city's air defences.

The towers are located in Augartenpark (command tower and flak tower), Arenbergpark (command tower and flak tower) and Esterházypark (command tower – the corresponding flak tower is the Stiftskaserne).

GUIDED TOUR OF PALAIS EPSTEIN ⑦

A sad anecdote from the early days of the Ringstrasse

Dr Karl-Renner-Ring 3, 1010 Wien
*Guided tours without appointment, fixed times, Monday to Saturday between
11am and 4pm*
www.parlament.gv.at/GEBF/EPSTEIN/

Throughout its turbulent history, the magnificent Epstein Palace, designed by Theophil von Hansen, successively housed the bank and residence of the Von Epstein family, the Reich administration in the Nazi era, the Soviet headquarters after the Second World War and the Vienna rectorate. Since 2005, it has been the Austrian Parliament building.

In addition to the monumental interiors, visitors can see the former servants' quarter, featuring the original parquet floor of the former ballroom, and a small exhibition on the history and current situation of this most elegant of the Ringstrasse palaces.

In the early 1870s, banker Gustav Ritter von Epstein had the building erected in record time. He probably treated himself to the most expensive building on the Ring, with a view of the Hofburg and the Schottentor gateway. This patriotic man who loved art and travel gave financial support to numerous charitable organisations as well as to Franz Joseph for his wars and the 1866 campaign against Prussia.

The ground floor housed the offices of the Epstein Bank. The first floor, which was already fitted with bathroom and toilet, was for

family use. The construction of the palace took two and a half years, but the Epsteins lived there for only two years because the stock market crash of 1873 put an end to their luxurious and glittering lifestyle. Financially ruined, they were obliged to leave the immense house and to accept the aid of the charitable associations that they had formerly subsidised. As misfortunes never come singly, Friedrich, the son, succumbed to laryngeal tuberculosis when he was only 17. Gustav von Epstein died in 1879 at the age of 51.

GERARD VAN SWIETEN'S STATUE ⑧

The real inspiration behind Dracula

Maria-Theresien-Platz, 1010 Wien
U-Bahn: line U2 / U3, Volkstheater station

The monument in Maria-Theresien-Platz in honour of Maria Theresa, by German sculptor Kaspar von Zumbusch, was supposed to enhance the reputation of the Habsburg monarchy, already weakened by 1888. Below the statue of Maria Theresa (Sisi's "predecessor"), her personal physician, Gerard van Swieten, stands on the plinth among other nobles and advisors.

This Dutch physician had acquired considerable power over the monarchy. For example, when in 1755 Maria Theresa learned that the people of Olmütz (Moravia) were worried about frightening noises emanating from the cemetery, she immediately sent her personal "ghost hunter" to the haunted region.

In the 18th century, although nobody turned a hair when phoney aristocrats held orgies with innocent girls, vampires were held responsible for illnesses and unexplained deaths. Maria Theresa promptly banned the occult practice of impaling or beheading dead bodies. After all, Dr van Swieten had certified that they were no longer alive. The condition and temperature of the soil, the lack of oxygen in the graves and the still unknown phenomenon of fermentation slowed decomposition and caused the chemical reactions responsible for the "noises" described by cemetery visitors. The doctor severely criticised the superstition of the local authorities and the Church, not to mention the ignorance of his Moravian colleagues.

Irish writer Bram Stoker paid tribute to van Swieten in his Gothic tale *Dracula* (1898), whose main character, Dr Abraham Van Helsing, is inspired by the Dutch doctor. Before opting for Transylvania, the author had set the scene in the Austrian state of Styria. In a first draft, he described the tomb of Countess Dolingen von Gratz, from the same region, pierced with a stake. The earlier vampire story *Carmilla* (1872, by Stoker's compatriot Le Fanu) takes place there too.

Van Swieten died at Schönbrunn in 1772 and was laid to rest in St George's Chapel at Vienna's Augustinerkirche (Church of the Augustinian Friars).

"Madame Emperor"

Although her husband, Franz 1 (Francis Stephen of Lorraine), was consecrated Holy Roman Emperor, Maria Theresa never actually bore the title Empress of Austria (the Austrian Empire was founded in 1804), nor Holy Roman Empress. She was Archduchess of Austria and Queen of Hungary and Bohemia, but that didn't prevent her from presenting herself as a crowned empress.

BOUQUET OF PRECIOUS STONES ⑨ AT THE NATURHISTORISCHES MUSEUM

Flowers for the emperor

Burgring 7, 1010 Wien
Open Thursday to Monday 9am–6.30pm, Wednesday 9am–9pm, closed Tuesday
www.nhm-wien.ac.at/en
U-Bahn: line U2, Museumsquartier station

While the Natural History Museum offers a wide-ranging selection of dinosaur skeletons, meteorites and other imposing objects, it also has a stunning bouquet of precious stones that tends to be overlooked in a stairwell.

"Never marry an idle man!" Maria Theresa once said to a lady courtier. The empress was referring to her husband, Holy Roman Emperor Franz I, who had little political power but plenty to fill his time. He had multiple interests, ranging from the theatre to alchemy, Freemasonry to mineralogy. In 1764 Maria Theresa offered him a unique gift: a bouquet of precious stones. She mentioned "a little surprise on the occasion of his name day". Until the 20th century, the feast day of the saint whose name someone shared was considered more important than their own birthday.

The bouquet is a miniature Baroque piece composed of 2,863 coloured precious and semi-precious stones (emerald, ruby, garnet, agate, chalcedony, jasper, lapis lazuli, turquoise, serpentine) artistically transformed into sparkling flowers and insects. The leaves, originally of pale green silk, have almost entirely lost their colour. Created by Viennese jeweller Michael Grosser in 1760, the bouquet is 50 centimetres high and weighs almost 3 kilos. In his memoirs, Goethe reports that a jeweller from Frankfurt, Johann Gottfried Lautensack, is thought to have done the preparatory work.

The bouquet of precious stones is the foundation of the Natural History Museum's mineralogy displays. On the death of Franz I at Innsbruck in 1765, Maria Theresa donated her husband's gemstone collection to the state. In the spirit of the Enlightenment, private imperial property was often made available to the public for research and teaching purposes.

PAPYRUSMUSEUM

A collection of antique papers

Heldenplatz, Neue Burg, 1010 Wien
Open Tuesday to Sunday 10am–6pm, closed Monday
www.onb.ac.at/papyrusmuseum.htm
U-Bahn: line U3, Herrengasse station

The Papyrus Museum has the most eclectic collection of writings ranging from worship of the dead to religion, through the magic rites, medicine and everyday life of the ancient Egyptians. It also has examples of early scriptures, commercial documents, mathematical calculations and excerpts from literary works.

The oldest papyrus on display is a copy of the Egyptian *Book of the Dead*, which dates back over 3,000 years. Literally entitled "The Chapters of Coming-Forth-by-Day", this is one of the most mysterious traditions of ancient Egypt and would have been inconceivable without the invention of writing. Formulae supposed to help the deceased in their passage to the afterlife were inserted in a mummy's bandages or copied onto papyrus and placed in the tomb. Once the text had been written by specially trained priests, no living creature was allowed to see it, either before or after the funeral. Archduke Rainer, a member of the Austrian imperial house who was popular because he was close to the people and a patron of the arts and sciences, presented his invaluable collection to his uncle Franz Joseph in 1899. It later became part of the Royal and Imperial Library.

The Papyrus Museum now belongs to the Österreichische Nationalbibliothek (National Library of Austria), although just a fraction of the collection – about 200 items – is on display. The ancient Egyptians wrote on papyrus: the word "paper" derives from the Greek term for the plant fibres. Cultural exchange between Egypt and ancient Greece is also at the heart of the museum's permanent exhibition, with its parchments and clay artefacts.

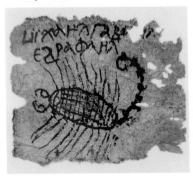

A particularly fine example is a papyrus fragment with lyrics and instrumental symbols from the first chorus of *Orestes*, Euripides' Greek tragedy. You can even listen to a modern interpretation of the music. The collection forms part of the UNESCO World Heritage site of the Historic Centre of Vienna, inscribed in 2001.

CHARLES BORROMEO'S INTESTINES ⑪

A saint against the plague

Museo Borromeo
Karlskirche, Karlsplatz, 1040 Wien
Open Monday to Saturday 9am–12.30pm and 1pm–6pm, Sunday and public
holidays noon–5.45pm
www.karlskirche.at/museo.html
U-Bahn: line U1 / U2 / U4, Karlsplatz station

A small, unobtrusive museum in the Karlskirche is devoted to the Italian saint Charles Borromeo (1538–84), who gained great importance in Vienna after the plague of 1713–14. A number of churches, altars and statues in the city are dedicated to him.

The Borromeo Museum contains an actual relic of St Charles Borromeo, apparently a piece of intestine. This type of "intestinal relic" is quite rare in the vast reliquary of the Roman Catholic Church. The exhibition devoted to the saint also displays a white cassock, a pair of red Baroque ceremonial shoes, a cardinal's hat and a mitre that once belonged to him. The certificate of authenticity accompanying these effects was handed over in 1713 by Empress Elisabeth Christine, wife of Karl VI.

Emperor Karl VI, Maria Theresia's father, had solemnly promised to build a church in memory of his patron saint at the end of the plague epidemic that was devastating Vienna. Charles Borromeo, a former Archbishop of Milan, was revered for his courage and involvement while the disease was rife in that city. He was also a fierce opponent of Protestant doctrine. The iconography of the church traces his entire life.

PRIVATE TOUR OF PALAIS TODESCO  ⑫

The house of Sigmund Freud's most famous patient

Palais Todesco
Kärntner Strasse 51, 1010 Wien
Guided tours by appointment
www.gerstner.at/wien/palais-todesco.html

Contact the management of the famous Viennese patisserie Gerstner to visit some of the sumptuous rooms of Todesco Palace on the Ringstrasse. You'll have access to ballrooms and banqueting halls, as well as a private study containing many objects from the world of Franz Joseph.

Sigmund Freud maintained that he "learned" psychoanalysis through sessions with his patient "Cäcilie M." and it was during her treatment that he developed his "investigation of the psyche". Cäcilie's real name was Anna von Lieben (born von Todesco, 1847–1900) and she came from a wealthy Austrian family. Freud regarded her as his "instructress".

Anna's parents, Eduard and Sophie von Todesco, occupied a monumental palace built between 1861 and 1864 by Ludwig Förster, opposite the Opera House. The interior design was commissioned from Danish architect Theophil Hansen. Sophie von Todesco received many guests, including writers Eduard von Bauernfeld and Ludwig Ganghofer, Burgtheater directors Franz von Dingelstedt and Heinrich Laube, Johann Strauss (son) and Hugo von Hofmannsthal. It was she who presented Strauss to his future wife, Henrietta "Jetty" Treffz, a well-known mezzo-soprano previously linked with Moritz, the brother of Eduard von Todesco. She dreamed of bearing the title of baroness.

Anna, who found it hard to cope with life in a golden cage, in 1871 married Leopold von Lieben, president of the Chamber of Commerce and 12 years older than her. She followed him and settled in the family palace on the Ring (Universitätsring 4). His sister-in-law Helene, wife of industrialist Rudolf Auspitz, also lived in Lieben-Auspitz palace, built around 1873 by architects Carl Schumann and Ludwig Tischler. The ground floor housed the famous Café Landtmann, while members of the family occupied the first floor – the most beautifully laid out of any Ringstrasse palace. The other apartments and floors were let, hence the term *Zinspalais* (profitable building).

Anna von Lieben, a woman of multiple talents, gave birth to five children but was never able to make use of her gifts as a mathematician and artist. She was diagnosed as suffering from hysteria and monitored by renowned psychiatrists such as Jean-Martin Charcot in Paris and Sigmund Freud in Vienna. Despite Freud's visits several times a week for therapy sessions, her condition only improved temporarily. She was never cured and died in 1900 at the age of 53.

VIENNESE SEWAGE SYSTEM

Return of the Third Man

Pick-up location: Karlsplatz / Girardipark, 1010 Wien
Open May to October, Thursday to Sunday 10am–8pm
Tour starts every hour; in English at 3pm only, all other tours in German
www.drittemanntour.at/
U-Bahn: line U1 / U2 / U4, Karlsplatz station

Thirty minutes you'll remember all your life", proclaims the brochure advertising the mysterious excursion into the city sewers. All the participants in this visit to the "Vienna Canal" seem satisfied when they finally emerge into the daylight.

The tour plunges you into a subterranean world, so dark and eerie that you can scarcely tell what's happening. Visitors are given a taste of the dank atmosphere of the classic movie *The Third Man*: incredible shadows, mysterious voices, deafening gunshots. Then the encounter with the "real" third man takes place. He is played by a collaborator of Wiener Kanal, a gifted actor.

The experience reveals a great deal about Orson Welles and the film, shot in Vienna in 1949, but also about the world of the sewer workers. Anecdotes include how director Carol Reed dumped quantities of Chanel No. 5 into the water to make the location as bearable as possible for his film crew.

Orson Welles, who plays Harry Lime, only briefly graced Vienna with his presence: the stench, the cold and the rats stretched his patience. He eventually had to be replaced by doubles, while a studio in England reproduced the background of the Vienna sewers. Producer Alexander Korda, on the other hand, originally filming in the occupied city, was truly inspired by the filth. While location-hunting in Vienna, he said he wanted to "rub shoulders with the misery of the city and seek out the lost souls".

The tour is not recommended for those with heart or back problems or with a tendency to vertigo, pregnant women and agoraphobics, as stroboscopic flashes and loud animations are also part of the show. Everybody else, equipped with helmet and headlamp, will be able to descend the original staircase from the film, 7 metres down below ground. The 1830s sewers remain almost untouched to this day.

Third Man Museum

Dritte Mann Museum, Pressgasse 25, 1040 Wien. Open Saturday 2pm–6pm.
For all those interested in everyday life in postwar Vienna, the museum is divided into four occupied sectors – as was the city.

MUMMIES IN THE THERESIANUM LIBRARY

Thanks to two Egyptian brothers, Theresianum boarders in the late 19th century ...

Favoritenstrasse 15, 1040 Wien
Open only to students and their families or on special days such as Tag des Denkmals (Monument or Heritage Day)
www.theresianum.ac.at
U-Bahn: line U1, Taubstummengasse station

The Theresianum, an elite Austrian private boarding and day school, has only accepted female students since 1989. Before then, only the library housed females – the mummies of two young women, probably from the late Ptolemaic period (between 200 and 100 BC).

They owe their presence in Vienna to the cordial diplomatic relations between Egypt and Austria, consolidated during the construction of the Suez Canal in the mid-19th century. It was in fact an Austrian, Alois Negrelli, who drew up detailed plans for the canal, before being appointed inspector-general of all the new Egyptian canals.

As the Egyptian brothers Ibrahim and Süleyman Bey had been boarders at the Theresianum at the end of the 19th century. Their father – an emir from the Nile region – donated the mummies to the school

as a sign of gratitude. They are still swathed with painted bandages.

The library owns another curiosity: a mummified crocodile. It is thought to come from Arsinoe, a town in ancient Egypt where sacred crocodiles were embalmed before finding eternal rest in a dedicated cemetery. Such mummies were often given to Europeans as gifts.

The food parcel lying in the showcase is certainly a joke. As the library's director explains, this way neither mummies nor crocodile should die of hunger ...

Curiously, mummies are to be found in libraries in many parts of Europe. Both mummies and libraries are regarded as an antidote to the passage of time, two different means for people to attain eternity and immortality. Or perhaps the opposite: a mummy devoid of its *Book of the Dead* is as nothing. Only the lines written therein will allow it to cross the threshold of the next world and begin a new life.

HEUMÜHLE (HAY MILL)

The oldest secular building in Vienna

Schönbrunner Strasse 2 / Heumühlgasse 9, 1040 Wien
U-Bahn: line U4, Kettenbrückengasse station

The *Heumühle auf der Wieden* is a 14th-century former watermill in an inner courtyard that can easily be reached via Heumühlgasse. Considered by the Viennese to be the city's oldest secular building, it was restored in 2008.

The building was originally called the Steinmühle (Stone Mill) and belonged to the Bürgerspital, a group of buildings dating back to 1326. The mill was twice ravaged by fire during the 16th century, but was always rebuilt, before finally falling into the hands of the Bishopric of Vienna during the reign of Ferdinand I.

The building you can still see today, which used to have a kitchen, living rooms and a bakehouse, probably dates from the 16th century. It has only been known as the Hay Mill since the 17th century. In 1856, the City of Vienna bought the land and title deeds from the archdiocese, and then filled in the watercourse for health and safety reasons. As the wheel no longer turned, the mill was used as a warehouse. Now privately owned, the building is rented out for seminars and other events.

FRANZ SCHUBERT'S LAST HOME

For two and a half months

Schubert Sterbewohnung
Kettenbrückengasse 6, 1040 Wien
Open Wednesday and Thursday 10am–1pm and 2pm–6pm
www.wienmuseum.at/de/standorte/schubert-sterbewohnung.html

Franz Schubert lived out his final days at No. 6 Kettenbrückengasse, in the apartment of his elder brother Ferdinand, also a composer. His piano, last sheet music projects and some handwritten letters are preserved in the museum now devoted to him in this magnificent Biedermeier-style house, as well as documents attesting to the family arrangements for his funeral.

This old Viennese residence was totally transformed in 1986, when the façades, windows, doors and roofs were renovated and the courtyard landscaped. The fountain, once in ruins, was given a new lease of life.

Schubert settled in this apartment on 1 September 1828 after spending some time in the city centre at his friend Franz Schober's

home. It is still unclear whether he succumbed to typhus or syphilis, but even as a sick man he never stopped working. His last piece was a setting of a poem entitled *Der Hirt auf dem Felsen* (The Shepherd on the Rock).

The composer died in the afternoon of 19 November 1828, at the age of 31, after two solid weeks of fever. The "nervous fever" indicated as the cause of death was probably an acute infectious disease.

Schubert wanted to rest with Beethoven for eternity ...

The tombs of Schubert and Beethoven used to be in the cemetery at Währing. When it was closed in 1873, the coffins of the two famous composers were transferred to the city's Central Cemetery, granting Schubert's wish to rest with Beethoven for eternity.

HOUSE OF ARCHITECTS SICCARDSBURG AND VAN DER NÜLL

A page from the city's gay history

Schadekgasse 4, 1060 Wien
U-Bahn: line U3, Neubaugasse station

Opposite Esterházy Park, a magnificent residence from the *Gründerzeit* (Founders' era, 1850–1914) has since 1957 carried an unusual plaque in memory of the architects August Siccard von Siccardsburg and Eduard van der Nüll, who lived there until the end of their days. But the nature of their relationship isn't mentioned.

Designers of one of the Ringstrasse's most famous buildings, they were driven to their deaths by a wave of animosity. "*Siccardsburg and Van der Nüll / Don't have any style / Antique, Gothic, Renaissance / They don't care!*", mocked the know-alls. There was talk of an "architectural Königgrätz", referring to the devastating military defeat and terrible humiliation a few years earlier at the 1866 battle between Prussia and Austria. Franz Joseph joined in with the general sullen mood, commenting on the opening of Vienna's *Staatsoper* (State Opera House) that it appeared a bit sunken – the road level had been altered in the course of construction and was a metre higher than the arches of the building. However, the error was attributed to the planning department rather than the pair of architects.

Eduard van der Nüll, then aged 56, couldn't face this criticism from

all quarters and hanged himself on 4 April 1868. The forensic report concluded that it was a case of "mental confusion". August von Siccardsburg collapsed at his drawing board two months later and died of a heart attack, unable to get over the suicide of his companion.

The two gay men had been inseparable since their student days at Vienna Academy of Fine Arts. Yet they managed to keep up appearances, in that Van der Nüll had married a year before killing himself. His wife Mary was in her eighth month of pregnancy.

The new Opera House was inaugurated with great pomp and ceremony less than a year later, with a performance of Mozart's *Don Giovanni*. The level of the street had been altered and the building itself aroused general enthusiasm.

The fate of the architects had finally touched the emperor, who henceforth refrained from expressing his personal opinion. The formula he used on many occasions is still quoted: "It has been very pleasant. I enjoyed it very much."

SALVATORIANER KOLLEG

Baroque Barnabite cloister

Barnabitengasse 14, 1060 Wien
Access difficult but sometimes possible; contact via website
www.pfarremariahilf.at/mariahilf/index.php?mid=Kontakt&cid=Kontakt

Even if not always easy to enter (see above), the Salvatorian College, connected to Mariahilfer Church by a corridor, is well worth a visit. It used to be a cloister of the Barnabite Order. The three-storey building, designed by architect Paul Ulrich Trientl, was erected between 1768 and 1777.

In summer the monks ate their meals on the ground floor. This refectory, now known as Salvator Hall, has a magnificent Baroque fresco.

The superb library on the first floor is distinguished by its vaulted ceilings and its grisaille (grey-toned) paintings. The collection includes works dating from the early 16th to the 19th centuries as well as the Barnabite college archives, which date back to the year 1692.

BLESSING OF EYES

Cure for styes, conjunctivitis and other eye problems

Hemma Kapelle
Mariahilfer Kirche
Barnabitengasse 14, 1060 Wien
www.pfarremariahilf.at
U-Bahn: line U3, Neubaugasse station

Once a year, on 27 June, a blessing of eyes is held in the Hemma Chapel, just to the right of the church entrance. Until very recently, St Hemma's ring was brought to Vienna from the Diocese of Krka (Gurk) in the Austrian state of Carinthia, so that believers could touch it, hoping to be cured of diseases of the eye. As this custom of seeking the saint's intercession has fallen into disuse over the years, the ring itself now remains in Carinthia. This gold ring decorated with corundum (a very rare gem in Europe) is undocumented until the 15th century, so can hardly have belonged to the noble-born Hemma of Gurk, Countess of Friesach-Zeltschach. Nowadays the priest gives the benediction in front of the portrait of the saint in the chapel.

The rich and powerful countess probably died on 29 June 1045. Little is known about her life. She is thought to have lost her husband and sons and shed so many tears that she is frequently associated with the symbolism of the eye.

Hemma is always depicted as a noblewoman with a voluminous headdress and holding a model of the twin-steepled Gurk Cathedral, a document and a rose.

Hemma of Gurk is also at the origin of many pagan customs. Thus, slipping under the sarcophagus in the crypt of Gurk Cathedral guarantees a trouble-free confinement and the Hemma Stone, also in the Gurk vault, has the power to grant wishes. Your wish, whether expressed in silence or aloud, will be fulfilled if you sit on the stone, which is surrounded by crutches and other abandoned prostheses.

Finally, the cathedral treasury has a hat and shoe that supposedly belonged to Hemma. These unique pieces really have no link with the saint, dating as they do from the early Middle Ages.

NEARBY
Crucifixion by Kaspar Gerbl, c. 1680

A life-size Baroque crucifixion scene, in a niche behind a grating and a glass plate, adorns the north-west façade of Mariahilfer Church. The crucifix dates from 1680, while the sculptures of the Virgin Mary and St John the Evangelist were not added until 1710. This work once graced the main gate of Vienna prison, located at No. 10 Rauhensteingasse (Innere Stadt) since the 14th century. Several levels of vaulted cellars, taking in the basements of neighbouring buildings, included an interrogation room – in other words, a torture chamber. Most often, the "poor sinner" was then driven along Liliangasse to the marketplace gallows. The prison was demolished in 1785, during the reign of Emperor Joseph II.

WESTLICHT

Photographers' mecca

Westbahnstrasse 40, 1070 Wien
Open daily 11am–7pm, Thursday 11am–9pm
www.westlicht.com/
Tram: 49, Westbahnstrasse / Kaiserstrasse stop; U-Bahn: line U6, Burggasse-
Stadthalle station

A vast loft designed by renowned architects Eichinger oder Knechtl, WestLicht provides a fascinating insight into the technique and art of photography. These premises, once a glass factory, are a stone's throw away from the first Institute of Graphic Education and Research, which saw the rise of a large number of renowned art photographers, both men and women. The atmosphere of creativity still reigns.

The impressive assortment of photographic apparatus, some on loan from private collectors, consists of nearly 800 historical and technical exhibits that trace the history of photography from its earliest beginnings to the digital age. Exhibits from many countries make this one of the most complete collections in the world. The main attraction is the first commercially produced camera, the *Susse Frères Daguerréotype*, dating from 1839.

Several times a year, the gallery puts on exhibitions of work by a wide range of photographers. For example, Ferdinand Schmutzer's historical portraits, Christine de Grancy's photojournalism and Mary Ellen Mark's documentaries have all been recently shown at the loft. 2015 saw a retrospective of iconic fashion photos by the influential Edward Steichen, who worked for *Vogue* and *Vanity Fair* magazines and organised "The Family of Man" event in the 1950s.

A must-see for keen photographers.

The OstLicht gallery in the 10th district (No. 27 Absberggasse) and the Leica Shop on Westbahnstrasse also belong to the WestLicht group.

CONDOMI MUSEUM

Patrons of protection

Esterházygasse 26, 1060 Wien
Open Monday to Friday 11am–7pm, Saturday 11am–6pm
www.liebens-wert.at/veranstaltungen/condomi-museum
U-Bahn: line U3, Zieglergasse station

Opened in 1994, the Condomi Museum traces the history of the condom through some 300 exhibits of the various products used around the world since 1930. Originally, sheep gut or fish bladders were the only protection against many diseases.

In partnership with the sex shop "Liebenswert – feminine Lebensart", the museum retraces over its 100 square metres the controversy over the installation of condom dispensers in Vienna and the need to camouflage the condoms in discreet packaging. And to ensure complete protection, a full body contraceptive is also on display.

The museum shop has an impressive collection of vibrators, with examples from the 1950s and 60s, once referred to euphemistically as "massage machines". You'll notice that only women are shown on their brochures ... The relaxed atmosphere and the vast choice make for a particularly instructive visit.

SANITÄRHISTORISCHES MUSEUM ㉒

The smallest room

Mollardgasse 87, 1060 Wien, in the vocational school
Visits by appointment, Monday to Thursday: Herr Kurt Pant, 01-982 92 78
U-Bahn: line U4, Margaretengürtel station
https://www.wien.gv.at/ma53/museen/san-his.htm

I n 1986, on the occasion of the 75th anniversary of the Mollardgasse vocational school, highly committed teacher Kurt Pant had the idea of founding a museum of sanitary ware. Such was the enthusiasm of his pupils that entire loads of old washbasins, toilet bowls and chamber pots were collected.

A site was found for the museum in the school cellar, on the two levels of the old boiler room. In addition to a heterogeneous collection

of various types of sanitary ware, it also possesses the last of the 1930s' washing machines from the Karl-Marx-Hof social housing complex and the order book of Sigmund Freud's plumber. Judging by the number of call-outs, the lavatories of the father of psychoanalysis were frequently blocked ...

One of the best-known WC designs is the Nautilus, in the form of the mythical mollusc. The museum has only one example, among the 300 objects tracing the history of sanitation technology since 1889. Bathroom fittings, water heaters, tools and drawings complete this collection of "teaching aids".

Like the schoolteacher Kurt Pant (now retired), Charles, Prince of Wales, has a keen interest in sanitary ware, but the public has no access to his collection.

BRAHMS' ROOM
IN THE HAYDNHAUS

A fervent admirer

Haydngasse 19, 1060 Wien
Open Tuesday to Sunday and public holidays 10am–1pm and 2pm–6pm
www.wienmuseum.at/de/standorte/haydnhaus.html

Joseph Haydn's former house – owned by Wien Museum since 1904 – has a separate room entirely dedicated to Hamburg musician Johannes Brahms (1833–97). He was a fervent admirer of Haydn and always tried to perpetuate the memory of his idol, who had died in 1809.

Brahms' famous apartment at No. 4 Karlsgasse in the 4th district (Wieden) was demolished in 1907 to make way for an extension to Vienna Technical University. The Haydnhaus has had a Brahms memorial room since 1980. Portraits of Brahms, as well as furniture and personal effects from his previous accommodation, are on display.

The garden in the inner courtyard is not to be missed. It used to be planted with fruit trees, according to many of Haydn's guests, but has now been completely redesigned by the City of Vienna.

HUNDSTURMER KAPELLE

Last representative of the Hansl am Weg chapels

Junction of Schönbrunner Strasse / St Johanngasse, 1050 Wien
Exterior always accessible, interior only during services (times vary,
information at the entrance)

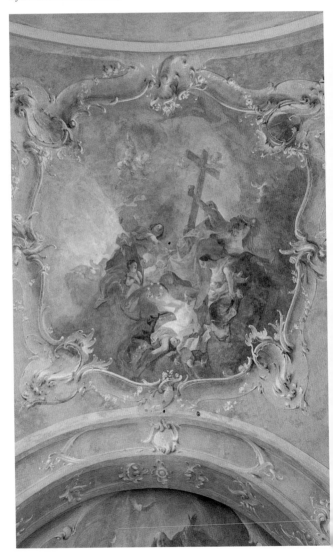

In popular parlance, the chapels that stretch along the fortifications are known as *Hansl am Weg* (Hans along the Way). They offered travellers both shelter and a place to pray. Although the chapel built in 1756 in Hundsturm, now a suburb of Vienna, is the last of these, it had been neglected for a long time. It was renovated in 2007, but now seems rather lost: the enclosure with its bridge and gates that once formed a harmonious architectural ensemble with the chapel have all gone.

Services are still celebrated in the chapel. The ceiling frescoes attributed to Franz Anton Maulbertsch were only rediscovered during recent renovation work. At the glass-clad entrance is a statue of St John of Nepomuk that has graced the interior since 1759. Originally, the building had eight life-size statues of saints. Three of them are still there, one is in Hütteldorf Cemetery (Penzing), and four have found a new home in the garden of a house in nearby Linzer Strasse.

A plaque mounted in the chapel in 2007 pays tribute to the victims of Nazism in the Margareten district.

The name Hundsturm (Hound Tower) dates back to 1850 and refers to an old building in the neighbourhood used for breeding imperial hunting dogs.

IDYLLE CERAMIC MURAL

The ideal Nazi family

Brandmayergasse 27, 1050 Wien
Tram: 6 / 18, Arbeitergasse / Gürtel stop

The ceramic mural on the end wall of the Brandmayergasse apartment block (1937–39), designed by the architect Peter Brich, is by Rudolf Böttger. The image is faithful to Nazi criteria for the ideal German family: father, mother and four children. The elder boy is wearing a Hitler Youth uniform and waving a swastika.

After coming under increasing pressure from the media, in 2002 the City of Vienna launched a competition for ideas to transform the artwork. The winning project was by Austrian artist Ulrike Lienbacher, who chose to cover it with a glass plate bearing the inscription *IDYLLE*, printed back to front to illustrate the falsely idyllic life of a family under the Third Reich. An explanatory notice in four languages was placed alongside.

Böttger, who was originally from Bohemia, assumed leading positions in the art and cultural policy of the Reich territory after the annexation of Austria. Following his expulsion from Czechoslovakia, he settled in Regensburg, where he lived until his death in 1973.

The building on Brandmayergasse, which was severely damaged during the Second World War, was restored by the architect Alois Strohmayer in 1945.

ÖSTERREICHISCHE GESELLSCHAFTS- UND WIRTSCHAFTSMUSEUM

"The Otto Neurath Method"

Vogelsanggasse 36, 1050 Wien
Open Monday to Thursday 8am–6pm, Friday 8am–2pm
www.wirtschaftsmuseum.at
Tram: 6 / 18, Margaretengürtel / Arbeitergasse stop

The leading Austrian economist Otto Neurath founded the Austrian Museum for Social and Economic Affairs in 1924, in association with the City of Vienna labour and social security department. Its objective was to present complex economic and social practices and their interrelations in a way that could be understood by all. Together with artist and graphic designer Gerd Arntz, Neurath developed the "Vienna Method of Pictorial Statistics", a symbolic way of visually representing quantitative information explained in the museum. Their approach consisted of replacing rows of unintelligible figures with immediately accessible graphic symbols.

The educational tour explains commonly used terms such as gross domestic product, inflation, money and currency. The EU and globalisation are among the key themes of the exhibition, which is aimed mainly at adolescents. The "100 Years of Life and Living" section traces the evolution of everyday life in Vienna, from the monarchy to the present. As a follow-up, 23 computers with interactive apps are available to visitors.

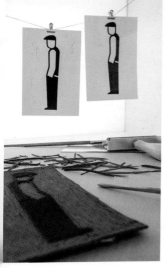

The museum was forced to close under the Austrofascist and then the Nazi regimes. Renamed the Isotype Institute in 1934, it became the Museum for Social and Economic Affairs in 1948.

The ensemble, housed in a former school, was conceived as a centre of public education. It holds regular free lectures on contemporary economic topics. The museum attracts over 100,000 visitors a year.

NEARBY

Kaffeemuseum

The building also has a Coffee Museum with an extensive collection of historic coffee machines, boxes and grinders, as well as documents and images. The coffee journey from plant to cup is presented in detail.

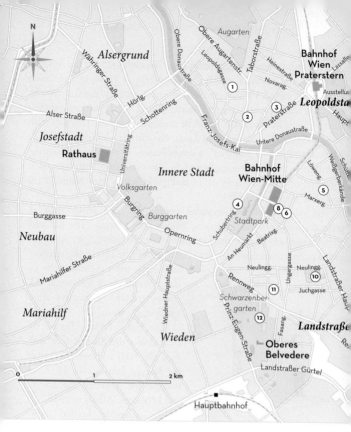

Leopoldstadt, Landstraße

MUMMIFIED HEAD IN THE WIENER① KRIMINALMUSEUM

Forensic experts at the Ringtheater

Grosse Sperlgasse 24, 1020 Wien
Open Thursday to Sunday, 10am–5pm
www.kriminalmuseum.at/krimwien.html

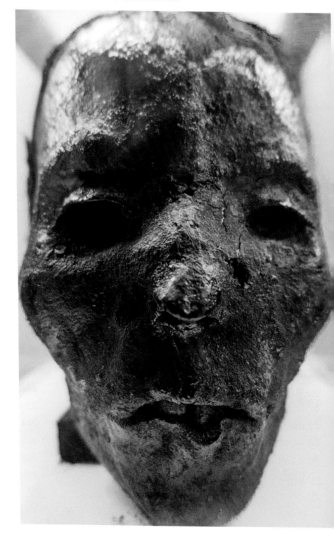

Room H of the Viennese Crime Museum, specialising in law, houses the charred body of a woman who died during the Ringtheater fire (see p. 440). Her head, the centrepiece of the collection, is particularly thought-provoking – "fascinating" or "macabre", depending on your point of view.

Squeamish visitors could instead look round the objects from the former Police Museum, but be prepared for large photos of murder victims dotted around the exhibition.

The many topics covered include the medieval legal system, the last executions in Vienna, serial killers of maidservants, poisoners, and the sinister mob lynching of the Minister of War, Latour (Theodor Franz, Count of Baillet von Latour) in 1848. There are also displays on the history of modern forensic pathology.

This type of scientific investigation developed towards the end of the 19th century, particularly after the tragic Ringtheater fire in 1881, which cost the lives of some 400 people. As the government offered to provide financial compensation to the families of the victims, forensic identification played a major role in distinguishing the true beneficiaries from the 700 claimants. Medicine and the police had rarely worked so closely together. The pathologist Eduard von Hofmann identified many of the bodies by studying their dentition – a revolutionary procedure at the time.

The Vienna School of Crime was set up around this time. Between 1870 and 1930, the Austrian police were leaders in their field.

Two other skulls of the fire victims are kept in the Department of Forensic Medicine at the University of Vienna, but this is closed to the public.

The former soap factory housing the Crime Museum was mentioned for the first time in a late 17th-century document, and the structure of the building reveals its age. It's one of the oldest in the 2nd district (Leopoldstadt).

PHARMACY OF THE KRANKENHAUSE ②
DER BARMHERZIGEN BRÜDER

The oldest Viennese hospital run by a religious Order

Taborstrasse 16, 1020 Wien
Open Monday to Friday 8am–6pm, Saturday 8am–noon
Tram: 2, Gredlerstrasse stop

Whereas the first Zum Granatapfel (Pomegranate) pharmacy, opened in 1624, is now an office space decorated with painted stucco, the present "new pharmacy" of 1803 is a superb place with remarkable Empire-style furniture. The parquet creaks and a sweet smell of waxed wood and herbs floats in the air. Although this pharmacy, specialising in cancer drugs and ophthalmological treatments, is intended for patients at the *Krankenhause der Barmherzigen Brüder* (Hospital of the Brothers Hospitallers), it's also open to the public.

This is Vienna's largest and oldest hospital run by a Roman Catholic Order. It was founded in 1614 by an Italian monk and renowned surgeon, Gabriele Ferrara. During the 19th century, the cloister was enlarged by architects Carl von Hasenauer, Otto Hofer and Anton Schönmann. Proving inadequate as soon as the work was completed, however, the building was again renovated and extended for over a decade during the 20th century. The clinic now boasts the most up-to-date dialysis centre in Europe.

In 2008 the square in front of the building, Johannes-von-Gott-Platz, was named in honour of the founder of the Hospitaller Order of St John of God in 2008. A stained-glass window in the cloister chapel shows the saint (1495–1550) healing the sick.

VIENNA'S WAY OF THE CROSS ③

The world's most emulated Way of the Cross

Pfarre St Johann Nepomuk
Nepomukgasse 1, 1020 Wien
Open daily 9am–6pm
U-Bahn: line U1, Nestroyplatz station

On the walls of the side-aisle of the parish church of St John Nepomuk, the *Kreuzweg* (Way of the Cross) by Joseph von Führich, a Viennese late Romantic artist, consists of 14 frescoes painted between 1844 and 1846.

This version of the Way of the Cross has been copied in over 100 churches scattered all over the world.

The life-size scenes are among the most important monumental paintings in Vienna. The artist's preliminary sketches, with the same dimensions, belong to the Albertina Museum (Innere Stadt). They are sometimes displayed at thematic exhibitions.

In his youth, Von Führich was an adherent of the Nazarene movement. These painters, all around 20 years old, were romantic religious artists with long hair and flowing tunics. Many of them had studied in Rome, where they were treated with derision by the locals, who called them Nazarenes because of their biblical mannerisms.

For the artist Von Führich, the conception and religious content of this Way of the Cross had a missionary dimension. He painted the frescoes during the summer months, but even at this time of year there was little natural light in the church. His pupil Adam Vogler assisted him, for his eyesight had worsened considerably during this immense task.

Unlike the Biedermeier-favouring art critics, Vienna churchgoers were enthralled by the frescoes. Believers were not put off by images of the Passion tinged with ancient medieval mysticism. Contemporary artists could do nothing to stop it: the immensely popular images were soon reduced, copied, engraved and printed. Just one year after the work was complete, printed reproductions were available for sale.

This success proved Von Führich right. The dramatic effect of the highly valued representations of devout Christians is still as strong as ever.

DEUTSCHMEISTER-PALAIS ④

Neo-Renaissance seat of a Grand Master

Parkring 8, 1010 Wien
Open only on special occasions, such as Heritage Days
www.ofid.org; www.tagdesdenkmals.at
Tram: 2, Weihburggasse stop; U-Bahn: line U4, Stadtpark station; line U3, Stubentor station

As Grand Master of the Teutonic Knights (*Deutschmeister*) from 1863 to 1894, Archduke Wilhelm Franz – one of the sons of Fieldmarshal Archduke Carl Ludwig of Austria – had this palace built between 1864 and 1868 to the plans of Ringstrasse architect Theophil Hansen. The building was the seat of the Grand Master from 1870 until the Anschluss.

The impressive five-storey neo-Renaissance building is open to the public on some occasions.

The main floor has several richly decorated state rooms: the monumental pillars and staircase are particularly impressive.

Hansen had to comply with certain rules in the construction of this palace: as the Grand Master of the Teutonic Knights cannot marry, there are no apartments for a spouse. Archduke Wilhelm did, however, have a son with actress Maria Lutz, later legitimised by Karl Rott, her future husband.

The vast, lavish stables, which could accommodate 24 horses, are spectacular – members of the Order always came to meetings on horseback.

After the Anschluss in 1938, the Teutonic Order was dissolved by the Nazis. The palace was requisitioned and the property transferred to the City of Vienna. Under the Third Reich, it became the Viennese headquarters of the SS (Schutzstaffel or protection squadron). In Franz Antel's film *Der Bockerer* (1981), Karl Merkatz plays the role of butcher Karl Bockerer, who is dragged from the staircase to the offices of an SS bureaucrat.

From the end of the war to 1974, the Federal Police Department occupied the former palace. As the building had begun to deteriorate, it has been restored at great expense. Some alterations were made: for example, the gravel-covered courtyard has been converted into a stone-slabbed atrium. The meeting rooms have been renovated in exactly the same style as the originals.

The building has been owned by the Organization of the Petroleum Exporting Countries since 1981 and currently hosts OFID, the OPEC Fund for International Development.

Archduke Wilhelm Franz of Austria (1827–94) was one of the few members of the Habsburg family to make his home on the magnificent Ringstrasse boulevard. However, this wasn't the outcome that Franz Joseph had intended when he started renovating the capital. Although the boulevard was supposed to be for members of his family and the aristocracy, it became a residential area for families who had made their fortune in industry and banking.

FÄLSCHERMUSEUM

True fakes!

Löwengasse 28, 1030 Wien
Open Tuesday to Sunday 10am–5pm
Tram: 1, Hetzgasse stop
www.faelschermuseum.com/Seite1_englische.htm

This private Museum of Art Fakes, established in 2005 and the only one of its kind unique in Europe, is concerned with forgeries but also with disentangling the true from the false. How to recognise a copy? What's the difference between imitation, fake and copy?

An unknown Chagall where the paint isn't completely dry, a brand-new Bruegel or another version of Klimt's *Judith* ... This "criminal" art museum is doing some intriguing detective work on forgeries. Are those who make the copies artists? Are imitations of any value?

Art forgers such as Han van Meegeren, Edgar Mrugalla, Lothar Malskat, Eric Hebborn and Tom Keating are featured here. You'll discover why an English master forger hid "time bombs" in his canvases and why another disappeared in suspicious circumstances ...

An entire section is devoted to Konrad Kujau, who sold the (fake) diary of Adolf Hitler to the German magazine *Stern* for nearly 10 million marks in 1983.

HEAD OF ST ELIZABETH OF THURINGIA ⑥

Authenticated with the mark of a golden band

Elisabethinenkirche
Landstrasser Hauptstrasse 4a, 1030 Wien
Open 19 November (St Elizabeth's Day) only
www.elisabethinen-wien.at
U-Bahn: line U3 / U4, Landstrasse station

The most important Christian relics in the City of Vienna, outside the Innere Stadt, are kept in an ornate silver-framed glass case in the oratory of the Church of St Elizabeth (on the left) – the skull and femurs of St Elizabeth of Thuringia, patron saint of charity.

Elizabeth, who was widowed very young and died in extreme poverty in 1231 at the age of 24, had long been venerated as a saint. She had given up all her possessions in order to found a hospital for the sick and the poor in Marburg, Germany. She was buried in the hospital church and canonised in 1235. Her coffin was later transferred to a shrine in the great new Church of St Elizabeth at Marburg, built by the Order of the Teutonic Knights in her honour. A barefoot Emperor Frederick II himself took part in the procession.

In 1539, the Protestant Landgrave of Hesse removed Elizabeth's magnificent coffin and appropriated the precious crown. Her skull and femurs were handed over to the Vienna Order of the Poor Clares in 1588, while her lower jaw is now on display in Besançon, France. The greater part of the body was nevertheless returned to Marburg, so that the Catholic saint rests in a Protestant church.

As the Poor Clares were devoted mainly to prayer and silence, their "useless" (i.e. non-practical) Order was abolished by Emperor Joseph II. The bones of the Countess of Thuringia were handed over to the Elisabethinen nuns (whose caregiving Order was not dissolved). They gave the saint a new crown, which she still wears today. There is no doubt about the authenticity of her skull, for the bone still bears the impression of the golden headband that noblewomen wore from childhood.

From secret code to Braille

Wittelsbachstrasse 5, 1020 Wien
Visits by appointment only
www.bbi.at/museum

The third floor of Vienna's Blindenerziehungsinstitut (Institute for the Blind), founded in the 19th century, has a remarkable collection that traces the history of blind people in Austria. The German philanthropist Johann Wilhelm Klein launched an entirely benevolent project to get them off the streets, so that they no longer had to beg or to work as musicians in sad taverns on the outskirts of town.

In 1804, Klein set up the first educational institution for blind people in a German-speaking country – it was to become the world's largest and most comprehensive collection on the subject.

The first book printed in raised lettering was published in 1796, thanks to the goddaughter of Empress Maria Theresa, the blind composer and pianist Maria Theresia von Paradis, who was famous throughout Europe. She had shown that blindness had nothing whatsoever to do with mental deficiency. The teaching material that was specially designed for her is displayed in the museum. Around 1800, education was regarded as the most precious advantage a person could have. Everyone should be able to benefit from a basic education so as not to become a burden on the community.

The museum focuses on the development of writing and learning styles for the visually impaired. Such objects as period "tactile" watches, sets of letters of the alphabet, globes, topographical maps and animal models are of great historical interest.

Louis Braille's system was established in 1825. Its ancestor is a rather similar alphabet used as a military code during the Napoleonic wars.

The evolution of the Braille typewriter is covered in detail. One unique machine, built in Turin in 1899, has the distinction of being adapted to both "normal" lettering and Braille. This type of relief printing began to be used in all languages.

The Institute for the Blind has occupied this address on Wittelsbachstrasse since 1898, when Anton Dreher, millionaire owner of the Schwechater brewery, donated the site.

The museum opened in 1910 with the Klein collection. The collection has been constantly expanded and it now possesses some 1,700 items relating to blindness.

PHARMACY OF KRANKENHAUS ST ELISABETH

A historic Baroque gem

Landstrasser Hauptstrasse 4a, 1030 Wien
Open only on certain occasions such as "Long Night of the Churches"
https://www.franziskusspital.com/
U-Bahn: line U3 / U4, Landstrasse station

The pharmacy of St Elizabeth Hospital is one of the few from the late Baroque period (1750) to have been fully preserved, and is certainly one of the most beautiful in the world.

It is still open, but not usually to the public, only meeting the needs of the hospital to which it is attached.

Unfortunately, the maker of the pharmacy's sumptuous furniture is as much a mystery as the fresco artist (18th-century Austrian painter and etcher Johann Cimbal?). The paintings depict angels holding medicinal plants or apothecary's utensils; Teresa of Avila (or according to other sources St Elizabeth) writing in a herbal; pious words drawn on the walls in Viennese dialect so that everyone can understand them; St Francis below a cross, a rose growing at his feet; a blindfolded woman – allegory of vice – injuring herself on the thorns of a rose.

The symbols commonly used by pharmacists and alchemists to represent the four elements, Earth, Fire, Water and Air, feature in little triangles.

Drawers exude the aroma of the herbs and remedies stored there over the centuries. The huge counter with its crucifix and apothecary's scale stands in the centre while cabinets are filled with glass, wood, tin and ceramic containers. Laboratory flasks are numbered to identify them when used within the hospital.

In another room, ostrich eggs and huge narwhal teeth, thought to be unicorn horns, are displayed below frescoes of the four continents that supplied the medicines. Europe is decorated with mortars and test tubes.

ELISABETHKAPELLE

A little-known memorial to an assassinated empress

Franz-von-Assisi-Kirche
Mexikoplatz 12, 1020 Wien
Chapel accessible during church opening hours
www.erzdioezese-wien.at/pages/pfarren/9015
U-Bahn: line U1, Vorgartenstrasse station

The Red Cross Society, whose first patron was Empress Elisabeth, dedicated a chapel to her memory in St Francis of Assisi (aka Kaiser Jubilee) Church in 1900, two years after her assassination in Geneva. The construction of this massive Romanesque-style basilica, begun in 1898 and completed in 1910, was originally intended to celebrate the 50th anniversary of the reign of Franz Joseph in December 1898. But the commemoration was more modest than expected, following Sisi's tragic death in September that year.

The chapel, designed and built by the architect Viktor Luntz, was consecrated in 1908. This little Art Nouveau gem, too often overlooked, is the result of a commission from the extremely conservative imperial house and was inspired by classical models: the Basilica of San Vitale in Ravenna, Italy, and the Palatine Chapel of Aachen Cathedral, Germany. The octagonal hall is decorated with gold mosaics and the marble covering the walls is reminiscent of early Christian baptisteries. To the left of the entrance, five steps and a grille separate the chapel from the rest of the church. A medallion depicts St Elizabeth of Thuringia, patroness of the deceased sovereign.

NEARBY

On the western face of the richly ornate façade, a sacred work still evokes Elisabeth and her patron saint, the Countess of Thuringia. A bas-relief by Theodor Charlemont shows the empress kneeling before the saint, who is welcoming her into heaven. As with all representations of Sisi, and in spite of her 60 years, she retains her youthful looks as if time held no sway.

ARENBERGPARK FLAKTÜRM

Code name: Valerian

Dannebergplatz, 1030 Wien
Open to the public during exhibitions

Two flak towers, immense reinforced concrete blockhouses, were built in Arenbergpark during the Second World War to protect the city and its inhabitants from air raids.

Vienna has three pairs of towers, each consisting of a combat tower for anti-aircraft guns and a command tower for observation and evaluation of data.

The largest of the flak towers, in Arenbergpark, was code-named "Valerian". Nine-storeys-high, it was built between December 1942 and October 1943. It has walls 2 metres thick, increasing to 7 metres on the upper floors. The lower levels were used as civilian shelters, the fourth floor as a hospital, the fifth for the heating and ventilation system, and the sixth for the Ostmark aircraft engine repair shops. The top floors housed the military, propaganda offices and the radio station Reichssenders Wien. There are hardly any windows.

The Arenbergpark combat tower, used by the Austrian Museum of Applied Arts (MAK) as a repository of their contemporary art collection, is itself considered as a work of art through the Contemporary Art Tower (CAT) project

The flak tower is open to the public during exhibitions, but visitors enter at their own risk because the security system is rudimentary. There are very few reminders of the war left.

RUSSISCH-ORTHODOXE KIRCHE ST NIKOLAUS ⑪

A church at the embassy

Jauresgasse 2, 1030 Wien
Open during Mass or by appointment
www.russischekirche.at/

Vienna's Russian Orthodox Church, built between 1893 and 1899 in the gardens of the Russian Embassy, was financed by private donations as well as funds from the Tsar.

Grigory Ivanovich Kotov, a Russian specialist in historic religious buildings, drew up the plans along 17th-century models. The upper church, completed under the reign of Tsar Nicholas II, is dedicated to St Nicholas of Myra, while the lower church (begun under Tsar Alexander III) is dedicated to the "Orthodox Grand Duke" Alexander Nevsky.

The cathedral (as it has been since the 1962 establishment of the Russian Orthodox Diocese of Vienna) has 10 bells, one of which – the last to be installed – was donated by the Red Army in 1947. It was cast from German cannon.

Between 1914 and 1924, the church was virtually unused because of the tense diplomatic relations between Austria and the Soviet Union. From 1927, the building was used as a warehouse by the Soviet Embassy. During the Nazi period, the group of buildings housed part of the Reichshochschule music conservatory as well as a boarding school.

In October 1945, after being closed for 31 years, the church was restored to its original function. It has recently been completely renovated, regaining its former glory.

The Russian Orthodox Church in Vienna has a significant collection of Christian relics, including those of St Nicholas, St Peter and St Paul (brought directly from Rome), St Martin of Tours, as well as St Alexander Nevsky and holy monks from the St Petersburg monastery. The sacristy also has a relic of the Cross from Venice, which had been brought from Byzantium by the Crusaders.

Nowadays the church services are attended by Ukrainians, Belorussians, Georgians, Macedonians, Moldovans, Austrians and Germans, as well as Russians.

HUNDRED-YEAR-OLD YEW

Vienna's oldest natural monument

Rennweg 12, 1030 Wien
Ask the porter at the European Patent Office, Monday to Friday 8am–4pm
Tram: 71, Rennweg stop; S-Bahn or O tram, Ungargasse / Neulinggasse station

The ancient yew which stands in the gardens of the Patent Office is said to be the last survivor from a grove of yews dating back to Roman times. This huge tree has enjoyed protected status since 1936.

Even assuming that the presumed age of this yew seems to owe more to myth than reality, the species is known to grow very slowly and can live for over 2,000 years.

Conifers prefer the shade, which is why they have been associated for centuries with the afterworld or limbo. Yew can also be toxic: a decoction of needles and branches was traditionally used as a laxative and for deworming.

As early as the 15th century, yew trees along the roads and in the villages were felled or burned to avoid poisoning horses and cattle. They were also torn up or chopped down because of their sanctity to many Germanic peoples. Furthermore, the Church looked askance at the needle-based preparation that could induce an abortion. For all these reasons, the yew has become scarce throughout Europe.

All yew trees in Austria have been protected for several decades now, and their little red berries still garnish the forests in autumn. The fleshy casing of the berries is the only non-toxic part of the plant.

RABENHOF THEATER

From social housing to the stage

Rabengasse 3 / St Nikolaus-Platz, 1030 Wien
Open during performances
www.rabenhoftheater.com
U-Bahn: line U3, Kardinal-Nagl-Platz station

Vienna is probably one of the few cities in the world with a theatre in the heart of a social housing complex. Built between 1925 and 1928, it was known as "Austerlitz-Hofes" in a tribute to Friedrich Austerlitz, the militant editor of the newspaper *Arbeiter Zeitung*. The large hall was a meeting place for the workers who lived in the affordable housing round about.

Renamed the Rabenhof in 1934, the complex is one of the most remarkable developments of the 1920s in "Red Vienna", as the city was known when a strong municipal government was trying to solve its social problems. The main hall was converted into a cinema in the 1930s, and then a major renovation around 1990 enabled the Theater in der Josefstadt (the oldest in Vienna) to use the venue too. Additional work carried out in 2008 aimed to restore its former splendour to one of the finest authentic halls of the interwar period.

Today, the Rabenhof is an independent theatre that has become a benchmark for political satire and cabaret. Among the other events organised here are theatre for young audiences, musical comedy and book readings.

The venue is regularly used as a set for the police procedural TV series *Kommissar Rex* and *Tatort*.

MUSEUM REMISE WIENER LINIEN

A spectacular setting

Ludwig-Koessler-Platz, 1030 Wien
Open Wednesday 9am–6pm, Saturday and Sunday 10am–6pm
https://www.wienerlinien.at/eportal3/ep/channelView.do?channelId=-46636

The Remise Transport Museum, which reopened in 2014, offers a journey into the fascinating universe of public transport in a major city, heading back in time to a page in Viennese history.

The museum, housed in Remise Erdberg, an immense brick hall dating back to 1901, now has the space to display an impressive collection of Vienna Line vehicles in a perfectly adapted setting.

Public transport over 150 years, from the horse-drawn tram to the opening of the metro, testifies to the changing city lifestyle and also teaches basic electrical engineering. But the thematic displays are not just for information: they also invite you to slip into the shoes of a 19th-century conductor and face the challenges of the job, design your own tramway and oversee the planning of the network, or even drive a subway train in the simulator.

The interactive museum currently has 40 vintage vehicles as well as a subway carriage accessible to visitors.

The former Remise hall, with all its facilities, can be hired for professional events or private functions.

A WALK ON THE "WILD SIDE"

Urban wilderness with a very special atmosphere

Maiselgasse / Baumgasse, 1030 Wien
U-Bahn: line U3, Schlachthausgasse station; Tram: 18, Baumgasse stop

Opening onto Baumgasse, parallel to Schlachthausgasse, Maiselgasse leads to the "wild side". It's also signposted Wiener Gstettn. Over the last few decades, this raised plateau has seen the proliferation of a variety of plant and animal life that gives it a very special atmosphere. A real urban wilderness.

The *Gstettn* (plots reclaimed by nature) overlooking the steep banks of the Danube are in sharp contrast to this densely populated suburb with its busy roads.

It was here that the second city wall (Linienwall) once met the river. Some vestiges of the wall are still visible near the dog-friendly park. A branch of the river flowed here before redevelopment, which led to the emergence of this high plateau, nearly 10 metres above the former riverbed.

The recently built neighbourhood of Neu-Marx is also visible on the horizon, at the site of the former slaughterhouse. Although the noise of the nearby motorway is inescapable, you can still hear birds chirping in this particularly attractive part of the city.

KIRCHE MARIA GRÜN

Energy boost for the sick and newlyweds

Aspernallee 1, 1020 Wien
Bus: 77A, Lusthaus / Aspernallee stop

A little off the main path through the Prater, near the Altes Jägerhaus restaurant, the Roman Catholic pilgrimage site dedicated to Maria Grün ("Mary on the Green") is considered to be a source of energy and fulfilment for those who love esotericism, sick people and newlyweds.

Numerous weddings are held here in spring and summer, and in the month of May, the "Long Night of the Churches" ends with a walk through the Prater towards Maria Grün Church.

As early as the 19th century, before the church was built in 1924, an image of the Virgin Mary decorated a tree, later to be replaced by a statue. So many pictures and religious symbols were added that the park management was obliged to remove many of them. The church itself eventually became a place of pilgrimage in 1937.

These days the site mainly attracts Croats from Austria's Burgenland province, as can be seen from the votive images in the side chapel. Since

1985 an organ has replaced the former harmonium.

The small square chapel next to the church dates back to 1931. It was built to protect the open-air altar from the elements. The rather kitsch symbols of the Way of the Cross, glass tomb and Mount of Olives in relief are from the same period.

The priest and chaplain of the Archdiocese of Vienna responsible for people living with AIDS has an office at the church. The AIDS Memorial (inaugurated in 2007) is also on this site: a red ribbon on a gravel bed and the phrase "Susanne 2004", in memory of a woman who died as a result of AIDS in 2004.

Rectangular, oval, differently coloured street nameplates: the forgotten history of Viennese place names and numbers

Vienna currently has around 6,800 streets that cover a total of 3,000 kilometres.

The shortest is Irisgasse in the Innere Stadt (1st district), which owes its name to the best-known funeral parlour in Vienna, Zur Irisblume, while the longest is the Höhenstrasse (17th to 19th districts), most of which was built in the 1930s as part of a programme to tackle unemployment.

As early as 1782, Emperor Joseph II ordered that names should appear on the façades at the beginning and end of each street. A nameplate from this era still exists in Blutgasse (1st district).

Street signs like those of today first appeared around 1860. The streets radiating outwards from Stephansplatz had rectangular plates, while the streets parallel to the Ringstrasse (the grand circular boulevard commonly known as the Ring) were fitted with an oval-shaped panel.

To facilitate identification of the different suburbs, districts 1 to 9 had a square plate, each with a distinct colour: red, violet, green, pink, black, yellow, blue, grey and brown respectively.

Later, all street signs were given a red frame. The inscription itself was red for squares and black for streets and roads.

Since about 1940, all the nameplates have been uniformly blue and white. Since the 1980s, only those places with special architectural merit have been given a copy of the historic plate dating back to the construction of the Ringstrasse.

Houses with the old numbering system, known as "constituency numbers", are still sometimes found. These were introduced during the 18th and 19th centuries to help in the administration of housing and plots of land.

The numbers were mainly used for military purposes and for collecting taxes or statistics (census of buildings and occupants).

As a single house could be allocated several numbers over the decades due to cadastral changes, the expression "house number" came to be a rough estimate rather than a precise indication.

Outside the Centre North

HELDENBERG MEMORIAL

"Three heroes found eternal rest here; two of them delivered battle, the third delivered shoes"

3704 Kleinwetzdorf
Open April and October 9am–5pm, May to September 9am–6pm
Closed in winter and on Mondays, except public holidays

The Heldenberg Memorial, in the grounds of the castle at Kleinwetzdorf, has been ridiculed since the 19th century in these lines: "Three heroes found eternal rest here; two of them delivered battle, the third delivered shoes." Count Joseph Radetzky von Radetz and Baron Maximilian von Wimpffen were both fieldmarshals. The third man, Joseph Gottfried Pargfrieder, was a major supplier to the imperial army and a millionaire of private means. The Walhalla of Regensburg (hall of fame in honour of illustrious figures of German civilisation) was the model for the Heldenberg Memorial.

To reach the crypt where the three men are buried, go through the entrance gate, with its sometimes formless figures by 19th-century sculptor Adam Rammelmayer, and follow the path up the hill to an artificial plateau. To left and right are statues of Radetzky and Von Wimpffen. Clio, the Muse of History, gazes at an obelisk on top of which a genie weeps, torch lowered. The military men are buried here, while Pargfrieder himself lies nine steps below them.

From the obelisk and entrance to the crypt, the Path of the Heroes (Heldenallee) and the Path of the Emperor (Kaiserallee) lead to the statue of a young Franz Joseph.

Pargfrieder presented himself as the illegitimate son of Joseph II, his ancestry and date of birth being unknown. He made his fortune as an official supplier to the army, providing food, clothing and shoes during the Napoleonic Wars. He acquired the Wetzdorf estate in 1832.

Radetzky was a nobleman but lived in poverty with his wife and eight children. His association with Pargfrieder was providential and saved him from several challenging financial situations. As Pargfrieder assumed Radetzky and Von Wimpffen's gambling debts, the pair agreed that he too should be buried at Heldenberg. Franz Joseph offered Radetzky, a key member of his General Staff, the opportunity to be buried in the Capuchin Crypt instead of the Heldenberg – an offer he refused. After Radetzky's funeral, Pargfrieder presented the entire park to the emperor.

The symbols on Pargfrieder's tomb (Sun, Moon, triangle with serpent, cross and four roses) suggest that he belonged to the Freemasons and the Rosicrucians. He had expressly refused any spiritual assistance at his death. The letters K. I. S. I. P. F. V. F. engraved on his coffin probably signify: "Joseph Pargfrieder son of the Emperor Joseph *vivi fecit*" (had built).

Although his body had been taken for burial on a cart pulled by cattle when he died in 1863, in the late 1970s Pargfrieder was exhumed in order to check whether his last wishes had been respected. He was in fact found to be seated, in a red-flowered silk dressing gown below his armour, embalmed with bitumen, a hat on his head. Josephine Pargfrieder, his daughter, married the "brick baron", Austrian industrialist Heinrich von Drasche.

MUSEUM GUGGING

Art Brut

Campus 2, 3400 Klosterneuburg – Maria Gugging
Open Tuesday to Sunday; winter 10am–5pm, summer 10am–6pm
http://www.gugging.at/en/
Bus: 239, Maria Gugging IST Austria stop

Klosterneuburg is home to the stunning Gugging Museum, which specializes in Art Brut (literally, "raw art"): artists such as Heinrich Reisenbauer and Günther Schützenhöfer live and work there.

The history of Art Brut (also known as Outsider Art) in Gugging began nearly 60 years ago, when psychiatrist Leo Navratil encouraged his patients from the clinic to draw and paint for therapeutic purposes. The doctor came to appreciate the surprising talent of some of the patients and began to encourage the most gifted among them.

Harald Szeemann, a Swiss curator, presented some of the patients' pictures at the "Documenta 5" event in Cassel in 1972. Their work has since been exhibited worldwide and the "Gugging Artists" are now recognised.

The psychiatric clinic was renamed the Gugging House of Artists in 2006. Patients' artworks are displayed over more than 1,300 square metres, directly where they were created. The permanent exhibition has a wide selection of paintings, drawings, reproductions and three-dimensional objects, and there are regular temporary exhibitions.

In recent years, women have lived and worked in what was originally a male-only artists' community. In the first room is a group portrait that includes Viennese artist Laila Bachtiar, a follower of the Gugging workshop.

The term "Art Brut" (raw art) was coined by French painter Jean Dubuffet. It refers to art on the margins of traditional artistic activity, and artists working outside generally agreed aesthetic standards.

TOMB OF JOSEPH VON HAMMER-PURGSTALL

Muslim inscriptions in a Christian cemetery

Weidling Cemetery
Lenaugasse, 3400 Klosterneuburg-Weidling
Open daily until nightfall

Built along the lines of Islamic tombs, the unusual funerary monument of Austrian diplomat and Orientalist Joseph von Hammer-Purgstall (1777–1856) stands next to the grave of Nikolaus Lenau, the Weltschmerz (World Pain) German Romantic poet. Two large stelae stand at the head and foot of the memorial. The headstone is engraved with a phrase commonly used at the time: "I flew at dawn / To rest with God."

Baron von Hammer-Purgstall's wife, banker's daughter Caroline von Henikstein, who had died several years earlier, had already been buried in this cemetery reserved exclusively for the nobility. Her husband had the following inscription engraved:

> *The much-lamented Caroline*
> *born 22 July 1797 von Henikstein,*
> *who died 15 May 1844.*
> *A woman noble*
> *in mind, soul and heart of a rare mother*
> *and wife tenderly loved by*
> *Joseph Freiherr Hammer-Purgstall*
> *born 9 June 1774, died 23.11.1856,*
> *who rests here with her.*

His own date of decease was added later. This tomb is not the only one of its kind: although this is a Christian cemetery, there are numerous Arabic, Turkish and Persian inscriptions in the centre. Poems by the 14th-century Persian mystic Hafez that Hammer-Purgstall had translated can be seen, as well as Islamic sayings designed for burial sites, with many references and much praise to Allah. There are also inscriptions in Latin, Greek, French, Spanish and English, all on the theme of death. The scholar himself had chosen the style of the tomb and the quotations to be engraved on it.

Behind the Hammer-Purgstall sepulchre is a small column with a rose ornament. This is the funerary monument of Rosalie, the couple's daughter, who died in childhood. Her father had a commemorative plaque made on the model of Eastern women's tombs, with this inscription: "The heavens gave her and took her back again. As Rose she lived as roses live."

Joseph von Hammer-Purgstall mastered an impressive number of languages and became an interpreter and translator. He courageously and confidently braved the censorship that was omnipresent in his day, arousing the hostility of Prince Metternich. His subsequent demotion gave him time to support the foundation of the Austrian Academy of Sciences and he became its first president, from 1847 to 1849. Goethe was inspired by Von Hammer-Purgstall's translations of Hafez to compose one of his own late works, a collection of lyrical poems in the Persian style, *West–Östlicher Divan* (*West–Eastern Diwan*), published in 1819.

A great nature lover, the Orientalist from Graz regularly spent his time hiking around Weidling and Klosterneuburg. The Austrian Oriental Society, founded in 1959, is formally named Österreichische Orient-Gesellschaft Hammer-Purgstall in recognition of his achievements.

AGNESBRÜNDL

A spring where your lucky numbers might come up

Jägerwiese 221, 1190 Wien
Bus 43A, Höhenstrasse / Rohrerwiese stop

Near the Plaine des Chasseurs restaurant, at the foot of the Hermannskogel, is another legendary site: Agnesbründl (Agnes' spring). From here you can see the town of Klosterneuburg and, on a clear day, the Czech border. Even though it feels a long way from the city, the cathedral is only 12 kilometres away.

Countless legends tell of the miraculous spring waters: anyone who embraces the portrait of Mary has their wish granted, for example.

Another legend says that if you sprinkle your eyes with this water, you'll see the winning lottery numbers for a brief moment.

According to a third legend, a forest fairy who had a child by a passing king met the daughter of Agnes.

Both the clergy and the authorities try to disperse the crowds that regularly gather here, in the first case to fight against superstition, and in the second to prevent demonstrations.

Mandrake roots have even been sold here to plunge into the water at nightfall, in the hope that would bring happiness ...

The annual Kirtag spring festival, which attracts all manner of prophets, clairvoyants and charlatans to the Agnesbründl, has been strictly controlled by the police since the 19th century.

The surrounding trees, and the spring to which healing powers are attributed, have always attracted crowds. Some say the place has significant telluric radiation. Trees growing crooked, in spirals or with other bizarre deformations also suggest the presence of radiesthetic (sensitivity to energy forces) phenomena.

Judging by the quantity of books and greeting cards found lying around the spring throughout the year, many people still hope for a miracle at Agnesbründl.

Weidling parish church

An image of the Virgin Mary that has been at Agnesbründl since the 19th century can now be seen in a niche of the ambulatory at Weidling parish church (No. 2 Hauptstrasse, 3400 Klosterneuburg-Weidling).

HERMANNSKOGEL

The measure of Vienna

1190 Wien
Grounds always accessible
Tower open from beginning of April to end of October, Saturday 1pm–6pm,
Sunday and public holidays 10am–5pm
Österreichischer Touristenklub (ÖTK); Tel: +43 (0)1 5123 844

The Hermannskogel, a hill in Döbling, is the highest natural point of Vienna (542 metres above sea level). During the Austro-Hungarian Empire, the hill was key to the measurement system and was used as a central reference point.

Since 1888, a medieval-style watchtower (27 metres high), built by Franz Ritter von Neumann in celebration of the 40th anniversary of Emperor Franz Joseph's reign, has stood on the summit.

The Austrian Tourist Club, which had organised a subscription to build the tower, still runs it, opening to the public on weekends during the season. The parapet at the top has a panoramic view of Vienna and the surrounding area.

Access to the Hermannskogel is via City Hiking Path 2 (departure and arrival in Sievering), which leads through a traditional leisure area with plenty of restaurants and Heurigen taverns. The round trip is approximately 10 kilometres and takes three to four hours. A highly recommended destination, even in winter!

SISI-KAPELLE AM HIMMEL

Mausoleum of a lottery scammer

Himmelstrasse, corner of Höhenstrasse
Gspöttgraben, 1190 Wien
Access: exterior any time, interior only during events

The Sisi Chapel was built between 1854 and 1856 in Am Himmel, a popular recreational area near the Vienna Woods, to the plans of architect Johan A. Garben. It is the oldest neo-Gothic monument in Vienna.

The chapel architecture is distinctively modern and romantic. But this is more than a chapel – it was commissioned by Johann Carl, Baron von Sothen, as a mausoleum for himself and his wife Franziska.

Baron von Sothen, son of a tobacco trader, had acquired his noble title from a German grand duke. In addition to his tobacco ventures, the baron also bought up used playing cards and cleaned them with spirits to resell in the Drahtgasse. He organised lotteries with houses as prizes, making vast sums of money in the process.

Von Sothen's multimillionaire status allowed him to acquire Cobenzl hill, where he could go hunting. He was gunned down in 1881 by the man in charge of the shoot, who was said to be seeking revenge after being dismissed. A more likely reason is that the retainer had grasped the secret of the baron's wealth. He was an expert swindler – carrier pigeons brought him the results of a lottery draw in the city centre while he placed his money on the winning numbers in the suburbs, where betting was still in full swing.

The gunman was condemned to death for murder but later pardoned by the emperor.

On the day of von Sothen's funeral, 20,000 people came along to make sure the crook was dead. They threw stones and rubbish at the coffin, in defiance of a police cordon. The industrialist's mausoleum bears a heartfelt inscription that goes something like this:

> *Here in this vault of the very best*
> *the worst of all crooks lies at rest.*
> *Don't show him a single sou*
> *or he'll rise up right beside you.*

The Sisi Chapel suffered major damage during the Second World War, and only a decision of the Austrian Federal Office of Historic Monuments saved it from demolition. The windows and doors were blocked up to discourage vandalism. In 2002, because the ground was drying out, the bodies of the von Sothens were exhumed: the following year, they were reburied outside the building.

On 24 April 1854, Emperor Franz Joseph married Elisabeth of Bavaria (known as "Sisi"), who became Empress of Austria. It was in honour of the new empress that Baron von Sothen dedicated his monument to the imperial couple's patron saint, Elizabeth of Thuringia (Elizabeth of Hungary).

CHOLERAKREUZ

Will-o'-the-wisp

Between Agnesgasse and the Dreimarkstein, 1190 Wien
Bus: 39A, Ährengrubenwegstop

On the way from Agnesgasse to the Dreimarkstein hill is a simple wayside cross, colloquially known as the Cholerakreuz (Cholera Cross), with a mosaic of the Madonna and Child on the front of the pillar. A legend relating to the cholera epidemic is linked to this monument.

There were many cholera victims at Sievering, an old wine-producing village now in the 19th district, and the dead were buried in a mass grave where this cross stands today. One of the dead seemed to be unable to find peace, for passers-by noticed a flame dancing above the grave. A boastful hunter declared to his drinking companions that he could give this poor soul some rest. He struck the flame with the butt of his rifle … and a shot rang out in the night. The next morning he was found dead at the foot of the cross, and was buried with the victims of the epidemic. The dancing flame was seen no more.

WASSERSCHLOSS HACKENBERG ⑧

A Döbling spectre?

Hackenberggasse 130, 1190 Wien
Always accessible (outside only)
Bus: 39A, Ährengrubenweg stop

Among the workers' housing and little gardens of the 19th district is an unusual building surrounded by a grassy sward, its walls covered with creeper. From a distance, with the lake waters lapping nearby, the domed roof, balcony and empty windows, the place resembles a scene from a horror movie.

Known locally as the Wasserschloss (Castle by the Water), it does seem to be a perfect film set. A series of *Kommissar Rex* was in fact filmed there in 2002.

This curious Romantic Secessionist building, listed as a historic monument, was originally a utilitarian construction by Eduard Bodenseher senior, architect in the Vienna planning office. It was built between 1908 and 1910 as a reservoir for the Second Vienna Spring Water Main. A large cistern stood just behind the building before it was eventually filled in, hence this extensive area of level ground. The tower itself was the chamber from which the sluice gate was operated, while the flat roof terrace was used as a lookout point.

Schutzhaus restaurant

After a stroll around Döbling, a good place to recover is the Schutzhaus restaurant in Hackenberg (No. 2 Am Neustiftblick), just a few steps from the tower.
Open every day.

BOUQUET OF ARTIFICIAL FLOWERS ⑨
AT GEYMÜLLERSCHLÖSSEL

Each flower consists of several butterfly wings

Pötzleinsdorfer Strasse 102, 1180 Wien
Villa: open May to November every Sunday 11am–6pm
Pötzleinsdorfer Schlosspark: open all day
Tram: 41, Pötzleinsdorf stop

In the first-floor salon of the small classical-style Geymüller villa is a rather striking bouquet of "artificial flowers", made in Prague around 1840.

Although at first glance this looks like any bouquet of dried flowers, a closer look reveals that the flowers are not actually made from petals. With extraordinary skill, each flower is composed of several butterfly wings.

Stuffed birds and a collection of wax fruit (a material that still has connotations of death) complete the floral arrangement.

Geymüllerschlössel is used as an exhibition space by MAK (Museum of Applied Arts) and is one of the few places in Austria open to the public specialising in Biedermeier decorative art

The villa was built in 1808 as a summer residence for Viennese merchant and banker Johann Jakob Geymüller. At the end of the 19th century, it was bought by textile manufacturer, Isidor Mautner, who turned it into a leading centre of the Viennese music and theatre scene. After the Nazi era and the end of the Second World War, the villa passed into the hands of the Austrian National Bank, which sold it to the state in 1948. The funds for this purchase were supplied by Franz Sobek, in return for the right to live there for the rest of his life. He had a fabulous collection of Viennese clocks that he left to the MAK, some of which can be seen in various rooms.

A beautiful garden with modern art installations is also open to the public. The ground floor of the villa hosts concerts in summer.

Pötzleinsdorf has been home to a Rudolf Steiner School since the 1990s.

Ringtheater statues

On the other side of the road is Pötzleinsdorfer Schlosspark (Pötzleinsdorf Palace Park), formerly owned by the same Geymüller. This park has sports facilities, playgrounds and grass-covered recreation areas. In the central alley stand four statues from the Ringtheater (burned down in 1881), nicknamed the "Singing Quartet".

URSULA'S HEAD(S)

Thousands of holy virgins

Treasure Room of Klosterneuburg Abbey
Stiftsplatz 1, 3400 Klosterneuburg
Open 17 November to 30 April 10am–5m, 1 May to 16 November 9am–6pm
Bus: 239, Klosterneuburg Stift stop

Klosterneuburg Abbey has a total of 12 *Ursulaköpferln* (Ursula Heads, see below), four of which are quite spectacular, on display in the Treasure Room. Most of the heads are in Cologne, Germany, but others can be found in southern Germany and Switzerland.

These heads are in fact skulls covered with fabric and decorated with multicoloured stones and a funerary crown. When unmarried women died, they were buried with this type of ornament: never having worn

a wedding headdress in life, it seemed only fair that they should have one for their funeral. This custom lasted until the mid-20th century in remote country areas.

These sophisticated ornaments (dating from the 18th century) were made by the women of the Laurenzerkloster St Jakob am Fleischmarkt in Vienna's Innere Stadt. Towards the end of the century, this monastery was closed and the premises converted into offices.

The term "Ursula Heads" refers to St Ursula and her followers, supposedly 11,000 virgins (there were only 11 originally). All these women are said to have been killed by the Huns in 3rd-century Cologne. Of course this is fantasy, especially as the legend has only been in circulation since the 10th century.

A lucrative trade in Christian relics emerged when the construction of the Basila Church of St Ursula in Cologne – built over an ancient Roman cemetery – brought to light a mass grave with a vast quantity of bones in 1106. It was assumed that these were the remains of the 11 martyrs, who became 11,000 simply through a translation error. Thousands of new holy virgins were thus "brought back to life". Their bones were sold all around Europe and became part of monastic collections. St Ursula's parish in Cologne made a fortune and was able to fund the construction of a new church.

St Ursula is still the patron saint of Cologne. A visit to the Goldene Kammer (Golden Chamber) of the church is highly recommended. The walls are covered by the world's largest mosaic designed from human bones, all of which come from the Roman cemetery.

JOHN THE BAPTIST PLATTER

Templars at Kahlenbergerdorf

Klosterneuburg Abbey Museum
Stiftsplatz 1, 3400 Klosterneuburg
Open 17 November to 30 April 10am–5m, 1 May to 16 November 9am–6pm
Bus: 239, Klosterneuburg Stift stop

On the first floor of Klosterneuburg Abbey Museum, an amazing wooden sculpture of a head rests on a platter – it represents the head of St John the Baptist, decapitated martyr, whose connection with Kahlenbergerdorf is today largely forgotten.

In the Middle Ages, what is now the Church of St George at Kahlenbergerdorf was dedicated to St John the Baptist. It was reconsecrated after the Turkish siege of 1683.

Kahlenberg is the only district of Vienna to have preserved a medieval custom associated with the platter of St John the Baptist, which was used to find drowned bodies. The platter was thrown into the Danube from the shore, and the place where it was carried by the current marked the probable site of a drowning. The search for the corpse began at the place where the platter rose to the surface.

The platter was also used to cure headaches and sore throats. Turning three times around the altar while holding it prevented migraines. In the old days, men would take off their hats and women their scarves before praying for a cure.

One day, a priest discovered the pagan origin of these rituals and the platter of St John the Baptist was banished from the church. So people just threw their hats into the air instead of doffing them. Some linguists think that the expression "*I hau den Hut drauf!*" ("I hang up my hat", meaning to abandon something) comes from this custom.

St John the Baptist is the patron of the Templars: almost all their churches are dedicated to him. This order of chivalry generally built circular, fortified churches with octagonal ossuaries, just like the Kahlenbergerdorf building. The ossuary below the church has been preserved and the round Romanesque construction is now the apse. The basement concealed secret tunnels leading to houses on the Danube.

LEOPOLDSBERG FUNICULAR ROUTE

 ⑫

What remains of the "Jerking Train"?

Lower station, opposite Hohe Heiligenstädter Strasse 196 (access via Donauwartesteig)
Upper station, Höhenstrasse after Josefinenhütte on the left, after the turn-off to Leopoldsberg
Bus: 38A, Elisabethwiese stop (upper station) / 239, Heiligenstädter Strasse 409 stop (lower station)

The hiking path along the Höhenstrasse road is often busy with young families on their way to the adventure park. After the turn-off at the Josefinenhütte chalet, on the left, you can see remains of old foundations on the ground, then a steep cavity cut out of the rocks. The upper station of the Leopoldsberg funicular was located here, while the lower station was near Kuchelau port on the Danube. You can also find the route by taking the Donauwartesteig as a starting point.

Contemporaries had dubbed this train the "Zuckerlbahn" ("Jerking Train"), because it always made a last hiccup before the final stop. The Leopoldsberg funicular was originally scheduled to open on 1 May 1873, at the Vienna International Exhibition. But on that date the illustrious visitors saw the site only: the train eventually went into service on 27 July 1873, carrying some 300,000 people during its first six months. The distance between Kahlenbergerdorf and Elisabethwiese was 725 metres. When one carriage was at the upper station, the other was waiting at the lower station, which had a ticket office and a fine staircase leading to the intermediate platform. This was the beginning of day trips.

Competition from the Kahlenbergbahn train and the disruption of a landslide sealed the fate of the Zuckerlbahn in 1876, and the installation was sold and dismantled the following year. The bricks from the control room of the upper station were reused in the construction of the Kahlenberg Stefaniewarte.

Swiss rack railways were used as models. The first in Europe, commissioned in 1871 in Switzerland, led to Mount Rigi in the canton of Lucerne. The world's third-oldest, the Budapest Cog-Wheel Railway leading to the Svábhegy (Swabian mountain) in Hungary, started operations in 1874 and is still in use today as tram line No. 60.

EMPRESS ELISABETH'S REFUGE

Art Nouveau for Sisi

Kahlenberg, 1190 Wien

KAISERIN-
-ELISABETH-RVHE

A little-known monument on the Kahlenberg, not far from the Church of St Joseph, is dedicated to Empress Elisabeth of Austria, murdered in 1898.

In 1904, architect, painter and artisan Oskar Felgel von Farnholz erected a statue framed by Art Nouveau motifs in memory of the empress. Her profile in relief is the work of Rudolf Bachmann. History does not record whether the keen walker Elisabeth once paused here during her rambles in the hills around Vienna. She liked to go out at night or very early in the morning.

Nearby is the Stefaniewarte (Stéphanie Observation Point), named after the wife of Crown Prince Rudolf, whom Elisabeth disdained as an inadequate match for her son. This tower, which dates from 1887, was designed by architects Ferdinand Fellner and Hermann Helmer. Some of the bricks were recycled from the control room of the Leopoldsberg funicular, which closed down in 1876.

SOBIESKI-KAPELLE

Polish national memorial

St Josephskirche am Kahlenberg
Josefsdorf 38, 1190 Wien
Open daily 9.30am–noon and 1.30pm–4.30pm
https://kahlenberg-kirche.pl/
Bus: 38A, Kahlenberg stop

Although the website and information boards at the entrance to the church are written in Polish, these are not the only Slavonic references: when you walk on the Kahlenberg towards the Sobieski Chapel, you'll see many Polish tourists and pilgrims emerging from their buses. Polish Pope John Paul II visited the site in 1983 on the 300th anniversary of the lifting of the Ottoman Siege of Vienna. Since 1906, the chapel has been run by Polish priests belonging to the Roman Catholic Resurrectionist Order.

The chapel is both a place of worship and a memorial, and is considered an extremely interesting part of the Baroque Church of St Joseph at Kahlenberg.

Entering by the side door, you arrive in a small antechamber dedicated to the events of the Turkish siege of 1683. Besides a souvenir shop, the Sobieski Chapel has pictures and engravings of the battle for the liberation of the Kahlenberg on 12 September 1683, when the Polish king John III Sobieski, commander-in-chief of the Catholic League, routed the Turks and rescued the city. The sabre he wielded during the battle is also on display.

The legend goes that Capuchin monk Marco d'Aviano celebrated a mass here with King Sobieski on the morning of the battle: the chapel has a strong sense of national identity for many Poles.

When the Polish Resurrectionists took over the chapel at the beginning of the 20th century, it was severely damaged and in need of restoration. Polish painter and decorative artist Józef Mehoffer was commissioned to transform the space into a memorial to Innocent XI (who was pope during the 1683 Turkish siege), King Sobieski and the other army commanders. The outbreak of the First World War in 1914, however, scuppered these plans and the money collected for

the renovation had to be used for other purposes. The chapel, by then in ruins, had to wait until the 1920s to finally see the renovation project come to fruition.

The superb frescoes by Johann Heinrich Rosen date back to 1930. The main image depicts the vision of Pope Innocent XI, the one on the left shows the Mass held by Marco d'Aviano, with the saints Joseph, Leopold and Johannes Capistran in the background, together with a Polish knight wearing the green flag of the Prophet Muhammad. The right wall is decorated with hundreds of coats of arms of the Polish nobles who took part in the battle.

KAHLENBERGERDORF CEMETERY ⑮

Tombs with a view

Willibald-Fischer-Weg, 1190 Wien

The little cemetery at Kahlenbergerdorf, not to be confused with the much older one at Kahlenberg, is attached to the parish church dedicated to St George. From here you can enjoy beautiful walks and a breathtaking view of Leopoldsberg. This cemetery amongst the vineyards was opened in 1878. It contains the tombs of a number of personalities, such as the actress Marisa Mell (died 1992), a native of Graz, who was a cult figure of Italian B-movies in the 1960s before dying in poverty; and the king of Viennese nightclubs Heinz Werner Schimanko (died 2005). Just beside Schimanko is an eye-catching tomb covered with graffiti.

The entrance to the mortuary was decorated in 1984 with two angel statues by sculptor Rudolf Friedl, who died in 2007 and is also buried here.

The road running along the bottom of the cemetery leads to a church, which used to stand in the middle of an earlier burial site (closed at the end of the 19th century). There are still some remains to be seen on the north side and in the choir of the church, where old headstones are built into the walls. There used to be an ossuary just under the choir. Many of the drowned bodies recovered from the Danube found their last home here.

The headstone of a former Freemason recalls the first children's home in Vienna, financed by the Humanitas Lodge (commemorative plaque at No. 1 Zwillinggasse). The depiction of the Templars' keys seems to show that they met at Kahlenbergerdorf before the Freemasons ever did.

In the vineyard above the church, another cemetery was opened in 1832 as a burial site for cholera victims. It was expanded several times until it too closed in 1878, leaving no trace.

VESTIGES OF COBENZL SKI JUMP ⑯

Soaring into the Vienna skies

Reisenberg, Ober-Grinzing, 1190 Wien
Bus: 38A, Cobenzl Parkplatz stop

The route of City Hiking Path 1 (Kahlenberg) takes in Mount Latisberg, better known as Cobenzl after the Austrian statesman Johann Philipp von Cobenzl, who had a country house there in the 18th century.

Cobenzl was also known for one of the biggest ski jumps in Vienna. The remains of this structure, whose stands could hold 20,000 spectators, can still be seen from the august terrace of the ruins of Schloss Cobenzl.

Although plans for the ski jump date back to 1919, work only started in 1928 and was completed in 1931. The winning jump in a competition organised by the Vienna Workers' Sporting Association was 38 metres. In 1940, the jump was rebuilt to allow for feats of 60 metres.

After the Second World War, Vienna attempted to regain its status as a ski-jumping capital. A competition was announced and the architect Adolf Hoch submitted an innovative model that included a 60-metre ramp, with a 25,000-seat atrium that placed spectators at the upper level. This project was also to have facilities for boxing matches and theatre performances in the summer season, but it was never carried out.

Cobenzl Castle once had a garden with fountains and grottoes. For a while it was run as a restaurant, then demolished after irreparable damage in the Second World War. In the 19th century, the castle had belonged to Baron Karl von Reichenbach (1788–1869), dubbed the "magician of Cobenzl". The baron conducted scientific research in the tradition of German physician Franz Anton Mesmer, who inspired therapeutic hypnotism. Reichenbach was particularly interested in the interactions between magnetism, electricity and radiation. He also collected meteorites. The materials he developed from alloys he found in them – kamacite, taenite and plessite – survived his other fields of research, which were already highly controversial during his lifetime. Yet a steel monument was erected as a tribute to his work.

Reichenbachgasse, in the 10th district, is named after Baron von Reichenbach.

After his death, the castle passed into the hands of Baron von Sothen.

CAMALDOLESE HERMITAGE

The hermits of Schweinsberg

Josefsdorf 18, 1190 Wien

Josefsdorf was once an independent municipality on the Kahlenberg, established in 1628 by the Congregation of Monk Hermits of Camaldoli, an order founded in Tuscany in the early 11th century by St Romuald of Ravenna. Originally, the mountain was called Schweinsberg (Pig Mountain), after the numerous wild pigs that lived in the oak forest.

The Viennese Camaldolese founded a small village consisting of a church, two farms and two rows of dwellings with 16 monks' cells. In 1781, Joseph II ordered the dissolution of contemplative orders which "wear neither footwear, nor offer service to the sick, do not preach and do not go to confession", such as the Carthusians, Camaldolese, Carmelites and Capuchins. So the Kahlenberg hermitage was dissolved and a restaurant opened in the hermits' hospice. Their cells were refurbished and sold, and the village was renamed Josefsdorf, in honour of the emperor.

Only one house has been preserved in its original state, north of the church at No. 18, although cells still exist in some of the other houses.

All these buildings are occupied private property. The old monks' cells can usually only be glimpsed over garden hedges or behind dividing walls.

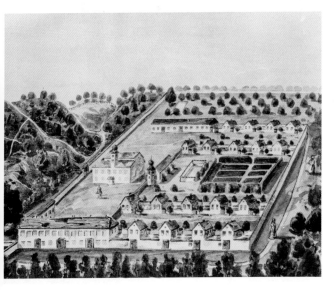

THREE OF BEETHOVEN'S HOMES IN VIENNA

Beethoven lived here ... or maybe he didn't

Wohnung Heiligenstadt *("Testamenthaus"), Probusgasse 6, 1190 Wien Open Tuesday to Sunday and public holidays 10am–1pm and 2pm–6pm*
www.wienmuseum.at/de/standorte/beethoven-wohnung-heiligenstadt.html
Bus: 38A, Armbrustergasse stop
Eroicahaus, *Döblinger Hauptstrasse 92, 1190 Wien*
Visits by appointment only, to be arranged two weeks in advance
www.wienmuseum.at/de/standorte/beethoven-eroicahaus.html
Tram: 7, Pokornygasse stop
Pasqualatihaus, *Mölker-Bastei 8, 1010 Wien*
Open Tuesday to Sunday and public holidays 10am–1pm and 2pm–6pm
www.wienmuseum.at/de/standorte/beethoven-pasqualatihaus.html
U-Bahn: line U2, Schottentor station; Tram: 1, 37, 38, 40, 41, 42, 43, 44, 71, D (Schottentor)

The German composer Ludwig van Beethoven settled permanently in Vienna in 1792. His reputation as a tenant preceded him. From his arrival until his death in 1827, he rented or occupied so many residences (80 moves) that it's almost impossible to figure out when and how long he lived in each. A difficult man to share a house with, he was unceremoniously evicted many times.

In 1802, Beethoven arrived at Heiligenstadt on the outskirts of Vienna, hoping that the healing spa waters would cure his gastritis. On 6 October 1802, he wrote the *Heiligenstadt Testament*, which is now in Hamburg National Library. This is a letter – never sent – to his brothers Carl and Johann in which he expressed despair over his progressive deafness. The newly laid-out apartment in Probusgasse has been designed as a "Viennese Beethoven Museum". The state-of-the-art exhibition space on the first floor follows the painful moves of the composer and his piano around Heiligenstadt, his illness, the disagreements within the family and the various cures on offer in the region. The wooden flooring from his last home on Schwarzspanierstrasse, preserved for decades, will finally be on view to the public here. It is not certain, however, that Beethoven actually lived in this pretty house with courtyard, which may not have been built until 1807. Moreover, there are indications that he spent the summer of 1802 in another house, albeit also in Heiligenstadt.

In summer 1803, Beethoven was working on his *Third Symphony* (the "*Eroica*") and living in a house called "Bierderhof" at No. 92 Döblinger Hauptstrasse. Two ground-floor rooms overlooking the street have been preserved, but nobody knows just how long the composer lived in this rural setting. Now only the original firewall remains, all the other elements of the building having been replaced at a later date. The Biedermeier-style courtyard is quite remarkable.

In late 1804, and by now a sick man, Beethoven moved into a house in Innere Stadt. The owner, Johann Baptist Freiherr von Pasqualati, was a great music lover and always kept a room at Beethoven's disposal. After several other moves, the composer returned in 1810 to the quiet street of Mölker-Bastei, on the old city walls. The entrance to the apartment he actually occupied is opposite the memorial, and the latest research indicates that it may have covered the entire floor, so these rooms in the Pasqualatihaus must really have been occupied by Beethoven.

KAHLENBERGERDORF FUNICULAR ⑲ ROUTE

Across the Viennese hills

Zahnradbahnstrasse 8, 1190 Wien

From the Zur Zahnradbahn (At the Funicular) restaurant, located in the Nussdorf building where passengers used to board the Kahlenberg rack railway, you can stroll along the old track. This station, as well as the nearby former toilet block, are classified as historic monuments. Tramline D loops between the two.

You'll find traces of the funicular behind the restaurant. The well-preserved lower section of the track runs through the vines. The upper section, also in good condition, begins towards Krapfenwaldl station.

This funicular from imperial days was supposed to come into service in time for the Vienna International Exhibition in 1873, but the opening was delayed until March the following year. The engine travelled the 5.5 kilometres of track at a maximum speed of 12 km/h. In summer, carriages were open and the glass was removed from the windows. The first-class carriages were fitted with comfortable leather seats. Over 260,000 people took a ride on this steam attraction in 1887.

By the time the First World War ended, the mechanism was worn out and obsolete, but the funicular ran until 1922. It was dismantled in 1925, with only two stations surviving until 1945 – Krapfenwaldl and Bergstation.

In the courtyard of Kahlenberg Church is a replica of an old carriage without a chassis. Inside, a small exhibition retraces the history of the funicular. Unfortunately, visitors are only occasionally allowed inside the carriage.

LEHÁR-SCHIKANEDER VILLA

Musicians of Nussdorf, a Heurigen village

Hackhofergasse 18, 1190 Wien
Visits by appointment only
Tel: +43 (0)1 3185 416
Tram: D, Nussdorf stop

Between the winegrowers' houses and the former brewery in Nussdorf is a gem of a villa containing mementoes of the two great musicians who lived there, Emanuel Schikaneder and Franz Lehár.

The Baroque façade on the garden side dates from the year 1737 and overlooks a large, steeply sloping park. The street side is more recent, reconstructed in the first half of the 19th century, and the building has been altered several times since then.

From 1802 to 1812 the villa belonged to Mozart's German librettist Emanuel Schikaneder, who hoped to enjoy a quiet retirement there. Things turned out otherwise: inflation ate up his savings and he descended into madness towards the end of his life.

The world-famous Austro-Hungarian composer of operettas Franz Lehár (Hungarian Lehár Ferenc) lived there from 1932 to 1944, during which time he wrote a single grand opera, *Giuditta*.

In the upstairs salon a number of paintings, autographs, photos and mementoes of Lehár's life are displayed, together with documents relating to Schikaneder's career.

The exhibition also includes some items that belonged to Anton Lehár, Franz's brother, who lived at the villa until his death in 1962.

The villa is currently privately owned and can only be visited by appointment.

VILLA MAHLER-WERFEL (Haus Ast) ㉑

A masterpiece by Josef Hoffmann

Steinfeldgasse 2, 1190 Wien
Tram: 37, Döblinger Bad stop
Closed to the public

The stunning Art Nouveau villa at the junction of Wollergasse and Steinfeldgasse is the work of renowned German architect and designer Josef Hoffmann, founder of the Vienna Secessionist movement. Constructed between 1909 and 1911, it is clearly distinguishable from his previous work.

The ground floor of the building is on two levels. The stripped decoration of the windows and the fluted façade give it an almost classical look.

The villa was acquired in the 1930s by the painter Carl Moll for his stepdaughter Alma, who had married the writer Franz Werfel (her third husband, after Gustav Mahler and Walter Gropius). Among the house guests of Alma Mahler-Werfel were personalities such as composers Alban Berg and Arnold Schönberg, polymath Egon Friedell and artist Oskar Kokoschka, as well as Nobel Literature laureate Gerhart Hauptmann.

The Werfels left Nazi Germany in the late 1930s for the United States. Alma eventually sold the villa, which is now the Embassy of Saudi Arabia.

"WASCHSALON" EXHIBITION

The new Vienna

Halteraugasse 7, Waschsalon 2, 1190 Wien
Open Thursday 1pm–6pm, Sunday 12 noon–4 pm or by appointment
http://dasrotewien-waschsalon.at/

The "Waschsalon" (Washhouse) No. 2 of the former public baths in Karl-Marx-Hof district runs a permanent exhibition on four main themes: the history of "Red Vienna" from 1919 to 1934; social housing and public amenities; clubs associated with the Social Democratic Party; and the festivities of the Viennese workers' movement.

In 1919, Vienna was the first megalopolis in the world to elect a social democratic administration. The experiment begun in the 1920s would encompass and reform all aspects of civic life, from social and health policies to town planning. An ambitious programme was financed by taxes on luxuries (e.g. horses, large private cars, servants) and the housing construction tax, known as the "Breitner tax" after the city councillor for finance Hugo Breitner. By 1934, about 380 housing blocks had been built, with over 64,000 apartments.

The exhibition highlights the conflicts between the "reds" (social democrats) and the "blacks" (conservatives), which culminated in the 1934 civil war. The rise to power of the Nazi Party (National Socialist German Workers' Party / NSDAP) is also documented.

KIRCHE ST JAKOB CRYPT

City of the Saints

Pfarrplatz 3, 1190 Wien
Visits by appointment
www.heiligenstadt.com

Cemeteries were historically regarded as loci sancti. The grounds of St James's Church contain many burial sites from different periods, hence the name of the parish that grew up around the church in the Middle Ages: Heiligenstadt (City of the Saints).

The crypt was excavated in the 1950s, revealing the foundations of a Roman fortress, an early Christian baptism site, and burial grounds dating from the great migrations of peoples into the territory of the then Roman Empire. One tomb is designated as that of St Severinus (died 482), a hypothesis since refuted. Current opinion is that the "Apostle of Noricum" died at Favianiae (site of a Roman camp, now Mautern) and that his body was taken to Frattamaggiore in Campania (southern Italy) for burial.

An empty Roman tomb in the curia garden suggests that the site chosen for the Heiligenstadt church was a disused cemetery. The Roman remains under the church also confirm that there were Roman houses along Limesstrasse, as the street is known.

In the 1980s, the skeletons of over 100 children were found on the east side of the church, the site of a 13th-century hospice destroyed in the Turkish siege of 1683.

While the renovated interior of the church is 19th-century Baroque, exterior is more austerely Roman in style. St James's is one of the oldest

churches in Vienna outside the city centre, dating back to the 5th century. There is a Romanesque window with modern glazing, a Gothic sacral chapel and a Gothic niche for storing holy vestments.

Today the church belongs to the Greek-Catholic Melkite (Melchite) community, one of the Byzantine Christian cults and the third most numerous in Lebanon. The term "melkite" derives from the Aramaic word for "royal".

SCULPTURES FROM
THE ROTHSCHILD GARDENS

The forgotten origins of Vienna's first football club

Döblinger Bad
Geweygasse 6, 1190 Wien

The four sculptures at Döbling Baths probably come from the former Rothschild Gardens: a sphinx, Poseidon (sea god), lion and Corinthian column.

Baron Nathaniel Meyer von Rothschild (1836–1905), who was particularly interested in gardening, owned a villa and grounds on Hohe Warte that were dubbed the "Rothschild Gardens". He had brought over English gardeners who in their spare time liked to play football – a new sport that was all the rage back home. Anxious to spare his gardens, the baron placed a stadium at their disposal on his land. The blue and yellow colours of the House of Rothschild were chosen by the players of First Vienna Football Club to mark their boss's generosity. These are still the club colours. After all, as the club chant goes: "If we wear blue-yellow it's not just decoration, our heart is also blue-yellow!"

The Rothschild Gardens were destroyed following the annexation of Austria in 1938. Some of the fixtures were moved to the southern section of Heiligenstadt Park in 1977. The head keeper's house (No. 6 Geweygasse, Döbling) was untouched and is now a scout club. Döbling Baths are right next to the house.

"Heilige Warte" is how fans refer to their football stadium, which bears the rather tortuous name of Care Energy – Naturarena Hohe Warte. The club's previous home was built in 1921: at the time, it was the largest and most up-to-date stadium in continental Europe.

First Vienna Football Club was officially founded on 22 August 1894 in the Schöne Aussicht restaurant (now the Pfarrwirt, No. 5 Pfarrplatz, Döbling). The English name is no coincidence, as the first Viennese players were English. As were the gardeners (see above).

ZACHERLFABRIK

Effective from Vienna to Philadelphia

Nusswaldgasse 14, 1190 Wien
Closed to the public but can be seen from outside
Tram: 37, Döbling stop

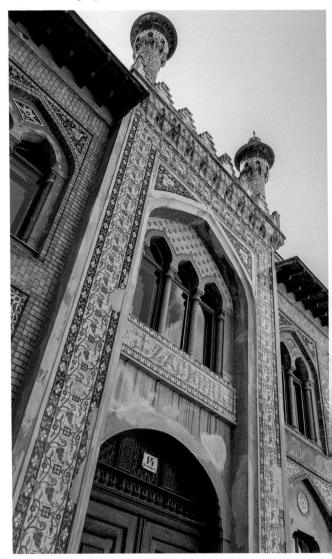

No. 14 Nusswaldgasse is a stunning multicoloured tiled building with cupolas and a minaret at the back. Originally a factory producing anti-moth powder, it was constructed in the years 1888 to 1892, a time when the hugely popular Oriental style was used to encourage trade.

Johann Zacherl, qualified in the casting of tin, travelled to Tbilisi, where he noted how the Georgians protected fabric from the voracious insects using a powder extracted from chrysanthemum-like flowers. The active element of this powder was pyrethrum. Zacherl launched himself into commercialising the insecticide, which he baptised "Zacherlin", or "True Persian Powder". He opened stores in Paris, Constantinople, Amsterdam, London, and even New York and Philadelphia.

It was Hugo von Wiedenfeld and Karl Mayreder who customised the manufacture of the insecticide for Zacherl's son, Johann Evangelist,

marketing it with ceramic tiles produced in Wienerberg. Young Zacherl managed the company until the first half of the 20th century, but the demand for its products gradually fell with the growth of the chemical industry. Production ceased after the Second World War.

In recent years, the former factory has hosted various artistic projects at the initiative of the Zacherl heirs. The programme is currently on hold, however, as the owners are not able to meet current building regulations.

The Yenidze cigarette factory in Dresden (Germany) also has stunning Eastern architecture.

Zacherlhaus

The Zacherl House at No. 5 Bauernmarkt in the Innere Stadt – designed by Josef Plečnik, a talented pupil of Otto Wagner – was sponsored by the same Johann Evangelist Zacherl who was responsible for the Zacherl factory. The façade, the work of Ferdinand Andri, shows St Michael armed with Zacherl insecticides – archangel triumphs over invaders! A light fitting in the form of an insect illuminates the oval staircase while publicising the company. Note the elaborate patterned roof. This building still belongs to the Zacherl family and houses offices and commercial premises.

SALON WERTHEIMSTEIN

The Viennese salonnières

Villa Wertheimstein/Döbling District Museum
Döblinger Hauptstrasse 96, 1190 Wien
Salon: open Saturday 3.30pm–6pm, Sunday 10am–noon
Park: open all day
Tram: 37, Barawitzkagasse stop

In the suburban Villa Wertheimstein (1834–5), now known as the Döbling District Museum, you can visit the original Wertheimstein ladies' lounge. At the invitation of Josephine von Wertheimstein, and later of her daughter Franziska, the scions of the upper classes came here in the 19th and early 20th centuries, including society portraitist Franz von Lenbach, architect Theophil Hansen, poet Ferdinand von Saar (who was madly in love with Franziska) and dramatist Eduard von Bauernfeld. The last two died here, much to the chagrin of their hostesses. Von Saar, who had an incurable disease that caused him great distress, shot himself in the head.

The building next to the villa is called Nonnenstöckl (Nuns' Court), recalling the time when it belonged to the Dominicans of Tulln. After the dissolution of the monastery, Viennese industrialist Rudolf von Arthaber bought the estate in 1833. He commissioned architect Alois Ludwig Pichl to rebuild this large country house in classical style, before reselling it in 1870 to Josephine's husband Leopold von Wertheimstein. The staircase had been painted with frescoes by the leading early Romantic artist Moritz von Schwind, and the park had a greenhouse filled with the tropical plants that were then so fashionable. The villa was already one of the curiosities of Vienna.

The Wertheimstein salon, with its antique furniture and portraits by Von Lenbach, illustrates the typically bourgeois lifestyle of the Wertheimstein family. The guest rooms where Von Bauernfeld and Von Saar stayed are included in the tour.

The vast park, with its winding stream, was a place of relaxation for the Wertheimsteins. Franziska von Wertheimstein and Ferdinand von Saar used to go for a stroll there in the morning. Franziska, who had no children and finally went mad, left the house and garden "to the people" of Vienna when she died in 1907.

At the entrance to the park is a plaque in memory of the benefactress. There is also a commemorative bust of her friend, Von Saar.

PAULINENWARTE WATCHTOWER IN TÜRKENSCHANZPARK

A former water tower, in memory of Pauline Metternich

1180 Wien
Open April to September, one weekend a month
www.wien.gv.at/umwelt/parks/anlagen/paulinenwarte.html
Tram: 41, Türkenschanzplatz stop

The elegant 23-metre "Pauline" watchtower was designed in the 19th century by building contractor Anton Krones senior. It was also a water tower, the metal tank of which has been preserved.

Inside, a flight of 57 steps leads to a platform with a 360° view over Türkenschanzpark, which was opened in 1888 by Emperor Franz Joseph himself. The style of the tower blends with that of the villas of the Association of Cottage Owners, which protects properties built in the neighbourhood at the end of the 19th century.

The tower is named after the most famous Viennese of her time (after the Empress Elisabeth): Baroness Pauline Metternich (1836–1921). Her charitable events were legendary throughout the empire and an invitation meant access to the heights of Viennese society. The baroness paid for most of the exotic plants in the park, so the watchtower was named in her honour.

The Pauline watchtower, which had stood derelict for a long time, was restored a few years ago and is now under the protection of Währing's Friends of Nature.

Türkenschanzpark has many monuments, hiking trails and a beautiful farmstead. The Priessnitz fountain is particularly interesting – a souvenir of farmer Vinzenz Priessnitz, the almost-forgotten inventor of hydropathy, or the "cold-water cure".

WASSERTURM WÄHRING

The dormant water tower

Anton-Baumann-Park, 1180 Wien
U-Bahn: U6, Michelbeuern-AKH station

Many people pass this utility every day without a second glance. Anton-Baumann-Park, constructed between 1836 and 1841 to a design by Bohemian architect Paul Sprenger, is nothing special and the tower itself looks like a neglected chapel. However, what you see here, on the Ganslberg hillside off the Beltway and surrounded by a playground, is a venerable water tower.

The classical-style tower was part of the Emperor Ferdinand Water Pipeline, fed by the waters of the Danube filtered at the Spittelau power plant. Unlike Favoriten's water tower, Währing's was not pressurised. Using a system of four hydraulic pipes, it evened out pressure variations in the pumps. The platform at the top of the tower was used as an observation post, overlooking the neighbouring districts as far as the Prater.

The hydraulic system soon reached the limits of its capacity and was replaced in 1873 by the First Vienna Spring Water Main. Währing tower was threatened with demolition several times. A residents' campaign in 1935 succeeded in having it classified as a protected monument. The name Ganslberg conjures up the legendary roast goose served by the nearby Edelmaier restaurant.

INSTITUT FÜR ASTROPHYSIK OBSERVATORY AND MUSEUM

Citizens against the mayor

Türkenschanzstrasse 17, 1180 Wien
Park: open Monday to Friday all day
Observatory and museum: visits by appointment
thomas.posch@univie.ac.at

For a long time the Sternwartepark (Observatory Park) was reserved, at least officially, for employees and students of the University Institute of Astrophysics, which owns the land. The building, opened in 1883, is still the largest enclosed observatory in the world.

Since spring 2013, some designated areas around the observatory have been open to the public. The whole Observatory Park is classified as a natural monument: it contains many rare plants and shelters badgers, foxes and butterflies, which benefit from the calm, protected environment.

This hasn't always been the case. In 1973, a political conflict over the park triggered an environmentalist consciousness in Viennese society. The municipal authorities had planned to build the University of Vienna's new Zoology Institute there. A press campaign was launched by the country's most widely read daily newspaper. "Murder!", shrieked a headline above an editorial condemning the felling of trees in the park. This led to the city's first popular referendum. Of the votes cast, 57.4% rejected the project and the mayor, Felix Slavik, had to resign. The power of private media magnates is clearly not negligible.

Today, public access to this oasis in the city is still limited. Visitors can only walk along the clearly marked paths during the opening hours of the University Institute of Astrophysics.

Visit the Institute of Astrophysics Museum

The Astrophysics Museum can be visited by appointment only. Mainly aimed at a specialist public, the museum has an extensive scientific library as well as a collection of telescopes and other astronomical instruments.

The key to a distinguished place

At the borders of Mollgasse, Gymnasiumstrasse, Philippovichgasse and Semperstrasse, 1180 Wien
Open Monday to Friday 7am–3pm (keys at No. 2 Mollgasse, MA 42 office)
U-Bahn: line U6, Nussdorfer Strasse station

The former Währing General Cemetery was the first to be turned into a park after 1918. At the time it was in service, from 1783 to 1874, the cemetery was not really "general" – instead, it was a burial ground for notables where a number of famous politicians and artists found their last home. As did the patients who died at the General Hospital.

The old Währing Municipal Cemetery, as it was also known, and its 58 interesting and well-maintained tombs, can now be visited by collecting the key nearby (see above). Sturdy trees embalmed in moss and ivy create an environment just asking to be photographed.

Here you'll find several memorable stories of well-known Viennese characters. The German librettist of the *Magic Flute*, Emanuel Schikaneder, lies here, as does Theodor Latour, the Minister of War who was lynched in 1848. His opponents, the four leaders of the 1848 revolution, Robert Blum, Cäsar Wenzel Messenhauser, Julius Becher and Herman Jellinek, were shot and thrown into a communal grave. Karl von Ghega, the engineer who planned the Semmering tramway, and Friedrich von Gentz, a German diplomat who played a major role at the Congress of Vienna, are buried here. At the age of 66, von Gentz had a liaison with the celebrated ballerina Fanny Elssler. She was only 19, and the couple lived in seclusion until his death in 1832.

Like almost all Vienna's cemeteries, the last resting place of Währing notables was made redundant by the opening of the Central Cemetery and was closed down.

The park was opened in 1923, and was first named Robert-Blum-Park, after one of the notorious revolutionaries. After the development of a leisure area in the years following the Second World War, the memorial stone of the 1848 revolutionaries was reinstated. The original name of the cemetery was forgotten.

WÄHRING JEWISH CEMETERY ㉛

Unique witness to Viennese social history

Schrottenbachgasse 3, 1180 Wien
Guided tours only, contact Israelitische Kultusgemeinde Wien (Vienna Israelite Community)
Tel: +43 (0)1 531 040; Email: office@ikg-wien.at
U-Bahn: line U6, Nussdorfer Strasse station

Opened in 1784 shortly after Emperor Joseph II's Patent of Toleration), the cemetery at Währing was at that time the main burial ground for Vienna's Jewish community. The cemeteries of Währing and St Marx are the last two built in the Biedermeier style. Interments took place there until 1884.

Währing is particularly interesting because it reflects the dilemma of many Viennese Jews, torn between assimilation and tradition. Baroness Fanny von Arnstein and her husband, the banker Nathan Adam Freiherr von Arnstein, are among the notables buried there.

The group of Sephardic tombs (Jews from the Ottoman Empire), with their oriental architecture and ornaments, tell us much about the social hierarchy of the Jewish community. Burials from the founders' era are ostentatious, sumptuous and innovative, just like the entrepreneurs of that time. Young architects were hired to illustrate the social standing of a tomb's occupant with splendid good taste. Representatives of the modern industrial society of the 19th century, such as the Epstein, Königswarter and Todesco families, are also buried here. Most of their headstones bear inscriptions in German. Note that the greater the degree of assimilation, the rarer the Hebrew inscriptions.

In 1941, under the Nazis, the City Hall decided to do away with the Jewish cemeteries in Vienna. Währing was turned into a green space,

complete with bird sanctuary. Any Jews still living in Vienna were asked to exhume the hundreds of bodies to submit them for "scientific" examination at the Museum of Natural History. The skeletons were only returned to the Jewish community in 1997 for a decent reburial.

Part of the cemetery was demolished during the Second World War to make way for a reservoir for fire-fighting. The Arthur-Schnitzler-Hof residential tower block was later built on this land.

Of the original 9,500 graves, about 7,000 remain today.

Celebrities united in death

Bei Währinger Strasse 123, 1180 Wien
Open Monday to Friday 8am–2pm (keys at No. 2 Mollgasse, MA 42 office)

Part of Schubertpark belonged to Währing Cemetery, where the composers Ludwig van Beethoven and Franz Schubert, and the writers Franz Grillparzer and Johann Nestroy, are laid to rest. Schubert, who had followed Beethoven's coffin in 1827, wanted to be buried near him, and his wishes were carried out in 1828.

Schubertpark was laid out in the mid-1920s in the geometric style then fashionable, with a fountain and a market for dairy products, both of which have long gone. On the other hand, just by picking up the keys of this normally closed park from the municipal office (see above), you can appreciate the fragrance of the roses and lavender that grow there.

The "gravediggers' row" funerary section runs along one wall of the park, entered by a classical gateway dating from 1827. Part of the access ramp still exists but it now leads to a car park in the basement.

The cemetery was in use for around 100 years from 1769 and housed 200 tombs. It was left to run wild after the opening, in 1874, of the Central Cemetery. Until 1912, when the City of Vienna acquired this land to create a park there, vaults were regularly opened and profaned by looters.

The authorities decided to keep 40 valuable tombstones, such as the "Crucifixion" ensemble by Balthasar Permoser, installed in 1785 and originally from the tomb of a court jeweller, Josef Friedrich Schwab, in the 3rd district. This late Baroque sculpture stands in the centre of the funerary section.

The buried celebrities were exhumed and moved to the Central Cemetery. Some old tombs can still be seen against the cemetery wall. One of the unfortunate designers of the Vienna State Opera House, Eduard van der Nüll, was buried here at Währing.

ENGELBERT WINDOW IN PFARRE- KIRCHE ST GERTRUD

Surprising glorification of an Austrian fascist

Gertrudplatz, 1180 Wien
Accessible during church opening hours
www.sankt-gertrud.at

When it was decided to enlarge the Baroque parish church of St Gertrude in Währing in 1934, thanks to subsidies granted to the Church by the "State of Corporations". Czech architect Karl Holey was commissioned to lengthen the nave. Some of the holy relics of St Engelbert (Archbishop of Cologne in the 13th century) were then transferred from Cologne to Vienna, in honour of the fascist chancellor Engelbert Dollfuss, assassinated by the Nazis in July of the same year.

The stained-glass window depicting the patron saint, by Viennese Jugendstil artist Leopold Forstner, was also dedicated to Dollfuss. It is inscribed with the legend, "Forgive them, for they know not what they

do" – a phrase attributed to both St Engelbert and Dollfuss the "martyr chancellor", as his supporters called him. So the saint was recycled to serve the personality cult of the murdered politician.

The fragments of St Engelbert's bones from Cologne were late in arriving at Vienna, so they couldn't be solemnly walled into the refurbished altar but instead disappeared into the cellars of the curia. Parish priest Klaus Eibl found them but refused to put them into place. The relics – two fragments surrounded by a piece of red silk – are now kept in a metal cabinet with a tiny viewing window.

In addition to the Engelbert window, St Gertrude's Church has a somewhat similar Theodor window, dedicated to another supporter of Austrofascism: Cardinal Theodor Innitzer, who inaugurated the enlarged church on 9 November 1934.

The spot where Chancellor Engelbert Dollfuss died is marked in the Bundeskanzleramt (Federal Chancellery) offices in Ballhausplatz, and is open to the public.

Outside the Centre West

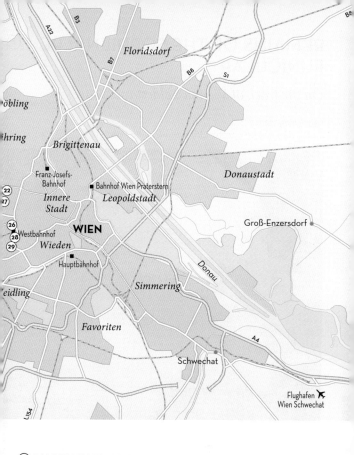

REMAINS OF THE SOPHIENALPE FUNICULAR

①

On the track of Vienna's oldest cable car

City Hiking Path 8
End of Karl Bekehrty-Strasse, Rieglerhütte, 1140 Wien

City Hiking Path 8 follows the track of the old funicular railway in the direction of the Sophienalpe mountain meadow. Vienna's oldest cable car, nicknamed the "Knöpferlbahn" (accordion train) because the carriages were pulled by a rope, was in service until 1881.

The climb starts at the Rieglerhütte, from where excursions on horseback can be arranged. Inside the chalet is a display of photographs of the attractions on offer in the 1870s. You'll see well-to-do Viennese wearing clothes as chic as they are uncomfortable, riding in wagons like horse-drawn carriages, on their way to the Sophienalpe restaurant. Day trippers of more modest means had to get there on foot.

The funicular guidelines said: "Carrying dogs and smoking is allowed if no passenger objects." In 1873, the year of the Vienna International Exhibition, the rocky Alpine plateau was transformed: in the fashion of London's Crystal Palace, balls and exhibitions were held there. But the magic eventually faded. Pictures of the event decorate the Sophienalpe restaurant, named after Archduchess Sophie, mother of Franz Joseph.

It takes three to four hours to walk the entire trail. There are forest and field sections, as well as a glorious panorama known as the "Franz Karl viewpoint", from where Sophie's husband used to admire his empire. The hiking circuit is clearly signposted and includes several pleasant refreshment stops.

SCHLOSS NEUWALDEGG CUSTODIAN'S HOUSE

The oldest landscaped gardens in Austria

Dornbacher Strasse 137, 1170 Wien
Visits: exterior only
Tram: 43, Neuwaldegg stop

The Baroque Neuwaldegg Palace is surrounded by the large green expanse of Schwarzenbergpark, with a superb view of the city centre. Just a stone's throw away from the Vienna Woods, it's perfect for a long walk or just a stroll. The privately owned palace houses the Franz Schubert Conservatory.

The palace, designed by Johann Bernhard Fischer von Erlach, was built at the end of the 17th century at the behest of Count Theodor von Strattmann and was known as the Gartenpalais Strattmann. In 1765, the estate was bought at auction by Count Franz Moritz Graf Lacy, who was a field marshal under Maria Theresa and adviser to her son Joseph II. As early as 1766, the valley of Dornbach (now in the 17th district) had its English-style landscaped gardens, considered the first of their kind in Austria and particularly popular with Viennese day-trippers. The small chapel in the park, modelled on an ancient temple, contains the tombs of Count Lacy and his nephew Georg Graf Browne.

At the beginning of the 19th century, both palace and park

were acquired by the princely Schwarzenberg family, who planned to use the land exclusively for forest pursuits. The landscaping was eliminated and the buildings now known as Schwarzenbergsche Meierei (Schwarzenberg Farmstead) were built at Neuwaldegg. The farmstead consists of several independent buildings and a house with wine cellar. The buildings have been restored and are accessible to the public (exterior only).

In 1914, a custodian's house was added in the courtyard – it seems to have stepped straight out of the 18th century, with steep mansard roof and covered porch. The depiction of the Virgin Mary on the façade dates from the early 20th century.

ADOLF LOOS AT HEUBERG ③

"One-wall" housing

Kretschek-, Schrammel-, Trenkwald-, Röntgen- and Plachygasse, 1170 Wien

Adolf Loos designed the Heuberg model colony in the years 1920 to 1922, with the support of Hugo Mayer. The two architects based their plans on a social housing policy that took account of the needs of future occupants, many of whom were unemployed or homeless.

Although only part of the settlement survives – there were originally 40 homes –the cost-effectiveness of building rows of two-storey houses with garden entrances is clear. In view of the economic hardship and food shortages of the time, the communal areas were conceived as productive gardens.

This "one-wall" terrace house system was developed and patented by Adolf Loos, then architectural director of the Viennese municipal Settlement Office. It is based on an exterior supporting party wall incorporating all services, with the end walls and infills built of wood, giving the living space a certain flexibility.

The collective housing movement in Vienna was inspired by British and German garden cities. The aim was to build low-cost individual homes that would ensure a sustainable lifestyle for their occupants.

Unfortunately, many of the houses in the Heuberg district have been altered beyond all recognition.

MONTLÉART MAUSOLEUM

The Angel of Wilhelminenberg

Savoyenstrasse 2, 1160 Wien
Bus: 46A, Wilhelminenberg stop

Along the winding road from Schloss Wilhelminenberg is a small neo-Gothic chapel where Prince Moritz de Montléart (died 1887) and his wife Wilhelmine (died 1895) are interred. The sarcophagus-shaped edifice was built by the prince's widow soon after her husband's death. The chapel is part of the estate of Wilhelminenberg – a name it should never have borne.

Although the forested slope where the castle stands was officially called Gallitzinberg, Prince Moritz, who had presented the estate to his wife on the death of his father, decided to rename it Wilhelminenberg – against the Ottakring community's wishes. He put up "Wilhelminenberg" signs all around the region, and the name soon became common usage.

On the death of her husband, Wilhelmine, who had no children and was by then disabled, decided to give away some of her possessions and devote herself to charity. She became known as the "Angel of Wilhelminenberg". When Ottakring decided to grant a substantial sum towards the construction of a hospital in 1888, on the occasion of the 40th anniversary of the reign of Emperor Franz Joseph, it was named Wilhelminenspital (Wilhelmine Hospital) in honour of the princess. It is still open today (No. 37 Montleartstrasse, Ottakring district).

WILLI FORST'S RUINENVILLA ⑤

The finest landscaped garden in Vienna

Dehnepark
Dehnegasse, 1140 Wien
Tram: 49, Rettichgasse stop; Bus: 47A, Wahlberggasse stop

For some it's a blot on the landscape, for others a curiosity worth a detour in the 5-hectare Dehnepark. The centuries-old trees, glittering pond, hiking trails, children's playground and forest make the park something special. Originally, the pretty little "castle" was designed as an artificial ruin in an orangery. It once belonged to Austrian actor and film director Willi Forst, who converted it into his "Ruinenvilla" in the 1930s.

The ruin had been erected at the end of the 18th century in the landscaped park of Princess Maria Antonie Paar of Liechtenstein. Laid out like an English landscaped garden, the park's many temples, pavilions and grottoes added a romantic touch in the Biedermeier style. These old-fashioned elements disappeared at the beginning of the 20th century, leaving only the Villa Forst as seen today.

The property next came into the hands of the famous confectioner August Dehne, after whom the park is named. His prosperous patisserie and chocolaterie was then on Michaelerplatz, before moving to the nearby Kohlmarkt in the 1880s. Meanwhile Dehne's lawyer son had sold the company to his eldest apprentice, Christoph Demel.

Willi Forst acquired the land in the 1930s. He had it fenced off and planned to live in the villa. There was no public access to the park, but from time to time Forst could be seen with a gun slung over his shoulder, tracking deer through the woods. The holes that inquisitive children sometimes made in the fence were always patched up the following day.

The former landscaped garden is now owned by the City of Vienna, which in 1969 bought out the surrounding lands left to run wild by Forst. The superb Dehnepark was opened to the public in 1973.

The villa, today once again a ruin, is sometimes occupied by homeless people or revellers. The wire fence is no defence against unwelcome visitors to the site, from where a narrow tunnel leads to the cellar.

ADMINISTRATIVE BUILDING ON BAUMGARTEN HEIGHTS

The most beautiful for the most needy

Baumgartner Höhe 1, 1140 Wien
Bus: 47A / 48A, Otto-Wagner-Spital stop

The Jugendstiltheater am Steinhof (Steinhof Art Nouveau Theatre), an administrative building belonging to the psychiatric institution now known as the Otto Wagner Hospital, Baumgarten (Penzing), has again recently been the venue for plays, concerts and other events. However, the authorities have declared it temporarily unfit for purpose.

Wagner is memorably quoted as saying that his vision for the hospital, opened in 1907, was "the most beautiful for the most needy". But it shouldn't be forgotten that in the 19th and early 20th centuries an asylum looked nothing like a modern hospital. It wasn't a question of curing patients, but rather of isolating them from "sane people". The Steinhof institution locked patients in. It was relatively easy to be admitted, but virtually impossible to get out again.

Of the buildings in the complex, Wagner was only responsible for the Church of St Leopold. The others were designed between 1904 and 1907 by chief architect Franz Berger in Baroque Art Nouveau style. The administrative building was a kind of multipurpose hall with auditorium, small stage à l'italienne (with wings) and seating for 600. There was also a gallery with lodges and a smaller hall. Art and culture were prescribed for the well-being of the mentally ill.

During the First World War, the buildings were converted into a military hospital. In the early 1930s, the Art Nouveau theatre fell into disrepair before it was renovated and reopened in 1970, as psychiatry was treading new paths and setting up new institutions.

Above the stage, a beautiful panoramic view of Vienna by Erwin Pendl (1875–1945) takes in the asylum buildings and the still unspoiled countryside of the 14th district, as far as the city centre.

KUFFNER STERNWARTE

Head in the stars

Johann-Staud-Strasse 10, 1160 Wien
Open Sunday and Monday from 9pm in all weathers, Wednesday and
Thursday from 9pm except rainy days
Sun observation, third Sunday of the month starting at 4pm
Tour of the institute: Sunday at 8pm; individual group visits can be arranged
Other events on the annual calendar
http://kuffner-sternwarte.at/index.php

The Kuffner Observatory, named after its philanthropic founder Moriz von Kuffner, industrialist and owner of the Ottakringer brewery, was built in 1886.

Although it was originally conceived as a private research institute by Franz Ritter von Neumann junior, the observatory, now run by the Ottakring authorities as part of further education (Astronomie Wien), is open to the public: a remarkable excursion into the universe of astronomy of past centuries. The immaculately preserved historical instruments, some faithfully restored, give an incredible view of the night sky.

Unlike a planetarium, you can look directly at the stars and planets, in particular through the large refracting telescope that dates back to 1886. Gas eruptions on the surface of the Sun, as well as the craters of the Moon, are clearly visible.

The former villa of the observatory directors, built in the same style as the research institute, is part of the complex. It can be viewed from the outside only.

Moriz von Kuffner had to sell his brewery in 1938 and emigrate to Switzerland, as the Nazis had appropriated the major observatories throughout the Austro-Hungarian Empire. He died in 1939 in Zurich.

Wien, XVI. Kuffner'sche Sternwarte.

REMAINS OF THE "HERO'S BUNKER" ON GALLITZINBERG HILL

A cuckoo's nest

Johann-Staud-Strasse
In the Vogeltennwiese near Jubiläumswarte (Jubilee Observation Tower)
Gallitzinberg, Ottakring, 16th district
Bus: 52B

The Gallitzinberg "hero's bunker", dating from 1940, has been partially demolished several times. However some vestiges of it can still be seen today around the Jubilee Tower: three sentry boxes, three or four water collection and purification points, and the ruins of a fuel tank.

The two-storey structure, 24 metres below ground, was only accessible at the end of a tunnel reached by a long spiral staircase. It is thought to have been built for the personal comfort of Baldur von Schirach, a Vienna *gauleiter* (district administrative officer) in Nazi Germany. There was even talk of a secret passage to his apartment in Neuwaldegg, but there is no evidence to support this.

This bunker fulfilled the dual role of a cable radio station and the Austrian air-raid warning centre. At the end of the war in Vienna, in April 1945, the site had been standing open for several months, and had been ransacked. The authorities finally intervened to blow it up. The entrances and exits were either condemned or sealed off.

In fact, von Schirach himself is unlikely to have manned the observation post (outside the bunker) during alerts, as has sometimes been reported. Notorious for his lack of courage, the man ironically

referred to as a "hero" would rush into Thaliastrasse, next to the bunker, to take shelter as soon as the "cuckoo" was heard. Far from being a warning siren, it was only a radio signal.

Thaliastrasse just missed being renamed Heldenstrasse (Hero Street). Today, this "centre of command" attracts a few more nicknames: the "Schirach bunker" or even the "hero's bunker".

Green peace

Mauerbachstrasse 45, 1140 Wien
Beginning of hiking trail
Bus: 249, Wien Hohe-Wand-Wiese stop

Gideon Ernst von Laudon (originally Loudon) is actually not buried in his idyllic forest tomb. His stone cenotaph lies opposite the castle, on the other side of Mauerbachstrasse. Nor is the monument at its original site. As the castle park was developed over the years, the cenotaph had to be moved several times. Although the fieldmarshal's last resting place is in the park, its exact location is unknown.

The most striking aspect of Laudon's neoclassical memorial, designed by Heinrich Fuger and Franz Anton Zauner, is the sentry: a life-size stone knight guarding the coffin. This work was dedicated to him by his widow Klara, as shown by the Latin inscription on the side: "Erected by wife and heirs, 1790". There is also a tribute to the military prowess of the Belgrade victor as recruit, leader and veteran. The gable-roofed tomb, adorned with sculptures of mythological figures, has images of Ottoman trophies: spears, horses' tails, a bow with quiver and arrows, as well as shields with representations of the Moon and Sun.

From Laudon's empty tomb, signs lead towards the "Rocks of the Turks" and the Laudon tombs. About 15 minutes' walk takes you to a small hill on which two more Laudon tombs can be seen – those of Johann Ludwig Alexius von Laudon (1762–1822) and his son, Olivier von Laudon (1793–1881). The first was Gideon Ernst's nephew. He took over the command of his uncle's infantry regiment and inherited his property, where he later died.

"Rocks of the Turks"

The path leading to the tombs of the Laudon heirs passes a picnic area with a fountain and the "Rocks of the Turks". They were originally intended to decorate Laudon's planned Turkish-style mausoleum, but this project never came to fruition. The rocks, part of the booty from the conquest of Belgrade in 1717, were built into a stone wall in the 19th century. The slab under the grimacing head, supposed to represent a Turk, has been mistakenly set upside down. The erection of a "worthy memorial in favour of reconciliation", constructed from the remains of a Muslim tomb and a city gate, has been on the cards since 1979, but unfortunately nothing has yet been done about it.

SCHLOSS LAUDON

Vienna's only waterside castle

Mauerbachstrasse 43, 1140 Wien
Private property
Gardens open to visitors
Bus: 249, Wien Hohe-Wand-Wiese stop

Laudon Castle, on the outskirts of Vienna, is now private property and is used for training Austrian civil servants. It was renovated in 1960 by Consul Alfred Weiss and then run as a luxury hotel until 1973. A stone in the garden commemorates the saviour of Castle Laudon – the owner of coffee and tea importers "Arabia". The 10-hectare park is perfect for a relaxing stroll: the splendid landscaped garden dating back to the 1770s has been partially preserved. In summer, sheep graze near two imposing statues of wild boar.

The castle was planned by Maria Theresa's fieldmarshal, Gideon Ernst von Laudon, for his retirement, and is built around a square courtyard surrounded by moats fed by the Mauerbach stream.

A new castle was built over the ruins of Hadersdorf (Penzing district) after the second Turkish siege in 1683. In 1708, the future mother of Maria Theresa (Elisabeth Christine of Brunswick) spent two nights there, as a plaque on the staircase reveals. Franz Wilhelm Schellerer designed the present castle in 1744.

Fieldmarshal von Laudon was known as a patron of the arts and sciences and famous for his extensive library. Some Bergl wall paintings dating from 1770 were moved to the castle's fresco room in 1963. They came from Donaudorf Castle, destroyed in the mid-1950s during the construction of the Ybbs-Persenbeug power station. The continents known in Bergl's time (18th century) – Europe, Asia, Africa and America – are represented allegorically. The predominantly female figures illustrate the peoples of distant countries. Collectively, they are a reflection of humanity as a whole.

The phrase *"Fix Laudon"* ("Cursed Laudon") refers to Gideon Ernst von Laudon. Maria Theresa is said to have uttered these words when she heard of Frederick the Great of Prussia's attack on the Habsburg province of Silesia in 1740.

UNDERGROUND WELL OF THE ALBERTINIAN WATER PIPELINE

Vienna's first piped water

Near Ernst Fuchs Museum
Hüttelbergstrasse 30, 1140 Wien

The striking building at No. 30 Hüttelbergstrasse, bearing the coat of arms of Prince Albert of Saxony, Duke of Teschen, is the site of the underground well of Vienna's first piped-water supply, known as the Albertinian Water Pipeline.

Prince Albert was the husband of Maria Christina, Maria Theresa's favourite daughter. She was a cholera victim, and one of her last wishes was that the suburbs of Vienna should be connected to running water. Albert completed the construction of the pipeline in 1805.

Four hundred cubic metres of water could then be transported daily from the Halterbach valley to Vienna. This fed 12 public fountains, including the Isisbrunnen (Isis fountain) in Albertplatz, the last of the line. The street and square named after Albert commemorate the duke's commitment to hygiene.

The pipeline was marked with finely carved stones with the initials HA (Herzog [Duke] Albert), a number and the year. Only a few of them have been preserved intact, but some can still be seen in Hüttelbergstrasse.

The City of Vienna took over the drinking-water supply in 1851.

ERNST FUCHS MUSEUM

An artistic genius in Otto Wagner's old home

Hüttelbergstrasse 26, 1140 Wien
Open from Tuesday to Saturday 10am–4pm and by appointment
www.ernstfuchsmuseum.at

The Otto Wagner Villa in Hüttelbergstrasse, built at the request of Crown Prince Rudolf, was owned by Ernst Fuchs from 1972 until his death in 2015. The flamboyant Austrian universal artist, who fathered 16 children with 7 different women, died at the age of 85 in his native city.

Fuchs is considered to be the leading representative of an artistic movement specific to Vienna, which goes back to the symbolism of the 1900s: Fantastic Realism. Many of his works have a strong religious or mythological symbolism.

The artist's superb private museum has occupied the ground and first floors of the villa since 1988. His paintings, sculptures and furniture are arranged chronologically in an exhibition space. Fuchs extended the derelict house and used it as a studio, although he lived and worked mainly in Monte Carlo. He also designed and built the Brunnenhaus (Spring House) in the garden with its "Nymphaeum Omega" fountain.

The architect of this opulent villa was Otto Wagner, who built it for himself and his young second wife between 1886 and 1888. A beautiful Art Nouveau hall was added in 1900 to the historicist-style summer residence with Palladian influences. This, the Adolf Böhm Hall, has the largest non-religious stained-glass windows in the city, designed by an artist friend of Wagner's, Adolf Böhm.

"Villa Wagner II"

At No. 28 Hüttelbergstrasse, another Wagner villa stands at the foot of the steep slopes of Hüttelberg. Dating from 1912–13, the style is resolutely sober and modern. The other villa proved far too large once the children had left home.

Villa Wagner II, fronted by an external staircase, is notable for its cubic shapes and angles in shades of blue. The mosaics above the door and in the loggia are by Kolo Moser. This villa is now private property.

HADERSDORF-WEIDLINGAU CEMETERY CHAPEL

Herzmansky crypt

Friedhofstrasse 12, 1140 Wien
Open from 3 November to end of February, 8am–5pm;
March and from 1 October to 2 November, 7am–6pm;
April to September, 7am–7pm;
May to August, every Thursday until 8pm

Perched on top of hill, the little cemetery of Hadersdorf-Weidlingau has a wonderful view of the Vienna Woods. It is overlooked by the chapel built in 1909 by Art Nouveau architect Max Hegele, the prolific artist who designed the "Lueger Church" at the Central Cemetery.

The cemetery chapel is actually a vast mausoleum for the Herzmansky family, founders of the eponymous department store that stood on Vienna's Mariahilferstrasse until the 1990s.

August Herzmansky was originally from the former Czechoslovakia. He arrived in Vienna in 1863 and opened a fabric shop. Its successful formula can be summed up in three words: "sales, fixed prices" (because before the advent of mass trade, prices were negotiable). His nephews Johann (Jean) and Eduard opened the renowned Herzmansky department store in the late 19th century. Since the unveiling of the mausoleum on 31 October 1909, they and their descendants have been laid to rest there. It is now also used as a hall for Christian confirmation.

The red and gold shrine of Eduard Herzmansky's family, also by Max Hegele, dates from 1909–10. Two years later, sculptor Theodor F.M. Khuen designed Jean Herzmansky's tomb. His splendid silhouette lies veiled, gaze turned towards the starry dark-blue sky.

TOLL CHAPEL

A picturesque little chapel in the undergrowth

Linzer Strasse 457, 1140 Wien, opposite toll office
Interior open for Mass (May to October, every first Saturday of the month at 8am)

Although a toll booth once stood at No. 457 Linzer Strasse, a flight of steps opposite now leads to "Our Lady of Sorrows", the former toll chapel partially hidden behind shrubs and bushes.

On 1 January 1892, a new city boundary was drawn up between Hütteldorf and Hadersdorf (14th district) to cope with the expansion of the city. Toll offices for levying consumer taxes were set up along this new frontier.

The Hütteldorf toll chapel has been standing at the foot of Bierhäuslberg since 1897. It replaced the Mariahilfer Chapel, demolished during urban redevelopment and whose stones were used in the new building. Commemorative plaques record the names of the generous donors without whom construction could not have been carried out. The largest contribution came from a funding association supported in particular by Beschorner, the Viennese manufacturer of metal coffins. The chapel, designed by Franz Ritter von Neumann, was finally built by architects Josef Kopf and Franz Gayer.

They opted for a simple Baroque building with a gabled façade and a wooden door decorated with floral arabesques in wrought iron. The 18th-century painting of the Virgin Mary is being restored.

Inside, a statue of St John of Nepomuk, patron saint of bridges and pathways, is a reminder that all toll chapels are dedicated to him. For several centuries, a pilgrimage route led past the chapel towards Mariabrunn.

The chapel used to stand in a grand park with an artesian well and ornate flower beds, now overgrown.

PALACE MILLER-AICHHOLZ
(EUROPAHAUS WIEN)

⑮

A perfect place to marry

Linzer Strasse 429, 1140 Wien
Interior can be hired for weddings and other events
www.europahauswien.at
Tram: 49, Hütteldorf / Bujattigasse stop

Nowadays, the orangery of the Baroque Miller-Aichholz mansion concentrates on hosting wedding parties, as guests greatly appreciate the idyllic park spread over 2 hectares. The garden lends itself particularly well to photo shoots, whatever the season. The long two-storey building is fronted by sweeping flights of steps. The glasshouse against the wall has been largely preserved in its original state and is thought to be the last Baroque example of its time in Vienna.

The ground floor of the mansion houses the original kitchens and cellars, while the first-floor rooms have mirrored ceilings with stucco decorations. The state rooms (great hall, Napoleon room, Prince Eugene room and Maria Theresa room) lead into the garden at the back and still have the original tiled stoves with rocaille ornamentation.

The place name dates back to 1894, when Austrian industrialist Heinrich von Miller zu Aichholz acquired it.

It was built about 1750 by one of the suppliers of Maria Theresa's army, who had made his fortune – Johann Georg Freiherr von Grechtler. He commissioned Baroque architect Johann Bernhard Fischer von Erlach to construct a hunting lodge at the Hütteldorf site that had been granted by the sovereign. The house later became the property of the Liechtenstein family. They were closely linked with the Esterházy family, who used it as a summer residence for over a century, when it came to be known as the "Esterházy hunting lodge".

The Miller-Aichholz family kept the building until 1938, but after the financial crash sold it to the Nazi police, who turned it into a rest home for civil servants.

The French High Commission was installed there from 1945 to 1955, during which time several canvases were damaged or painted over.

In 1955, the year the State Treaty was signed with the occupying powers and Austria regained its independence, Palace Miller-Aichholz was the site of the first occupation in the country. Members of the ÖVP (Österreichische Volkspartei / Austrian People's Party) affiliated to the young Austrian workers' movement gathered there to protect it from further damage. Since 1962 it has been Vienna's Europahaus (House of Europe), and can be hired, along with the new developments, for conferences, workshops and various functions. All the buildings belong to the Republic of Austria.

The glorious park is dotted with ancient trees, which are listed as natural monuments.

RAPIDEUM

"Father of the Rapid Spirit" honoured

Stadium Allianz, Gerhard-Hanappi-Platz 1, 1140 Wien
Open Monday to Saturday 10am–6pm, match days 10am to one hour after the finish
www.skrapid.at/de/startseite/verein/geschichte/
rapideum-und-stadionfuehrung/
U-Bahn: line U4, Hütteldorf station

The statue in front of the entrance to the new Allianz Stadium of SK Rapid Wien football club, opened in July 2016, represents Dionys Schönecker (1888–1938).

Although only an average player, he was a key figure in this legendary club, established in 1897, as coach and manager. During Schönecker's 28 years of service, from 1910 to 1938, SK Rapid won the championship twelve times, the Cup three times and the Mitropa Cup (Central European Cup, precursor of the European Cup) once.

The Rapideum museum isn't only aimed at football fans: it also deals with social conditions in the Penzing district, sports fashions, fan clubs, integration, conformism and resistance. All this is interactively explained through three broad themes that summarize the club spirit: Together – Fighting – Winning. The uninitiated will discover the special "Rapid quarter-hours" and how they are celebrated, mainly during matches abroad.

Models of the former stadiums of Hütteldorf, Pfarrwiese and Hanappi-Stadion are also on display, as well as kit, memorabilia, boots, cups, etc. belonging to legendary players and coaches such as Josef "Pepi" Uridil, Franz "Bimbo" Binder and Johann "Hans" Krankl.

Visitors can also relive some memorable games from the club's back catalogue.

FORMER "LANTERN OF THE DEAD" ⑰ AT PENZING

To preserve the memory of the dead and keep demons at bay

Einwanggasse 31, 1140 Wien
Bus: 51A, Cumberlandstrasse stop; U-Bahn: line U4, Hietzing station

In front of the St-Jakob-Kirche (parish church of St James) in Penzing district, near a busy crossroads, stands an octagonal pillar bearing a tabernacle with a crucifixion scene in bas-relief.

The pillar, dating from the late Gothic period (15th century), is the only one of its kind in Vienna. Originally, it served as a "lantern of the dead", where a light shone at night to indicate the cemetery adjoining the church.

The lanterns are a remnant of an era in which stone columns pierced with small openings were erected in churchyards in order to preserve the memory of the dead. But this custom recalls still more ancient rites, when lanterns were lit to keep away the spirits and demons that haunted the shadows but lost their power as soon as the light touched them.

KIRCHE ST ANNA BAUMGARTEN APSE PAINTINGS

Karl Lueger centre stage

Gruschaplatz, Linzer Strasse 259, 1140 Wien
Open for Mass or by appointment
www.pfarre-baumgarten.at/termine
Tram: 52, Gruschaplatz stop

During his mayoral investiture speech, Karl Lueger promised his Roman Catholic advisers some new churches. One of these was built between 1906 and 1908: St Anne's Church at Penzing. The Hans Zatzka paintings in the apse are part of the tradition of founders' images. They depict St Anne in the company of the church benefactors and, of course, the Mayor of Vienna.

Architect Moritz Otto Kuntschik is easily recognisable from the tools of his trade laid out at his feet. Karl Lueger, honorary president of the Baumgarten builders' association, kneels in his imperial ermine mantle (not counted among the mayor's attributes). Behind him stand a young girl and the moving spirit behind the foundation of the church, Anna Zehetner. Another donor, Raimund von Götz, prostrates himself before the mayor. The foreground is dominated by Lueger's patron saint, the ubiquitous Charles Borromeo.

On the left of the apse is a group of local citizens whose contributions helped to complete the church project along with Erich Graf Kielmannsegg, the governor of Lower Austria, accompanied by St Francis of Assisi, patron saint of Emperor Franz Joseph.

In the centre, two angels bear the coats of arms of Baumgarten and Vienna and a model of the church being offered to the Holy Family.

Note in this painting the absence of the usual allegory of the City of Vienna, as for example in the chapel of Hietzing Hospital. Here Mayor Lueger is acting as the city father, representing terrestrial concerns to the heavenly powers.

ENKELKINDER UND AUTOMATENMUSEUM

Ferry Ebert, king of vending machines

Beckmanngasse 7, 1140 Wien
Visits by appointment only
Tel: 0664 130 04 05; Email: ferryebert@hotmail.com

Heralded by an immense Austrian schilling shedding tears over the main entrance, the Museum of Grandchildren and Vending Machines displays some 50 items that represent the activities of the Austrian vending-machine pioneer, Ferry Ebert. Ebert retired in 1999, on the eve of the schilling being scrapped in favour of the euro, as converting his countless machines scattered throughout the country was not financially viable.

The museum now occupies Ebert's former office in Penzing (14th district). There you can see the legendary condom distributor which attracted the wrath of his more conservative contemporaries. One day he was even threatened with a rolling pin by a restaurant owner, furious at seeing her husband use the machine just like the customers ... In the 1980s Ebert was chased by three priests and the infamous Martin Humer, known as the "pornographer hunter", as he planned to install his notorious machines on the University of Linz campus.

Before starting his career as "king of the vending machine", Ebert worked for the tyre manufacturers Semperit, which also produced rubber toys and condoms. His first condom dispenser was installed in the late 1950s, not in Viennese public toilets but at an inn at Tragöss, a town in the Austrian state of Styria. This new concept was a huge success because it preserved the anonymity of customers who had previously been obliged to stock up at the chemist's. Nevertheless, throughout his career, Ebert concentrated on the sale of confectionery (PEZ chewing gum, Manner Original Neapolitan Wafers) before expanding into lottery tickets and storybooks.

Today, he emphasises his role as a grandfather, writing books and reading fairytales in kindergartens and schools, and dedicating his museum to grandchildren everywhere.

Ferry Ebert will sometimes sell one of his machines for a very special present. Unfortunately, the PEZ distributors of the 1950s bearing the face of Gerda Jahn, the PEZ lady now over 70 years old and a member of the Vienna Master Hairdressers' Association, were all sold long ago.

FERDINAND SAUTER'S MEMORIAL ⑳ TOMB

The Last Refrain

Hernals Cemetery
Leopold-Kunschak-Platz 7, 1170 Wien, group B, row F, No. 23
Open daily 3 November to end of February, 8am–5pm
March and 1 October to 2 November, 7am–6pm
April to September 7am–7pm (until 8pm Thursday, May to August)

A simple portrait medallion identifies the headstone of rhyming and drinking virtuoso Ferdinand Sauter (1804–54). The stone, engraved by Karl Philipp, was erected here in 1930, nearly a century after the death of the "people's poet".

Viel genossen, viel gelitten,
Und das Glück lag in der Mitten.
Viel empfunden, nichts erworben,
Froh gelebt und leicht gestorben.
Fragt nicht nach der Zahl der Jahre
Kein Kalender ist die Bahre.
Und der Mensch im Leichentuch,
Bleibt ein zugeklapptes Buch.
Darum Wand'rer zieh'doch weiter,
Denn Verwesung stimmt nicht heiter.

The unusual epitaph under the portrait was penned by the dead man himself:

> Much won, much lost,
> And luck lay in between;
> Much felt and nothing gained
> Content in life, in death no pain.
> Do not ask the number of years
> There is no calendar in the bier.
> And the man in his shroud,
> Remains a closed book.
> So, wanderer, on your way,
> There's nothing serene about decay.

This son of a council member, born at Salzburg, found rest in neither life nor death. In his youth he travelled around as an apprentice salesman, from Salzburg to Vienna via Wels, but he soon lost his various shop jobs – not always his fault. He moved into the notorious Viennese district of Hernals and then to Ottakring, where almost every building housed a tavern and where poverty, sickness and prostitution were the norm.

A favourite tavern was Zur blauen Flasche (At the Blue Flask) in Neulerchenfelder. It was one of the oldest cheap eating places in the district, famous for the lengthy panegyric Sauter recited there on New Year's Eve 1853. However, he is best known as the author of satirical and political verses such as *Geheime Polizei* (Secret Police) – he supported the revolutionaries in 1848.

Sauter's life was marked by tragedy: he lost his father, mother and brother very early. After breaking a leg in 1839, he walked with a limp until the end of his days. He was a cholera victim, suffering from terrible diarrhoea that led to dehydration and organ failure.

In 1917, journalist and playwright Rudolf Holzer wrote a part for stage star Alexander Girardi: the actor was to take on the tragi-comic role of Ferdinand Sauter in the play *Das Ende vom Lied* (The Last Refrain). Girardi died six months after the first performance.

Sauter, the author of numerous melancholy songs now part of folklore, died in utter poverty. For several years, his body lay in the section of the old Hernals Cemetery reserved for cholera victims. When it closed down in 1872, the "new Hernals Cemetery" was being built. The poet was transferred there in 1878.

Sauter, the unquenchable poet who had also known hunger, surely wouldn't have imagined ever reposing in such a grand tomb.

His elder brother, Anton Sauter, was a noted Austrian botanist.

WIENER RETTUNGSMUSEUM

We're on our way!

Gilmgasse 18 (access via Halirschgasse 12), 1170 Wien
Visits by appointment
Contact: post@ma70.wien.gv.at
S-Bahn: S45, Hernals station; Tram: 43, Hernals stop

You can book a visit to the Viennese Emergency Services Museum (which has around 300 exhibits) to immerse yourself in the history of the city's rescue services from their earliest days. The exhibition rooms are in the Hernals station, which dates from the early 20th century and is now classified as a historic monument. The building was once a community hospital used only in epidemics.

Stretchers, early defibrillators, uniforms, helmets decorated with crests, medical and technical equipment, communication devices and emergency vehicles, some of them several decades old, are among the artefacts on display.

It all began with the Ringtheater fire of 8 December 1881, which resulted in hundreds of deaths. The very next day, Johann Graf Wilczek and Jaromir Freiherr von Mundy started a volunteer rescue association. On 1 May 1883, a first-aid station was set up in the Innere Stadt. At the time, it had four ambulances, three teams of horses, two vehicles for transporting psychiatric patients and another two for infectious cases.

Stretchers were kept in strategic parts of the city, in order to be ready for accident victims.

Apart from Vienna Rescue, since 1977 the emergency services have involved the Austrian Red Cross, the Labour Samaritan Alliance and the Johanniter-Unfallhilfe (St John Ambulance), among other organisations.

Vienna now has 12 units equipped with 40 ambulances. Every day, the emergency services receive an average of 440 calls.

PALAIS ROTHSCHILD'S BALLROOM ㉒

Dancing with the Rothschilds

Elterleinplatz 2 (Kalvarienberggasse 28A), 1170 Wien
Visits by appointment with Tanzschule Strobl
www.tanzschule-strobl.at

Visit the Strobl dance school on the first floor of No. 28A Kalvarienberggasse in the Hernals district, and you'll find yourself in a Baroque, mirror-lined ballroom, straight out of the year 1882.

This immense, irregularly shaped hall, designed by French draughtsman and decorator François-Antoine Zoegger, is now used for dance classes and as a venue for concerts and social events.

The 18th-century building was at one time an educational institute for army officers' daughters. The interior fittings of the ballroom are from a later period: in the 19th and 20th centuries, they graced Alphonse Rothschild's palace which used to stand at 16–18 Theresianumgasse (4th district). A glass plaque in the ballroom commemorates this palatial neo-Renaissance townhouse built by Alphonse's uncle, Nathaniel Rothschild. Alphonse had to abandon his precious art collection during the Second World War after the Nazi police requisitioned his home. Badly damaged by bombing, it was demolished in 1954.

The site, now a training centre for the Austrian Chamber of Labour, belongs to the Social Democratic Party of Austria (SPÖ). But some fittings from the fabulous Rothschild salon were salvaged and reinstalled at the Hernals building, where the Strobl holds its classes and the 17th district SPÖ meets.

BRAUEREI OTTAKRINGER

Beer fountain and malting room

Ottakringer Strasse 95, 1160 Wien
Visits by appointment only (see website)
www.ottakringerbrauerei.at/de/home/
Tram: 2, Johann-Nepomuk-Berger-Platz stop

A visit to Vienna's last working brewery will inevitably end in a tasting session of the different types of beer in the traditional malting room This is well deserved, after the hundreds of steps in the various buildings …

This experience lets you discover the complex procedures involved in brewing.

The brewery's former drying tower is a landmark in Ottakring district. Built around 1907, it is 40 metres high with a hollow interior consisting of four drying levels, with racks on which the barley is left to dry after a soaking period in the cellar. Note that the rotating hood always moves with the wind. The tower, now classified as a historic monument, was in service until 1974.

Only barley-based beers are brewed at Ottakring. Depending on the variety, the beverage ferments from three to twelve weeks. Among the company's range of products are unfiltered beers, called *Zwiclk*, marketed as *Ottakringer Zwickl* (light) and *Ottakringer Zwickl Rot*, a darker brew.

After acquiring his brewing licence in 1837, master miller Heinrich Plank had the brewery built on the present site. He later sold it to the brothers Ignaz and Jacob Kuffner, who came from what was then Czechoslovakia in 1850. Moriz, Ignaz' son, contributed to the development of the brewery as well as Ottakring district and was a great supporter of art, culture and social issues. He was also a keen astronomer. Being Jewish, he was obliged to sell the brewery in 1938 and flee Austria.

The brewery has had its own artesian well since 1891. This brings water from a spring near Wilhelminenberg.

The oldest building still in use is in the south section and dates from 1902. It is one of the oldest reinforced concrete buildings in Vienna.

Ottakringer brewery also hosts events and the malting room has become a "must" for banquets. Although the founder Heinrich Plank originally owned a dance floor with a brewery attached to it, now it's the opposite: the brewery premises also have a dance floor … how times change.

FAÇADES BY OTTO RUDOLF SCHATZ

Open-air museums

Franz-Novy-Hof, Koppstrasse 97–101, 1160 Wien
U-Bahn: line U3, Ottakring station; Bus 48A, Possingergasse stop
Gemeindebau Hohenbergstrasse 24–32, 1120 Wien
U-Bahn: line U6, Meidling station; Bus 15A, Hohenbergstrasse stop

On the facade of No. 4a Pfenninggeldgasse in the Franz-Novy-Hof courtyard (named after politician and trade unionist Franz Novy), Otto Rudolf Schatz's monumental mural entitled *100,000 New Viennese Apartments* (1957) tries to encapsulate Vienna municipality's construction plans at the end of the Second World War. It shows several architects, both men and women, with models of the future buildings.

The inscription reads: "At the place where the creators meet / the seed grows 100,000 times / because men, space and time are associated / always in the general interest."

The first stone of the 100,000 new apartments was laid in 1957, even though this municipal scheme had been mooted during the First Republic (1919–38).

After the war, Schatz was kept busy, with the support of cultural adviser Viktor Matejka. In the 1930s, he had belonged to the avantgarde artists' group known as Hagenbund. As his wife was Jewish, he had to flee to Czechoslovakia after the annexation of Austria. He was, however, arrested in 1944 and taken to the "semi-Jewish" civilian work camp of Bistritz bei Beneschau before being freed in 1945 by the Red Army.

Back in Vienna, Schatz designed a mosaic for West Vienna station. Although he won first prize, the work was never carried out.

Instead, he was commissioned to design the façades for a new social housing complex. Two Schatz works dating back to the 1950s can be seen at Nos. 24–32 Hohenbergstrasse in Meidling. Sgraffiti on the two side walls of the courtyard show four female figures, considered to be allegories of the four elements: Fire and Earth to the east and Water and Air to the west.

MAILÜFTERL

The Austrian ancestor of the computer

Technischen Museum Wien
Mariahilfer Strasse 212, 1140 Wien
Open Monday to Friday 9am–6pm, Saturday, Sunday and public holidays
10am–6pm
U-Bahn: line U4, Schönbrunn station; Tram: 52 / 58, Winckelmannstrasse stop

Lording it over the media section of Vienna Technical Museum, one of the first computers in the world to run entirely on transistors (and not ephemeral electronic tubes) isn't called the Whirlwind or Typhoon, like its American contemporaries of the 1950s: its inventor more poetically named it the *Mailüfterl* (May Breeze). It was officially presented to the public in May 1958.

By today's standards, the *Mailüfterl* is a grey giant, 2-metres-high and several metres wide. With no screen or keyboard, it worked with perforated tape – keeping it going for several hours was quite a challenge.

At the time, transistors meant real progress. IT systems became smaller, more reliable and less expensive to manufacture.

The *Mailüfterl* was built by the Austrian electrical engineer Heinz Zemanek and his team for research purposes. The inventor had taken the liberty of tinkering around in the laboratory: as a university assistant, he had "no boss", as he later explained at a ceremony in his honour.

The international prominence of the *Mailüfterl* led to the introduction of computer technology in Austria and contributed to the unprecedented advance of automation in the 1960s and 70s.

Computing pioneer Zemanek died in July 2014 at the age of 94.

BILLARDMUSEUM WEINGARTNER ㉖

The difference between carambole, pool, billiards and snooker

Neubaugürtel 11, 1150 Wien
Open by appointment (see website)
www.billard-weingartner.at/billardmuseum.php
U-Bahn: line U3 / U6, Westbahnhof station

etween the traditional Viennese café Weingartner at No. 6 Goldschlaggasse and the eponymous billiards and games shop, Heinrich Weingartner's private Billiard Museum is the only one of its kind in Austria. The owner, a former Austrian champion player now over 70 years old, is a world snooker legend and still attends tournaments. He even publishes his own specialist journal. He opened his shop at the age of 24 and began collecting everything relating to his favourite pastime. The museum opened in 1992.

The centrepiece of the collection dates back more than 200 years: a complete set of elephant ivory billiard balls on which tarot card figures are engraved.

This captivating museum also has around 150 antique pool cues, 11 antique tables, 800 artworks and 2,000 postcards on the same theme.

The images taken from satirical journals are particularly interesting: very instructive about the changing fashions in billiards. A well-stocked library shows the great interest in this game that was formerly the reserve of the aristocracy. Some of the books were published as early as the 17th century.

Of course, Herr Weingartner also points out the difference between carom (or carambole) billiards, pool, English billiards and snooker.

HERNALS LENTEN MARKET

"Bamkraxler" at the Kalvarienberg

Kalvarienberggasse / St Bartholomäus-Platz, 1170 Wien
Held every year from Lent and throughout Easter

Every year, from Ash Wednesday to Easter Monday, the oldest Lenten market in Vienna is held at Hernals. It runs from Elterleinplatz to the Church of Kalvarienberg. Many of the vendors' stalls ranged along the pedestrian streets offer "*Bamkraxlers*": carved wooden figurines that epitomise this unusual market. These colourful little characters with bells are attached to a stick, in remembrance of the tree that Jericho tax collector Zacchaeus climbed in order to catch a glimpse of Jesus on the way to his Crucifixion, as recorded in Luke's Gospel.

The first pilgrimage of St Stephen to the Protestant village of Hernals near Vienna took place in 1639, on a road supposed to imitate Jerusalem's Via Dolorosa (Way of Sorrows). The first stone of Kalvarienberg, on the slopes to the right of the church, was laid 300 years ago.

From 1709 to 1714, the wealthy bourgeoisie of Hernals built a horseshoe-shaped "educational" flight of steps around the church: penitents pass the seven deadly sins before reaching the Crucifixion at the top. On the way back down to the courtyard are the seven heavenly virtues that counteract these sins: humility (pride), liberality (avarice), chastity (lust), meekness (anger), temperance (gluttony), brotherly love (envy), diligence (sloth).

Under Joseph II, penitence processions were forbidden, but they soon reappeared with the participation of local restaurants and folk singers under the name of Hernalser Kirtage (Hernals Festival).

The covered section of the market is the work of Viennese architect Richard Jordan and dates from the late 19th century.

MUSEUM FÜR VERHÜTUNG UND SCHWANGERSCHAFTSABBRUCH

Everything you always wanted to know about reproduction

Mariahilfer Gürtel 37, 1. Stock, 1150 Wien
Open Wednesday to Sunday 2pm–6pm
www.de.muvs.org
U-Bahn: line U3 / U6, Westbahnhof station

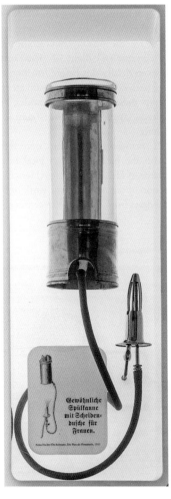

MUVS, Vienna's Museum of Contraception and Abortion, which opened in 2007, recalls the not-so-distant time when abortion could be fatal for the women who underwent it and led to prison for those who practised it.

The museum aims to make available scientifically accurate and up-to-date information on fertility, contraception and pregnancy tests, especially for young people.

It consists of two exhibition rooms, one dedicated to contraception (with masses of information about its history) and the other to abortion. Both are innovative in their field. Above all, it's a question of education – for both men and women. There are condoms, IUDs and suchlike, displayed like works in an art gallery.

Can frogs detect pregnancy? You'll find out here.

What was the real purpose of the bidet, an essential complement to any bathroom at the end of the 19th century? It definitely wasn't for bathing babies ...

This must-see museum is a private institution. Its comprehensive website has a wealth of information on fertility, contraception and possible abortion options.

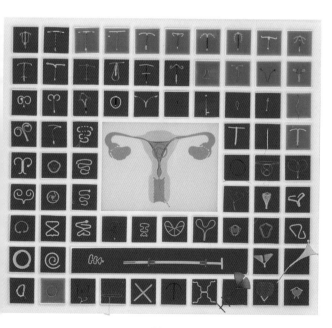

MUMMY OF ANTON MARIA SCHWARTZ

The apostle of Vienna's working class

Kalasantinerkirche
Pater-Schwartz-Gasse 10, 1150 Wien
Open annually during the week of 10–17 September
U-Bahn: line U6, Gumpendorfer Strasse station

Hidden behind the altar of the Kalasantinian Church, the mummy of Anton Maria Schwartz (1852–1929), founder of the Congregation of Christian Workers, is preserved in this ordinary church in the street named after him.

During his lifetime, the young workers' pastor fought for Sunday as a day of rest, an eight-hour day, leave for apprentices, trade union rights and the establishment of a social security system.

Surprisingly, Pastor Schwartz was first buried at Hietzing before being exhumed two months later and transferred to "his" church. Although his body was preserved immediately after death, the pastor was not embalmed in the usual way: by this time new and effective methods were available. As in the case of Mayor Karl Lueger and Emperor Franz Joseph, chemicals were used to preserve as much as possible of the bodily remains. The pastor's face and hands were covered with skin-colour and black wax.

This procedure was not intended to introduce a new saint whose "undamaged remains" could have been interpreted as a divine sign. Modern conservation methods should rather be associated with the culture of remembrance: preserving the body was tantamount to paying a special tribute to the deceased's achievements.

Pastor Schwartz founded the Congregation of Christian Workers of St Joseph Casalanz in 1889 in homage to the Spanish priest Joseph Casalanz (1557–1648), who came to Rome to promote training for young people. The diocese of Vienna, suspecting competition with the social reform work of German pastor Adolph Kolping, refused to approve the community for many years. It was only in 1939, 10 years after Schwartz's death, that it was officially recognised by the Vatican.

Anton Maria Schwartz was beatified by Pope John Paul II in 1998. His festival is celebrated on 17 September.

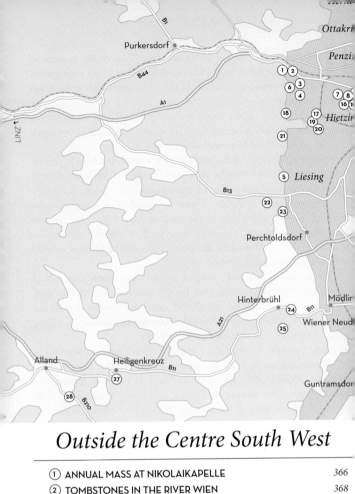

Outside the Centre South West

ANNUAL MASS AT NIKOLAIKAPELLE

Church service with hunting horns

Lainzer Tiergarten, Nikolaitor, 1130 Wien
Accessible during Lainzer Tiergarten opening hours
www.lainzer-tiergarten.at/oeffnungszeiten.html
Chapel open every year around 20 September, feast of St Eustace
www.hietzing.at/Bezirk/geschichte2.php?id=418

Take the Nikolaitor (Nicolas gate) into the Lainzer Tiergarten nature reserve, go past the playground and turn right at the next fork to find one of the oldest sacred buildings in Vienna. The late-Romanesque chapel on the hill was built in honour of the patron saint of water, Nicolas Episcopus. He was invoked as protection from the devastating floods of the River Wien, tributary of the Danube.

A small fortified nobleman's residence probably stood on the chapel site between the 11th and 16th centuries. The architectural style of the chapel suggests that it was built during the second half of the 12th century. Partly destroyed in the 13th century, it was later rebuilt, as evidenced by the bases of its Romanesque columns and medieval vaults. At that time, the "Nichlas chappelle" as it was called, belonged to the Bishopric of Passau.

The chapel suffered major damage in the two Turkish sieges of 1529 and 1683. Josef Heinrich Breitenbücher, pastor of Hütteldorf and first auxiliary Bishop of Vienna, had it repaired at his own expense in 1735. It was neglected during the time of Joseph II and Maria Theresa's reforms, but benefited from extensive renovations between 1835 and 1837. In the imperial hunting days, the chapel was dedicated to

St Eustace, patron saint of the hunt. Some Viennese still refer to it as the Eustachiuskapelle. There was once an altarpiece depicting the saint returning from the hunt.

In 1945, the building was plundered and no longer bears any sign of royal protocol. A marble altar and some wooden pews are still there, however. Every year around 20 September, a church service with hunting horns attracts crowds to the former shrine. St Eustace's Chapel now belongs to Mariabrunn parish in the 14th district.

TOMBSTONES IN THE RIVER WIEN ②

Recycled in death

Between Hütteldorf and Bräuhausbrücke subway stations, 1140 Wien
Always accessible (even in flood)
U-Bahn: line U4, Hütteldorf station

It is not "on Busento's grassy banks" in southern Italy – as in German poet August von Platen's *The Grave of Alaric* – but on the banks of the Wien at Hütteldorf that the dead seem to lie at rest. However, just as the King of the Visigoths was never buried in the Busento River, no remains of historical celebrities lie here.

As part of the consolidation of the riverbed in the 19th century, abandoned tombstones and various building materials were "recycled". Although, in order to avoid future problems, they had to be inserted face down, a few mistakes were made due to negligence. Sharp-eyed walkers might notice the odd relic from a Viennese cemetery. Some inscriptions are still legible, with details of the life and occupation of the deceased.

The lack of archives on this subject means not knowing exactly where the stones came from, but they would have belonged to several cemeteries in the western part of the city.

In the post-war period, it was customary to reuse tombstones from former cemeteries, as they were inexpensive and readily available building materials.

The walk along the River Wien also leads to interesting urban graffiti and then to the zone of alluvial deposits planted with reeds, the habitat of various wild animals. With a bit of luck, you might even see a beaver. Take your wellies.

KIRCHE OBER-ST-VEIT CRYPT

Clever astronomical calculations

Wolfrathplatz 1, 1130 Wien
Open occasionally (see website)
www.pfarre-oberstveit.at/kontakt/pfarrkanzlei

The pretty crypt below the altar of the church dedicated to St Vitus in Ober-St-Veit, a neighbourhood in Heitzing district, is reached by a wooden trapdoor from the central aisle. The hexagonal crypt has an octagonal central pillar and an altar that dates from the Baroque period, when it was the burial site for the lords of the nearby castle.

Sunlight is "directed" into the crypt according to precise mathematical and astronomical calculations. During the winter solstice, at sunrise, the rays shine across the vaulted ceiling directly onto the central column. As the weeks pass, the spot of light moves along the ceiling ridge to illuminate the whole column, at 9am precisely, on 21 March. In the following months, the rays reach the crypt floor and advance towards the east window until finally, on the day of the summer solstice, the ray of light lies exactly halfway between the window and the column.

Some researchers believe that the skills used to build this church were acquired during the construction of the Stephansdom, although this cannot be proved.

The Slavic god of light Svantovit was venerated on the site of the present-day Ober-St-Veit Church, which already housed a Slavic place of worship at the time of the great migrations. During the summer solstice, people danced until they dropped in honour of Svantovit. The Christians renamed the god of light and dance "Vitus" and ascribed 15 June as his feast day, known as Vidovdan (Day of St Vitus) in Serbia. The Roman Catholic Church used to rename the divinities and sacred spirits of new conquered territories in order to include them in its list of canonised saints.

It's no coincidence that there's a hard rock band called *Saint Vitus*: martyred in a boiling cauldron, St Vitus (also known as St Vith) comes to the rescue of those experiencing epileptic fits, consumed with rage or in a dance ecstasy. In ancient Greece, epilepsy was considered a sacred disease, a punishment or gift of the gods, and associated with genius.

TRAZERBERG WACHTTURM

A Viennese viewpoint

Hochschule für Agrar- und Umweltpädagogik
Trazerberg, Angermayergasse 1, 1130 Wien
Open during college hours
www.agrarumweltpaedagogik.ac.at/hochschule/kontakt-lageplan/service.html

Trazerberg watchtower, in the grounds of the University College for Agrarian and Environmental Pedagogy in Angermayergasse, probably had many functions which have not yet been clearly established. The tower has undergone so many renovations over the years that its medieval origin is also conjectural.

On the other hand, it was certainly built for military use. A spiral staircase winding to the left leads up to the battlements. As a sword was generally wielded in the right hand, this layout was intended to disadvantage any assailants coming up the steps. They would be forced to attack with the left side of their body facing forward, while the defenders above could fight with swords in their right hands.

It's thought that in the Middle Ages the tower was used as an observation post to spot enemy troops and sound the alarm. From the highest point of Trazerberg, you could see across the city as far as the River Wien. In an emergency, a fire was lit on top of the tower to alert the city defences.

RUINS OF MAURERBERG BARRACKS ⑤

Military shooting range

Beim Pappelteich, Anton-Krieger-Gasse, 1230 Wien

Among a profusion of trees and shrubbery, near the car park on Anton-Krieger-Gasse, are the ruins of Maurerberg barracks, including a stone wall several metres long. They belonged to the airborne intelligence regiment founded after 1938, and were intended to be the "most beautiful and most majestic barracks in the military district of Vienna". Research carried out by architect–historian Andreas Nierhaus shows that Rudolf Weiss, a student of Otto Wagner, was the architect behind the unfinished project.

Near the barracks, on the site of the celebrated 1970s Church of the Most Holy Trinity (better known as the Wotruba-Kirche, after its designer Fritz Wotruba), stood a group of huts that burned down at the end of the war. The remains were cleared away in 1949.

There were barracks on Mauerberg long before the Nazis came to power, however. The "Castle of Angels", a monastery originally belonging to the Jesuit Order, hosted soldiers from 1775 to 1918. The building was demolished in the 1920s and the area between Engelsburggasse and Kaserngasse is now residential.

The castle, part of the monastery before it was rebuilt in 1777 as a barracks, was razed to the ground in 1895.

The two barracks, one in the "*château*" and the other in the "*bourg*" of Mauer, had their own shooting range in the woods from 1834. It was abandoned in 1918, but could be visited until 2000, when the last pieces of concrete from the ruins were removed.

The Zur Schiessstätte (Shooting Range) restaurant ensures that the past history of the "wild mountain", as Maurerberg is also known, is not forgotten. This is a good starting point for long walks through the Vienna Woods.

JOHANN BERGL PAINTINGS

Elephants in America

Schloss Ober-St-Veit
Wolfrathplatz 2, 1130 Wien
Open only as part of Hietzing district festival
www.hietzing.at

The ground floor of the eastern wing of the castle at Wolfrathplatz is open only as part of Hietzing district festival. It contains four splendid rooms decorated by Johann Wenzel Bergl (1718–89). The building, which took its present form in the 18th century, was always the property of the Church except between 1762 and 1779, when it belonged to Maria Theresa, who spent no less than 80,000 guilders on refurbishing it. She commissioned this work from Bergl, her favourite painter. As at Schloss Schönbrunn, his brief was to give the walls a breath of exoticism. The concept of a *Sala Terrena* – large rooms open to the garden – is perfectly illustrated by this castle. There is a breathtaking view of the park, with its majestic trees and a fishpond. In poor weather, garden parties could be held in these ground-floor reception rooms, which gave the illusion of extending into a beautiful landscaped garden.

Bergl worked by applying his lush colours onto linen panels which were then fixed to the walls, when he would continue painting over the ceilings of the various rooms. Having chosen India as the dominant theme at Schönbrunn, he opted for the Americas at Ober-St-Veit. While his Indian frescoes focus mainly on splendidly exuberant fauna and flora, his later composition includes people, both European and American. The first room, which is particularly successful, shows a black tribal chief with a feathered headdress, seated in a sedan chair borne by two white men. A Baroque parasol protects him from the sun. In the background, a shipload of European explorers has just landed. This distant paradise is still unspoiled. In the Europe of those days, the idea prevailed that "savages" led a contemplative life and lived in perfect harmony with nature.

The walls of the four rooms are covered with "typical" fruits and animals from the Americas: cocoa beans, lemons, parrots, butterflies, flying fish, turtles, monkeys, snakes and llamas rub shoulders. Only the elephant and the rhinoceros seem out of place in this America according to Johann Bergl.

There was originally a fifth room designed by Bergl, at the end of the corridor. Unfortunately, his artwork has not been preserved and the room is now a kitchen.

Ober-St-Veit Castle, which now belongs to the Roman Catholic Church, is a Redemptoris Mater (Mother of the Redeemer) seminary.

The former library on the second floor of the castle is now a chapel. The wall and ceiling frescoes, painted in the 18th century by an unknown artist and now restored, represent the sequence of spring, summer and winter. The fourth ceiling is a personification of the Habsburg dynasty as established during the reign of Maria Theresa, who had decided to enlarge the room by a quarter. The royal couple, Emperor Franz I and his wife, appear in medallions over the doors.

VILLA BEER

An architectural gem from the 1930s

Wenzgasse 12, 1130 Wien
Opening to the public after refurbishment
Tram: 58, Wenzgasse stop

While Mies van der Rohe's design for Villa Tugendhat was for Brno, and Frank Lloyd Wright's Fallingwater house was built near Pittsburgh, the Austrian footwear manufacturers Julius and Margarethe Beer commissioned their new Viennese residence in the rural suburb of Hietzing. Villa Beer is today seen as an icon of modernist architecture, illustrating the best of the collaboration between Oskar Wlach and Josef Frank in the late 1920s.

The 700 square metre villa, built in 1929 over three floors, also has a garden with swimming pool. The owners wished to live in the countryside but with the impression of being in town – hence the "central square", with grand piano and acoustics that allow the music to be heard throughout the house. In the architectural journal *Der Baumeister* (The Builder), designer Frank, who supplied the furniture and fabrics at Villa Beer, summed up this innovatory lifestyle in an article entitled, "The house as path and place".

The imposing building has an asymmetrical façade with a mixture of round, square and rectangular windows. Inside is a series of dynamic

spatial effects: dramatic staircases, projecting landings and concealed doorways. The built-in cupboards, balustrades, part of the floors, radiator covers and lamps have been preserved in their original condition.

The Beer factory produced rubber soles. Just as building work was completed, power struggles in the rubber industry plunged Julius and Margarethe Beer into financial difficulties and they were forced to rent out the villa: opera singers Richard Tauber and Jan Kiepura stayed there for a while. The Beers emigrated to New York in 1940 and Julius died shortly afterwards. Margarethe returned to Austria after the war. Elisabeth, her younger daughter, died in Maly Trostenets extermination camp in Belorussia.

The upper storey of the villa housed the maids' rooms, and they had their own bathroom – the luxuries extended even to the staff!

The villa of Franz Joseph's lover

Gloriettegasse 9, 1130 Wien
Private property, closed to the public
U-Bahn: line U4, Gloriettegasse station; Bus: 56B /58B, Tiroler Gasse stop

Repeated on the façade of Villa Schratt – a magnificent building with a roof in the Eastern style then in fashion – are the intertwined initials KS for Katharina Schratt, one of the former owners of the premises.

Besides his capricious wife Empress Elisabeth ("Sisi"), the Austrian Emperor Franz Joseph kept several mistresses. Two of them are worth a mention, given the duration of their relationship with him – Anna Nahowski and Katharina Schratt. Both had a villa near Schloss Schönbrunn placed at their disposal, and both are buried in the nearby Hietzinger Friedhof (Hietzing Cemetery).

When Sisi introduced the Burgtheater actress Katharina Schratt to Franz Joseph, he was not yet 25 years old. In 1886 he began a relationship with "Madame", as he called her, that was to last 30 years. Katharina, wedded to Hungarian diplomat Nikolaus Kiss von Ittebe, gave birth to a son, but her marriage was not happy.

In 1893, the emperor gifted her this property in Gloriettegasse. She commissioned architects Andreas Streit and Eduard Frauenfeld to alter the layout, raising the ceilings to a height of 3 metres and adding a laundry, a maid's room and a luxurious bathroom with WC. Here the celebrated Viennese actress received any number of distinguished visitors and awoke the emperor in the early hours: Franz Joseph began his day at 4 o'clock in the morning.

A bowling alley runs alongside what is now Weidlichgasse and in 1894 an outdoor swimming pool was built in the garden. But today only a small pavilion remains: the Second World War bombs did extensive damage. The copper boiler used to heat the water for the pool was melted down during the war and the renovation carried out in the 1950s was more like an identical reconstruction.

Katharina Schratt was laid to rest in 1940 in Hietzing Cemetery (No. 15 Maxingstrasse, section 19, 108), in the vault of the Kiss von Ittebe family. She died at the age of 86. Her husband Nikolaus and son Anton were buried at her side.

The villa of Anna Nahowski, the emperor's other lover, stands nearby at No. 46 Maxingstrasse.

OTTO-WAGNER-HOFPAVILLON HIETZING

A breakthrough for modernism

Schönbrunner Schlossstrasse, 1130 Wien
U-Bahn: line U4, Hietzing station
Open Saturday and Sunday 10am–6pm
www.wienmuseum.at/de/standorte/otto-wagner-hofpavillon-hietzing.html

Franz Joseph only used his ultra-sophisticated private railway station twice. But this did not matter to its designer Otto Wagner, who was primarily interested in showcasing his work. This architectural gem reopened in summer 2014, after extensive renovation and restoration.

In the 1890s, the City of Vienna launched a large-scale infrastructure project with the construction of the Stadtbahn metropolitan railway. Wagner was in charge of the overall design of this new means of mass transport. On his initiative, a private pavilion was specially planned for the emperor and his court at Hietzing station. The building, completed in 1899, was in Art Nouveau style, with a unique exterior and opulent interior decoration – its imperial magnificence was a breakthrough for modernism.

Inside the pavilion are eye-catchingly unexpected red silk hangings and carpets, while sinuous philodendron motifs dominate the decoration. Trapezoidal windows, another of the architect's "specialities", make optimal use of indirect natural light. The low lighting is designed so that the precious fabrics do not fade. The upper part of the cupola is made from frosted glass.

This pavilion is an impressive compendium of Otto Wagner's artistic style, which paved the way for 20th-century modernist architecture.

A canvas painted from a vantage point of 1,600 m

The immense oil painting, dated 1899, is by Carl Moll, an important artist in *fin-de-siècle* Vienna. This aerial view of the city was painted in an airship at an altitude of 1,600 metres.

Eagles hover over the panorama, which extends from Schönbrunn Palace and Gardens to the Ringstrasse.

The painting is beyond any shadow of doubt a portrayal, not of Franz Joseph, as might have been expected, but of the rise of the capital during his reign.

ALCHEMICAL FRESCO AT SCHÖNBRUNN ZOO

Mysticism in the world's longest-surviving zoo

Tiergarten Schönbrunn, Maxingstrasse 13B, 1130 Wien
Open January 9am–4.30pm, February 9am–5pm, March 9am–5.30pm, April
to September 9am–6.30pm, October 9am–5.30pm, November and December
9am–4.30pm
U-Bahn: line U4, Hietzing station

The geometry of Schönbrunn Zoo in the palace gardens derives from the interests of Holy Roman Emperor Franz I, Freemason and Rosicrucian. Members of these fraternities met regularly in the Alchemist's (or Emperor's) Pavilion that the emperor, who had a profound interest in the sciences, had had built in 1759 at the precise centre of his menagerie. He had a laboratory set up in the basement to carry out his scientific experiments, cherishing the idea of piercing the mystery of the philosopher's stone.

The frescoed ceiling of the pavilion dome is by court painter Josef Ignaz Mildorfer. Through scenes from Ovid's *Metamorphoses*, the artwork illustrates the basic principle of alchemy, according to which every element on Earth comes from one and the same original matter. The celebrated philosopher's stone is also depicted.

Each of the animal enclosures was provided with a hut or "lodge" in the Masonic tradition, designed so that people could view the animals, but also, conversely, so that the animals could look at them.

The 12 animal enclosures – for the 12 signs of the zodiac – are arranged radially around the central Emperor's Pavilion, the 13th and final lodge intended for men. Its octagonal shape symbolises the eternal cycle and power. It rests on a square plinth which represents the four elements and the four virtues of Plato, illustrated on the arched doorways: Prudence, Courage, Temperance and Justice. Three

pathways lead to the centre of the menagerie.

Alois Kraus, the zoo manager, broke the quasi-magical ambience to build an extension in 1889, the year of the "Mayerling incident", the apparent murder–suicide of Archduke Rudolf and his lover, Mary Vetsera. Almost all the animal enclosures were destroyed by bombing in 1945 – only the pavilion remained intact.

Every year, on 13 May and 31 July, the pavilion is the site of an astonishing spectacle: the rays of the morning sun pass through the two-headed eagle on the roof of Schönbrunn Castle and across the central window, flooding the building with light for over 10 minutes. 13 May is Maria Theresa's birthday and 31 July is the anniversary of the founding of the imperial menagerie.

THE BERGL ROOMS
AT SCHÖNBRUNN

European yearnings for the exotic

Schloss Schönbrunn
Schönbrunner Schlossstrasse 47, 1130 Wien
Open only during guided tours
www.schoenbrunn.at/kontakt.html
U-Bahn: line U4, Schönbrunn station

The former summer apartments of Maria Theresa in Schönbrunn Palace, as well as the Bergl Rooms (later occupied by Archduke Rudolf, heir to the throne), are now open for guided group tours. An enchanting universe of palms and exotic fruits, tropical paradises and ancient temples is waiting to be discovered ...

The colours of the tropical world aimed to bring the ceilings and walls of the cool ground-floor rooms to life. The empress, who increasingly suffered from the heat in the summer months, particularly appreciated her garden-facing suite when the upstairs rooms became too oppressive.

Nine exotically decorated rooms are named after a Bohemian artist dear to the heart of Maria Theresa, Johann Wenzel Bergl (1718–89). This former pupil of Paul Troger – the Austrian artist whose illusionistic ceiling frescoes were hugely influential – skilfully merged painted interiors with the landscape beyond the windows, dissolving the confines of the room into romantic scenes. Birds and animals seem to emerge from the undergrowth, while balustrades, pergolas and vases evoke a human presence in the heart of nature. No doubt Bergl was also inspired by the luxuriant palace greenhouses and benefited from the advice of botanist Franz Stefan.

The generation that succeeded Emperor Franz I and his wife found Bergl's paintings too old-fashioned and hid them behind grey hangings. They were again on display by 1891, but not until the 1960s were they finally renovated.

The fantasy landscapes painted on the walls of Rudolf's sister Gisela's apartment, included in the tour of Schönbrunn Children's Museum, are also by Bergl.

CITRUS FRUITS FROM SCHÖNBRUNN

Sunshine over Schönbrunn

Kronprinzengarten Schloss Schönbrunn
Schönbrunner Schlossstrasse 47, 1130 Wien
Open only for special events, such as "Citrus Days", usually in May
www.schoenbrunn.at
U-Bahn: line U4, Schönbrunn station

Schönbrunn Palace Orangery, open only for special events such as Zitrustage (Citrus Days), usually in May, is unfairly overlooked, despite being the largest orangery in Europe after Versailles.

Go through the Kronprinzengarten garden to reach the Baroque greenhouse, with its vast windows. It houses 400 citrus fruit trees in all possible shades of yellow and orange.

Many of them have a very distinctive shape, such as the "Hand of Buddha", a variety of Asian cedar that resembles a many-fingered hand. This variety, popular in gourmet restaurants, has been grown at Schönbrunn since the early 2000s.

Citrus cultivation at Schönbrunn goes back to the 18th century, when the multitude of varieties reflected status as the fruits were presented or served to distinguished guests.

Today, the national gardens take care of the 400 trees. 30 historical species are represented among the hundred varieties. Some of the original trees are 180 years old: oranges, lemons and a mandarin. Empress Elisabeth probably smelled the perfume of their flowers.

Guided tours, lectures and exhibitions are held during the Citrus Days. There are always a few cuttings for sale, and tastings of jams, drinks and perfumed products make a pleasant finale to the programme.

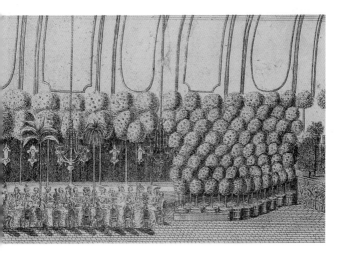

ZAUBERKASTEN MUSEUM

The kingdom of sorcerer's apprentices

Schönbrunner Strasse 262, im Hof, 1120 Wien
Open every first Sunday of the month 10am–4pm, or by appointment
www.zauberkasten-museum.at

Faced with the hundreds of exhibits in the Magic Set Museum, you realise that a set can take many forms. Boxes, chests, trunks, entire cabinets, conceal the strategies and tools you'll need, after completing your apprenticeship, to perform any kind of magic trick. Rings and coins, playing cards and cups, vases, marbles and false compartments complete the set. All that's missing are the conjurers and their skill in diverting the attention of spectators.

The first magic sets were made in the toy stronghold of Nuremberg, towards the end of the 18th century. Goethe gave one to his grandson, to improve his "mental dexterity, which we Germans don't possess in abundance". The tricks are often passed down unchanged from generation to generation, and are as successful now as they were in the past.

Manfred Klaghofer opened this museum after spending 15 years assembling the world's largest collection of magic sets. Formerly a professional conjuror, he was a member of the Zauberkistl, the Vienna Magic Circle. A video shows him performing traditional tricks, some of which have been known since the Middle Ages.

The magic sets come from all around the world, though mostly from the United States; some of them are almost 300 years old. The range includes books of magic, dating from the 18th century to the most recent acquisitions. As the books and films of the Harry Potter saga triggered a craze for sorcery and magic, models of Harry and Hermione straddling

their faithful hippogriff – half horse, half eagle – had to be brought in to complete the collection.

The museum also has thousands of archived pieces in storage, which can be viewed by the public only at special themed events or on request.

"BRENNPUNKT" – MUSEUM DER HEIZKULTUR WIEN

The warmest museum in Vienna

Malfattigasse 4, 1120 Wien
Open October to May from Monday to Wednesday, 9am–noon and 1pm–4pm,
Sunday 10am–4pm, and by appointment
www.wien.gv.at/kultur/museen/brennpunkt
U-Bahn: line U4, Längenfeldgasse station

The Brennpunkt (home) Museum of the History of Heating, which opened in 2010, is one of Vienna's most successful museum ventures. This collection, which is devoted to the history of home heating, is attractively modern and original.

The 10 rooms give a detailed explanation of how the heating system works in a large city. The social and cultural changes behind different methods of keeping warm are deciphered and the many interactive consoles are both instructive and entertaining. This unusual collection includes technology that has disappeared elsewhere: old boilers, industrial kitchen equipment, steam heaters for schools, hospitals or horticultural installations… Traditional stoves are ranged along the main corridor of this underground museum. The emphasis is on daily life: in bathrooms and kitchens, in public baths, laundries and toilets. How have home comforts and ambient temperatures evolved over the last 200 years? What temperature do we find pleasant? What was it like in the Biedermeier era?

Thermal energy, power sources, the future of energy supply … all these questions are addressed in the context of building an energy-saving house.

As it belongs to a vocational school, the museum is closed in summer.

HAYDN MEMORIAL

The incredible story of Haydn's head

Haydnpark
Gaudenzdorfer Gürtel, 1120 Wien
Tram: 62, Marx-Meidlinger-Strasse stop; 6 / 18, Arbeitergasse / Gürtel stop

Haydn's modest original tombstone, attached to a section of wall in the former cemetery at Hundsturm (in use between 1783 and 1874), bears the following inscription: "Haydn, born in 1732, died in 1809. *Non omnis moriar* [I will not die completely]. A tribute from his pupil Neukomm, returned to Vienna in 1814." Sigismund Ritter von Neukomm and the composer were related, but when Neukomm had Haydn's Greek-style memorial erected, he was unaware that an important part of his deceased brother-in-law was missing.

Josef Karl Rosenbaum, former secretary to Prince Esterházy, his friend Johann Nepomuk Peter and several others, including the gravedigger, actually stole the corpse's head three days after the funeral. Rosenbaum and Nepomuk Peter were followers of phrenology. This pseudoscience, founded by Viennese doctor Franz Joseph Gall, is based on the theory that the shape and structure of the skull reflects a person's character – even their intellectual superiority or genius. The thieves were clearly determined that nobody should know of their infamy, as they planned to keep the precious trophy in a mausoleum in one of their gardens.

When the Esterházy family, Haydn's patrons over many years,

asked for the mortal remains of the court composer to be transferred to Eisenstadt in 1820, the theft was discovered. Rosenbaum sent several items from his skull collection as a replacement, including the head of a young man, then the head of a man of similar age. The real skull was preserved by the Rosenbaum family before being handed over to the famous pathologist Carl von Rokitansky, whose son presented it to the Gesellschaft der Musikfreunde in Wien (Vienna Society of Friends of Music) in 1895.

Hundsturm Cemetery was renamed Haydnpark in 1926. Haydn's is the only tombstone to have been preserved.

Not until 5 June 1954 – more than 145 years after the composer's death – did the sculptor Gustinus Ambrosi open the coffin to the sound of the imperial anthem, to finally reunite the head with its owner. Haydn's mausoleum can now be seen at the Bergkirche (Hill Church) of Eisenstadt.

SCHOKOLADENHAUS
(Chocolate House)

A truly unusual home

Wattmanngasse 29, 1130 Wien
Bus: 56A / 58B, Tiroler Gasse stop

Although some Viennese also know it as the Lebkuchenhaus (Gingerbread House), this Art Deco residence owes its different nicknames to its dark brown majolica façade. Designed in 1914 by architect and interior designer Ernst Lichtblau, who studied under Otto Wagner, it was awarded the Prize of the Municipality of Vienna for Outstanding Buildings in the same year.

At first glance, the design of the façade is more akin to Josef Hoffmann's style than Wagner's. Its harmonious combination of straight and curved shapes, on both flat and relief surfaces, teems with detail. The majolica work is by German sculptor Willy Russ, who chose to intertwine floral and figurative motifs. The date "1914" is clearly visible on the wall to the left of the front door.

The multi-tiered cornice has raised ceramic panels featuring plants and birds of incredible ornamental richness. The gutters tumbling down on both sides are also remarkable. Ernst Lichtblau's window sashes seem to presage the architecture of the 1920s.

After the Anschluss, Lichtblau was forced to emigrate to the United States, where he inspired an entire post-war generation of American designers.

Many of his Viennese buildings are now listed monuments (notably a semi-detached house on the Werkbundsiedlung housing estate).

LOCKERWIESE ESTATE

Red Vienna's houses with gardens

Camillianergasse / Faistauergasse, 1130 Wien

"We're doing fine here," says one of the residents of the Lockerwiese housing complex when asked about the quality of life in his neighbourhood, which was renovated in 2014. This was probably already the case in 1928, when this complex of "decent lodgings" – as they were known at the time – was built between Wolkersbergenstrasse and Versorgungsheimstrasse.

The aim was to provide basic houses, with enough space and a small garden, running water and inside toilets. There were also communal facilities: kindergarten, mothers' support centre, mobile clinic, gymnasium, library and grocery store. These public institutions were crucial in the eyes of the ruling Social Democratic Party. They were grouped around the market square on the main road, Faistauergasse, which still emphasises the "countrified" aspect of the estate. The tobacco shop hasn't moved since 1932, when the buildings designed by Karl Schartelmüller were completed. The architect built another row of 120 houses in 1938 before adding a sports field and four apartment blocks in the years 1950–51. The former library is now a retirement home.

The sgraffito entitled *The World of Work* (1929, restored in 1949) is by Georg Samwald.

The apartments are still managed by the City of Vienna, and there is a long waiting list. Many well-known artists have lived on this estate, as noted on signboards. For example, the actress Senta Berger lived here at the end of the Second World War, and the actor/writer Helmut Qualtinger learned his lines in his garden, while his first wife, Leomare, grew up in this neighbourhood.

The name "Lockerwiese" (wide prairie) refers to the open fields on which the estate was built.

FANITEUM

Love, memory, grief

Hanschweg 1, 1130 Wien
Limited opening hours; church open during celebrations
http://www2.karmel.at/

It isn't easy to see inside the Faniteum. Since 1974 it has belonged to the Discalced Carmelites, who run Karmel St Joseph's convent there. Although it's rarely possible for the public to attend Mass, when the occasion arises the small church is well worth a visit.

In front of the church, a triple-arched loggia has been designed so that, in fine weather, you can see the Stephansdom.

The Faniteum is close to Ober-St-Veit Cemetery, but you have to walk further up to reach the walls of the Lainzer Tiergarten nature reserve, a former Habsburg hunting ground in the Vienna Woods, where the unusual convent stands.

The impression of being suddenly thrust into Italy is no coincidence: that was precisely the effect sought by Graf (Count) Karol Lanckoroński. The Tuscan-style church, surmounted by a cupola, was modelled on the 15th-century Pazzi Chapel in Florence.

When Lanckoroński's wife, Francisca (Fanita), died in childbirth a year after their marriage, the count decided to raise a mausoleum – the Faniteum – at the place where he had hoped his family would grow up.

As burial regulations changed while the vault intended for them was being constructed, the remains of Fanita and her stillborn baby could not be placed there in 1893. Private funerals outside official cemetery grounds were prohibited, so the two bodies now rest in Hietzing Cemetery.

The bas-relief in the ancient Greek-style church recalls the sad fate of the Lanckoroński family. A father holds his dead son in his arms while extending a comforting hand to his wife. Before the Carmelites took over the building, it was variously used as a girls' convalescent centre, a military hospital and a children's home.

Karol Lanckoroński remarried twice. He too is buried at Hietzing.

Graf Karol Lanckoroński-Brzezie (1848–1933), the giant with the red beard, encyclopaedic knowledge and sharp voice

This nobleman is still very well known in Poland, his native land, although almost forgotten in Vienna where he lived and studied the history of art, amassing a vast collection of works – one of the largest in the city. He undertook archaeological expeditions, accompanying celebrity painter Hans Makart to Egypt and establishing himself as a protector of heritage and monuments. At his request, August Stauda, documentary photographer of old Vienna, recorded the places due to be demolished or completely redeveloped.

Count Lanckoroński generously supported many artists and sculptors such as Viktor Tilgner, Kaspar von Zumbusch and Arnold Böcklin, as well as the writers Hugo von Hofmannsthal and Rainer Maria Rilke. His art collection was seized by the Nazis in 1939 and stored in Altaussee salt mine, Styria. After the war, most of these works were taken to Poland, where they remain today. The family residence, Palais Lanckoroński on Jacquingasse (Landstrasse district), was severely damaged during the war and later demolished.

LAINZ CARE HOME

Karl Lueger and the angels of death

Jagdschlossgasse 59, 1130 Wien
Open daily 9am–6pm; church open for celebrations
Tel: +43 (0)1 8046 1410
Email: Provinzialat@kamillianer.at / Kloster.Wien@kamillianer.at

Any Viennese over the age of 30 who hears the words "hospital" and "Lainz" in the same breath immediately thinks of the "angels of death" – nurses who murdered their patients. This huge hospital complex had to be renamed in 1994, changing Versorgungsheim Lainz (Lainz Care Home) to Geriatriezentrum am Wienerwald (Vienna Woods Geriatric Centre). In the late 1980s, a huge scandal erupted when several nurses were implicated in over 42 murders.

Initially, the Lainz complex was a model care centre for the elderly. The number of old people living on their own was already growing in 1900 as the population was ageing, but there were no social services to cope with them. Over an exceptionally short period (1902–04), architects Rudolf Helmreich and Johann Nepomuk Scheiringer designed a modern complex of 31 pavilions with a church and a pleasant park. With its brick architecture, the complex is often held up as a symbol of western Vienna.

In the church dedicated to patron saint Charles Borromeo, the right panel of the altarpiece shows Mayor Lueger himself, wrapped in an ermine mantle and posing before the personification of the City of Vienna. Behind him, an old man kneels in thanks for the care home. In the centre panel are the Virgin Mary and Charles Borromeo; while on the left, the mayor's parents are accompanied by an angel.

The mayor was not present at the 1906 unveiling of his bust in the park – a clever move designed to bolster his reputation, as he let it be known that only modesty had prevented him from taking part in the ceremony.

The care home closed in 2015. The buildings and church are classified as historic monuments.

The geriatric centre possessed the oldest light railway system in all Austria. The rails can still be seen in many places but no trains have run since 2011.

"My dear mayor, the only thing I ask is that you live a long and healthy life"

The Christian Democratic Union, to which the elected official Karl Lueger belonged, liked to put about the following anecdote. During a visit to his protégés at the Lainz Care Home, he is said to have asked the residents to voice any complaints and requests. An old woman answered: "My dear mayor, the only thing I ask is that you live a long and healthy life."

DREIFALTIGKEITS-KAPELLE TRIPTYCH

When Jesus blessed Karl Lueger ...

Hietzing Hospital
Wolkersbergenstrasse 1, 1130 Wien
Chapel open all day

Pavilion IV, the former nurses' home of Hietzing Hospital, is now the hospital chapel dedicated to the Holy Trinity (Dreifaltigkeits). Hans Zatzka, Mayor Karl Lueger's favourite artist, painted the triptych for the altarpiece, which was unveiled in 1913 when the building was opened.

The theme of the altarpiece is the art of medicine. In the centre, Christ is blessing a patient in bed. The prone man clearly bears the features of Lueger in his youth. The panel on the right shows several patients accompanied by a guardian angel, the left panel a female figure symbolising the city of Vienna in its ancient form of Vindobona. The woman wears the crown of the city and holds a framed picture of Lueger with his mayoral chain.

Hietzing Hospital, originally known as the Kaiser-Jubiläums-Spital (Emperor's Jubilee Hospital), was built between 1908 and 1913 by the architect Johann Nepomuk Scheiringer to provide modern care for Vienna's 2 million population. The 60th anniversary of Franz Joseph's reign was celebrated in 1908, while Lueger was still mayor (he died in 1910). The Habsburg crown in the chapel symbolises the emperor, whose role is shown as insignificant compared with the sacred figure of the mayor.

NEARBY
Statue of Roland

A fountain by Viennese sculptor Joseph Heu stands in the hospital grounds. At its centre stands the Mayor of Vienna in the guise of a knight in armour, leaning on his sword and seeming to admire his "work". The image is evocative of Roland, Duke of Brittany and member of Charlemagne's retinue. Roland is thought to have died in 778, during a bloody battle against the Basques. Later, he was depicted as the brave hero and defender of Christianity in the famous *Chanson de Roland*. Publicity for the inauguration of the Emperor's Jubilee Hospital in 1913 described Karl Lueger, whose anti-Semitic statements later attracted controversy, "looking eastwards in an attitude of defiance, faithful guardian of the German culture of ancient Ostmark".

HOHENAUER TEICH POND

The empress's bathing pond, an earthly paradise

Lainzer Tiergarten, Lainzer Tor, 1130 Wien
www.lainzer-tiergarten.at/oeffnungszeiten.html

About 10 minutes' walk from the Lainzer Tiergarten main gate (Lainzer Tor), a little earthly paradise lies in the Vienna Woods. Opposite the wild sheep and deer enclosure, Hohenauer Teich – the pond in which Empress Elisabeth used to bathe in the night or very early in the morning – extends over almost 2 hectares. From the banks you can see Sisi's country retreat, Hermesvilla, which is only about 20 minutes away. The pond is fed by the Lainzer Bach stream, which you'll cross several times while hiking through the reserve. There used to be a dam too. The water is still of good quality, but Lainzer Tiergarten is now a protected nature reserve, and the swimming facilities are only for carp, mallard and mandarin ducks. Near the pond are a children's forest playground, a lawn and an enclosure for aurochs. This species of wild ox has been extinct since 1627, but around 1928 veterinarians succeeded in creating a new species of auroch from ancient breeds of cattle.

"Offshoot of the Great Wall of China"

The former imperial hunting ground of Lainzer Tiergarten once covered a much larger area of forest. Early members of the Habsburg family were very fond of hunting. The "deer parks", as they were known, were surrounded by palisades so that the court could hunt the game confined within. This fencing on the edge of the forest extended from Kahlenbergerdorf in the north (now part of the 19th district, Döbling) to beyond Lainz in the west. The stone wall (over 24 kilometres long) that encircles the Lainzer Tiergarten nature reserve was not built until the 18th century: the great Austrian dramatist and satirist Johann Nestroy called it an "offshoot of the Great Wall of China".

"*Armer Schlucker*", the Viennese expression commonly used to describe a "poor wretch", is linked to Lainzer Tiergarten park. The story goes that a Lower Austrian contractor Philipp Schlucker (1747–1820), in all innocence, priced a job so much lower than his competitors that the imperial court had no choice but to give him the work. Emperor Joseph II was completely satisfied with the result, and saved Schlucker from penury by offering him the post of contractor to the forestry service. He also gave him a plot of land in the Baden region.

Hirschg'stemm restaurant, which dates back to the Enlightenment, is still in Lainzer Tiergarten. Built in 1782, it was originally the forest ranger's house.

KALKSBURG MURALS

Among thieves and Jesuits

Promenadeweg 5, 1230 Wien
Silver Chamber: open only during special events, Open Days or Monument Day
Park: open all day
www.kalksburg.at
www.tagdesdenkmals.at
Bus: 254, Wien Kalksburger Kirchenplatz stop

Kollegium Kalksburg is a private Roman Catholic college that not only specialises in old Viennese bawdy songs but assists recovering alcoholics. The property is surrounded by a vast park: a former English-style landscaped garden of which there are few traces today. There remains a round structure that was originally found in a lake and a Chinese temple, partly renovated, at the edge of the wood. A walk through the garden leads to a secluded pond.

Kalksburg was once the haunt of a band of brigands, until in 1463 some members of the local bourgeoisie managed to apprehend their leader and destroy their fortress. From 1609 the site belonged to the Jesuits and then to court jeweller Franz Mack (1730–1807), who bought up the grounds surrounding the buildings. He was knighted under the name Edler von Mack.

The "Silver Chamber", now the meeting place of the inter-faith charitable organisation B.R.O.T., dates from this period. Its superb panoramic frescoes with pastoral motifs dating back to around 1800 have been restored.

Prince Albert of Saxony spent time in Mack's residence while he was in mourning for his beloved wife Archduchess Maria Christina (Mimi, who died in 1798). He often walked in the park, where his friend Mack had set up a place of contemplation dedicated to her. You can still decipher some weathered letters: "He sought consolation and left the city, and came to you, Mack, in your refuge in Kalksburg...".

By the mid-19th century, the estate had again come into the hands of the Jesuits. Their educational institution has been welcoming young people to Kalksburg since 1856 and the college adopted its current form in 1897.

"Heap of stone"

Promenadeweg 12a, 1230 Wien

The road to Kalksburg College passes Liesing pond in front of the ruins of a villa dating from 1786.

This building, conceived as an artificial cliff pierced with caves, was commissioned by Mack the jeweller, who was appointed Grand Master of the Masonic Lodge of St Joseph in 1785. This "heap of stone" is one of the rare "ruined" villas that were fashionable during the Enlightenment. The privately owned property is classified as a historic monument.

MIZZI-LANGER-WAND

23

Viennese climbing pioneer

1230, Rodaun, access by St Christiana school car park, Willergasse 55
Bus: 60A, Willergasse / Schule stop

The Mizzi-Langer-Wand is a climbing wall named in honour of Marie Langer-Kauba (1872–1955), a mountaineering and skiing pioneer. The wall is on the southern slope of the Zugberg, above Kaltenleutgebner Strasse. The rock faces of the disused Rodaun limestone quarry, 40 metres high, are used to practise most levels of difficulty. The Grosses Dreiect and Kleines Dreiect (Big Triangle and Small Triangle) and the Feserl Uberhang (Feserl Overhang) are among the best-known climbs. In good weather, the site is very busy at weekends.

As female climbers have so far been in the minority, naming a climbing wall after a woman who took up this sport in the 19th century is rare enough.

In 1905, Langer, who came from a middle-class family, was the only woman to take part in an alpine ski race at Lilienfeld in Lower Austria. A year later, she became the manager of the oldest sports shop in Vienna, probably founded by her father, at No. 15 Kaiserstrasse. Her portrait is still over the front door. In 1897, she married Johann

Kauba, who helped her to run the Mizzi-Langer-Sporthaus. The shop is still open (under the name Bergfuchs) and is popular with climbers who want to equip themselves with outdoor gear to tackle Austria's mountains.

The shop's catalogues were known for their many illustrations of the mountaineer and alpine painter Gustav Jahn, but especially for photos of Mizzi Langer herself, who often posed on skis or in the mountains.

SEEGROTTE HINTERBRÜHL

24

Europe's largest underground lake

Grutschgasse 2a, 2371 Hinterbrühl
Open April to October 9am–5pm, November to March 9am–3pm (guided tours only)
www.seegrotte.at
Bus: 364 / 365, Hinterbrühl Seegrotte stop

Hinterbrühl Lake Grotto, a disused gypsum mine, has the largest subterranean lake in Europe, fed by seven springs and covering an area of 6,200 square metres. A boat trip across this body of water, about 60 metres below the surface, is highly recommended.

The museum on the upper level chronicles the beginning of the mineworkings in 1848, when the so-called Wagner's hill began to be excavated for gypsum. The mineworkings were shut down in 1912 following an underground blasting operation that burst open a spring and flooded the galleries, creating the lake. An international team of cavers discovered the unique spectacle 20 years later and the grotto was reopened as a tourist attraction.

The pithead where the miners took their breaks can be visited, as well as the stables for the horses that pulled the gypsum wagons towards the surface. The horses were all blind, as sighted animals would have been too frightened by the darkness and the flickering gas lighting.

As in all mines, there is a shrine dedicated to St Barbara, built in 1864 by the miners for their comrades involved in accidents. One of the legends surrounding Barbara, as the patron saint of miners, is that a rock opened up to protect her.

Other points of interest on the cave tour are the slag heap, mine shaft and headframe (winding tower).

An underground annex of Mauthausen camp, where the world's first jet aircraft was built

In 1944–45, an annex to the Mauthausen concentration camp was set up in the upper level of the mine.

The galleries were kept dry by continuous pumping and one of these pumps can still be seen. 1,800 prisoners worked here day and night as part of an aircraft production project, including the world's first jet.

Scale models and original aircraft parts are on display. A slideshow tells the story of the National Socialist factory, Wiener Neustadt aeronautical workshops.

In 1945, a commando unit dynamited the factory. Those prisoners who were still able to walk had to return to Mauthausen on foot, while the injured were executed by kerosene injection. Few survived their underground labour or the concentration camp. A commemorative plaque in Hinterbrühl cave records these horrors.

A scene from the Disney film *The Three Musketeers* (1993) was shot in this cave. The boat in which Cardinal Richelieu attempts to escape is still there, as well as a Hollywood-style dungeon.

HUSARENTEMPEL

Where Prince Rudolf went to commit suicide with his beloved

Kleiner Anninger, 2340 Mödling

The so-called Hussars' Temple in the Föhrenberge Nature Park (496 metres above sea level) is Austria's oldest monument. This classical building, designed by Joseph Kornhäusel (1813), can be seen from around most of the Viennese basin. The notable who had it built, Johann von Liechtenstein, wanted to erect a "temple to military glory" in recognition of the Austrian victory at Aspern-Essling (1809). Some of the soldiers who died that day lie below the "temple". Two classical urns and a tomb can be seen through a screened window. The commemorative plaque is often covered with sheaves of flowers.

From the temple terrace, the view pans out over the battlefields of Aspern and Essling.

In 1888 Crown Prince Rudolf came up here in desperation with his beloved Mizzi Caspar, whom he asked to commit suicide with him.

Mizzi refused and informed the Chief of Police of this incident. Rudolf ended his days a few months later at Mayerling with another of his mistresses.

In 1945, Soviet soldiers defaced the illustrations of soldiers on the temple frieze. Many of them are still damaged.

The town of Mödling maintains the Hussars' Temple as a tomb of honour, illuminated at night.

Ludwig van Beethoven, who was a great walker and often strolled around the region, noted in 1819: "Went to the Liechtenstein soldiers' monument."

RUDOLF'S MEDALLION

A medallion brought from Greece

Wiener Strasse 17, 2361 Laxenburg
Bus: 200, Laxenburg, Wiener Strasse stop

Crown Prince Rudolf, only son of Empress Elisabeth and Emperor Franz Joseph, was born on 21 August 1858 in Laxenburg. There are few memorials to him there and even his medallion portrait travelled far before arriving here to be set into the wall of the Rauchhof building.

After his suicide at Mayerling in 1889, it was forbidden to mention the name of the deceased prince at court. Bravely, his mother Elisabeth had the Achilleion summer palace built in Corfu (Greece) in homage to Rudolf – something that would have been unthinkable in Vienna.

She commissioned a funerary monument from sculptor Antonio Chiattone, well-known in his time, consisting of a broken cannulated column with a seated genie and the notorious medallion portrait.

When Elisabeth sold the Achilleion, the monument was moved to Mayerling and then to the gardens of the Rudolf Foundation's Vienna

hospital, where it was badly damaged during the Second World War. The medallion was still intact, however, and after 1945 it was displayed in the Landstrasse Museum (now the 3rd District Museum) before being taken to Rudolf's birthplace in Laxenburg in 1979.

The imposing Rauchhof, now converted into an organic farm, is one of the oldest buildings in Laxenburg (17th century). It is named after the owners: Rhau, Rauh or Rauch, who came from the German Vogtland to Austria.

TOMB OF BERTHOLD VON TREUN ㉗

The "blond blue-eyed hero"

Stift Heiligenkreuz
2532 Heiligenkreuz
Open daily for guided tours only (see website)
www.stift-heiligenkreuz.org/kontakt-adressen
Bus: 365, Heiligenkreuz Stift / Badner Tor stop

Renovation work on the cloister of the Cistercian Abbey of Heiligenkreuz (Holy Cross) in 1893–94 revealed a tombstone dating back to the Middle Ages that has always been an enigma for historians. On the back of this stone is carved the name "Berthold von Treun".

Although this aristocrat was in the service of Duke Frederick II of Austria, "the Quarrelsome" (1211–46), the carved relief on the front seems much older: it shows a well-dressed man with a strange creature at his feet.

It was this sculpture that inspired the racist ideology of Adolf Josef Lanz (1874–1954), a monk at Heiligenkreuz. His biographer Wilfried Daim describes Lanz (who left the Cistercian Order shortly after the discovery) as "the man who gave Hitler ideas". He was known as "Jörg Lanz von Liebenfels", the author of pamphlets on the *Ostara* (pagan spring festival) filled with racist and misogynist tirades that met with some success until 1918.

The identity of the tombstone sculptor is still unknown. Lanz was sure that it had been made by a Templar and that the creature was a simian monster symbolising the Evil One. The "blond blue-eyed hero", as Lanz described him, was crushing the monkey as a symbol of the inferior races (or perhaps the physical and material impulses that drag man down).

Lanz later founded a "New Order of the Knights Templar" and asked to be buried beside his "Templar" in Heiligenkreuz, a wish that was not fulfilled because he ended up in the ecclesiastical cemetery of Penzing.

The body buried at Heiligenkreuz is almost certainly not that of a Templar.

MARY VETSERA'S COFFIN

A companion in death buried five times

Museum of Karmel St Joseph's convent, Mayerling 3, 2534 Alland
Open in winter on Saturday, Sunday and public holidays 9am–5pm, in summer
open daily 9am–5.30pm or by appointment
Tel: +43 (0)1 2258 2275; Email: information@karmel-mayerling.at
Bus: 365, Mayerling Altes Jagdschloss stop

The last lover of the unfortunate Crown Prince Rudolf is often described in literature as his "companion in death". The epithet is spot on because she died with the heir to the throne of Austria, and has been buried five times.

The coffin now in the cloister at Mayerling was not found until 2007 in Heiligenkreuz monastery. The remains of Mary Vetsera had been buried for the penultimate time in 1959, the year she received a new coffin as the result of a subscription organised by a society lady. Although the lady wished to remain anonymous, her grandfather is known to have been in the service of Emperor Franz Joseph.

Mary's former coffin, made by Beschorner (suppliers to the imperial house), had been stored for decades in the abbey. It dated from the year of her death in 1889 and had been ordered by her sister Johanna. As Rudolf's lover, Mary had at first been buried in a simple wooden coffin in Heiligenkreuz cemetery. In May 1889, Johanna had Mary reburied in the vault where she now rests. She lay there in a splendid copper coffin until 1945, when Soviet soldiers opened and desecrated the vault. The cemetery was restored, but Mary had to wait 14 years for another coffin.

Her body was exhumed again in 1991 by a furniture merchant from Linz, Helmut Flatzelsteiner, who stole the remains to personally investigate "the mystery of Mayerling".

There is really no mystery, however: on 30 January 1889, Rudolf shot the young woman with a revolver before committing suicide a few hours later.

The Abbot of Heiligenkreuz went to the Institute of Forensic Medicine and brought the infamous deceased back to his cemetery.

The "mortuary chamber"

After the events of January 1889, Franz Joseph had the Mayerling hunting lodge converted into a convent, which was settled by nuns of the Discalced Carmelite Order. The room where Mary and Rudolf died is now the chapel. The almost life-size statue of the Madonna – *Mater Dolorosa* (Sorrowful Mother) – by Viktor Tilgner is said to have the features of Empress Elisabeth, Rudolf's mother.

Outside the Centre South

REMINDERS OF THE CEMETERY AT MATZLEINSDORF

Famous painter and plague victim

Waldmüllerpark
Ada Christen-Gasse 2B, 1100 Wien
Open Monday to Friday 7am–3pm (collect key from municipal office in charge of the gardens, Stadtgartenamt, Antonsplatz 12)
Tram: 62, Kliebergasse stop

An enclosed graveyard in Waldmüllerpark, and a stone gazebo and pergola at the main entrance, are the last reminders of the former Roman Catholic cemetery at Matzleinsdorf.

Curiously, there is a certain poetry to this old graveyard converted into a park. A visit to the funerary grove is particularly poignant in autumn or winter, when its hundred or so tombs of historical or artistic interest are cloaked in fog or covered with snow.

This became a burial ground in 1679, the year of the terrible plague, when victims had to be hurriedly disposed of. But it was not until Joseph II became emperor that the site officially became a cemetery, opened in 1785. During the 18th and 19th centuries, many renowned artists were buried there, among them the painters Heinrich Friedrich Füger, Karl Russ, Johann Nepomuk Ender, Johann Peter Krafft and the "Raphael of dogs", German artist Johann Matthias Ranftl, well known for his striking canine portraits. Most tombs of famous artists were moved to the new Central Cemetery in the 19th century.

The funerary grove's mission is to commemorate the original purpose of this place. Ferdinand Georg Waldmüller, Austrian master painter of the Biedermeier period (1815 - 48), is one famous personality whose tomb has been preserved there – unlike that of Italian composer Antonio Salieri (1750 - 1825), who now lies at rest in group 0, row 1, grave No. 54 of the Central Cemetery.

SPINNERIN AM KREUZ

Memories of a place of execution

Triester Strasse 56, 1100 Wien
Tram: 1, Männertreugasse stop

Some kind of cross or stone column has stood on the hilltop of the Wienerberg, now in the 10th district of Favoriten, for at least 600 years. The Spinnerin am Kreuz (Spinner at the Cross), erected near a place where criminals were executed (mostly by hanging), was probably used as a "lantern of the dead".

All the themes illustrated on the monument – the Crucifixion, flogging, crown of thorns and Ecce Homo – relate to the death of Christ. But these are not the original sculptures, which had to be removed because of heavy traffic pollution and are now on display in Favoriten District Museum.

The name of the monument has changed several times over the centuries: the Column of the Wienerberg Suppliants (referring to the executions that took place there); the Spinner's Cross; then, in 1804, the Spinner at the Cross. At that time, executions were still being carried out, a macabre practice that continued until 1868. An impressive number of summarily buried skeletons was found in the neighbourhood during building work in 1927. The column was restored several times during the 19th century and completely renovated after 1945.

The legend that relates the tale of the spinner goes back to the time of the Crusades. A merchant's wife, after he had left for the Holy Land, had come to the site of the cross every day to sit and work at her spinning wheel, praying for her husband's safe return. She pledged to use the money she earned by spinning wool to donate a stone piety column. She worked tirelessly for three years, until one day a lone injured man, walking with a cane, stopped at this spot. The woman recognised her husband at once. She kept her promise to have a monument built, and it was named in her memory.

A similar monument in the north of the city, dating from 1382 to 1384, may have been modelled on the Spinner at the Cross.

At the Viennese Crime Museum in the 2nd district, you can see a wax model of an execution scene at the Wienerberg.

WASSERTURM FAVORITEN

One of the world's most beautiful?

Windtenstrasse 3, 1100 Wien
Interior: open by appointment or during special events
www.wien.gv.at/wienwasser/bildung/wasserturm

The Favoriten water tower, designed by architect Franz Borkowitz, was built between 1898 and 1899 on the Wienerberg hill in Vienna's 10th district. The interior of this splendid brick tower (standing 67 metres high) can be seen by appointment or during special events. Climb to the top to reach the wide circular passage, which has fine views.

Inside, the building has a steel water tank with a capacity of 1,000 cubic metres, reached via a spiral-shaped ramp over 200 metres long.

The tower formerly supplied water to the highest points of the 10th and 12th districts, as the pressure of the nearby Wienerberg water tower was insufficient. The population of these districts was growing rapidly and the demand for drinking water had increased exponentially. In 1910, with the commissioning of Vienna's second water supply system, use of the Favoriten tower was restricted to peak demand and emergencies. It was taken out of service in 1956.

Nowadays the building has found a new use as a water-themed cultural venue and exhibition space. Outside you'll find an aquatic playground and discovery trail.

Wien X. *Favoriten.* Wasserturm.

FK AUSTRIA WIEN MUSEUM

The unbeatable Wunderteam

Horrplatz 1, 1100 Wien
Open Monday to Friday 9am–6pm, Saturday 9am–1pm
http://www.fk-austria.at/en/stadium/museum/
U-Bahn: line U1, Altes Landgut station

Open since 2009, the Austria Vienna Football Club Museum traces over a century of the team's history with an extensive collection of photographs, trophies and memorabilia of famous players. Most of the objects on display come from the private collections of ex-footballers and their fans.

The emphasis is on the legendary career of one of the greatest stars of the "Violets", Matthias Sindelar (1903–39). You can see his boots, photos, identity card and the well-known poem by Friedrich Torberg, dedicated to the player known as the "Paper Man" because of his slight build:

> *He was an unparalleled player*
> *Full of wit and artifice*
> *His game of lightness and elegance*
> *Was always a game, never a fight.*

Sindelar died in the company of his Jewish girlfriend Camilla Castagnola from "carbon monoxide poisoning due to a defective chimney", according to the public version, which has continued to fuel speculation. Many people believed – and still believe today – that the couple committed suicide.

The National Socialists turned the footballer's funeral in the Central Cemetery into an official ceremony, in an attempt to rehabilitate the "Mozart of football". The anniversary of his death is commemorated every year on 23 January. The Franz Horr stadium has a central stand dedicated to this mythical sportsman.

The museum tour ends on a very special note in the Hugo Meisl Memorial Room. It holds the original furniture of the Karl-Marx-Hof apartment where Meisl – future player, coach, referee and manager – lived with his family in the 1930s. Many exhibits from the heyday of the Austrian *Wunderteam* are presented as a tree of life to illustrate the outstanding journey of Hugo Meisl, the Jewish merchant's son born in Bohemia in 1937 who became such a famous name in Austrian football.

SCHLOSS NEUGEBÄUDE

Turks, tulips and a menagerie

Otmar-Brix-Gasse 1, 1110 Wien
Guided tours at fixed times, private visits by appointment
www.schlossneugebaeude.at
Tram: 6, Zentralfriedhof 2, Tor stop; Bus: 73A, Hörtengasse stop

The monumental Renaissance-style Neugebäude Castle was built by Emperor Maximilian II in the mid-16th century between the Simmering district and the former hunting lodge of Ebersdorf, on the edge of the Central Cemetery. It is now an event venue offering a wide range of entertainment: romantic open-air cinema, Easter and Christmas markets, a medieval festival, theatre, cabaret and refreshments. It also has some hidden attractions.

Since 2010, the "Lower Garden" of 12,500 square metres has been redesigned on the footprint of the historic imperial garden. The original beds and pathways have been preserved. Water games with fountains provide freshness in the shade of 70 plane trees, and an avenue lined with lilacs is an invitation for a stroll. The rocking animals and elephant slide are reminiscent of the former palace menagerie, considered to be Vienna's first zoo.

Lions and other wild beasts were kept within the grounds of this magnificent building, a work of art in terms of architecture, sculpture, painting, landscaping and water features. The name "Neugebäude" (New Building) was simply meant to distinguish it from the old castle of Ebersdorf.

A portico leads to the courtyard and garden through a passage under the castle – subterranean but with refined natural lighting. The regular alignment of the trees filters the light to produce a particularly successful chiaroscuro effect.

A Renaissance-style grotto, the oldest to have survived in the entire German-speaking region, leads into the garden. Halloween parties are sometimes held there.

Neugebäude is a stone replica of the canvas fortress of Sultan Süleyman the Magnificent, erected on this exact spot in 1529. With its towers and wide walls, the castle does seem to draw inspiration from the Ottoman style.

Tulips, originally from Persia, were cultivated for the first time on European soil at Neugebäude Castle, before "tulipmania" took hold and they became a symbol of the Netherlands.

Some parts of Neugebäude were used in the construction of the gardens at Schönbrunn Palace, summer residence of the imperial family under Maria Theresa, and the imposing castle was reduced to an ammunition depot. The zoo was also transferred to Schönbrunn.

OUROBOROS ON THE CHOLERA CROSS ⑥

Eternal life for Simmering epidemic victims

Zehngrafweg, behind Thürnlhofstrasse 19, 1110 Wien

A small fenced-off patch of grass and flowers, with a stone cross in the centre – this is the discreet tribute paid to the many victims of the Austro-Prussian War (1866) and to those who died from the epidemics that raged throughout the 19th century. The "cholera cross" carries a marble plaque recounting the sad events that took place here. Between 27 August and 7 September 1866, 40 soldiers from the "Graf Nobili" infantry regiment succumbed to cholera. Casualties of the terrible sanitary conditions at the Ebersdorf garrison, they were buried here.

The cross is decorated with an *ouroboros*, a snake eating its own tail, which represents eternal life and divine enlightenment (see p. 434).

The Ouroboros: a symbol of divine illumination

The figure of a coiled serpent biting its own tail is sometimes found in iconography and literature. This symbol is traditionally known as the Ouroboros, a Greek word derived from the Coptic and Hebrew languages – *ouro* is Coptic for "king" and *ob* Hebrew for "serpent" – meaning "royal serpent". Thus the reptile raising its head above its body is used as a symbol of mystical illumination: for Eastern peoples, it represents the divine fire they call Kundalini.

Kundalini is the origin of the association that Western medicine of the Middle Ages and Renaissance made between, on the one hand, the body heat that rises from the base of the spine to the top of the head and, on the other, the *venena bibas* ("ingested venom" mentioned by Saint Benedict of Nursia) of the snake whose bite can only be treated by an equally potent poison. Just as the Eastern techniques of spiritual awakening, Dzogchen and Mahamudra, show how a meditating person must learn to "bite his tail like the serpent", the theme of the Ouroboros and ingested venom is a reminder that spiritual awareness can only result from a devout life: by elevating your consciousness onto a mental plane surpassing the ordinary, you search within to truly find yourself as an eternal being.

The Greeks popularised the word *ouroboros* in its literal sense of "serpent biting its tail". They acquired this image from the Phoenicians through contact with the Hebrews, who had themselves adopted it from Egypt where the Ouroboros featured on a stele dated as early as 1600 BC. There it represented the sun god Ra (Light), who resurrects life from the darkness of the night (synonymous with death), going back to the theme of eternal return, life, death, and the renewal of existence, as well as the reincarnation of souls in successive human bodies until they have reached their evolutionary peak, which will leave them perfect, both physically and spiritually – a theme dear to Eastern peoples.

In this sense, the serpent swallowing itself can also be interpreted as an interruption of the cycle of human development (represented by the serpent) in order to enter the cycle of spiritual evolution (represented by the circle).

Pythagoras associated the serpent with the mathematical concept of infinity, coiled up as zero – the abstract number used to denote eternity, which becomes reality when the Ouroboros is depicted turning around on itself.

Gnostic Christians identified it with the Holy Spirit revealed through wisdom to be the Creator of all things visible and invisible, and whose ultimate expression on Earth is Christ. For this reason, the symbol is associated in Greek Gnostic literature with the phrase *hen to pan* ("The All is One"); it was commonly adopted in the 4th and 5th centuries as a protective amulet against evil spirits and venomous snakebites. This amulet was known as Abraxas, the name of a god in the original Gnostic pantheon that the Egyptians recognised as Serapis. It became one of the most famous magical talismans of the Middle Ages.

Greek alchemists very quickly espoused the figure of the Ouroboros (or Uroboros) and so it reached the Hermetic philosophers of Alexandria – among them, Arab thinkers who studied and disseminated this image in their schools of Hermeticism and alchemy. These schools were known and sought out by medieval Christians. There is even historical evidence that members of the Order of the Knights Templar, as well as other Christian mystics, travelled to Cairo, Syria and even Jerusalem to be initiated into the Hermetic sciences.

MUSEUM DER BESTATTUNG

Vienna: 1.7 million living souls and 5 million dead ...

Central Cemetery
Gate 2, beneath Chapel of Rest 2
Simmeringer Hauptstrasse 234, 1110 Wien
Tram: 71, Zentralfriedhof 2, Tor stop
Open Monday to Friday 9am–4pm

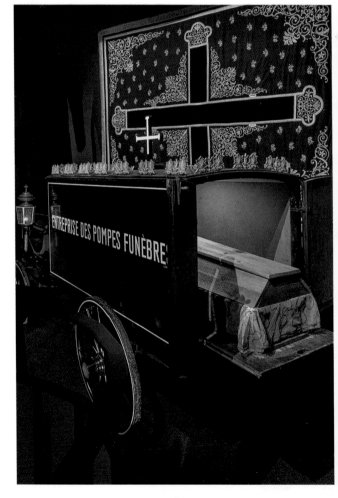

The Funeral Museum, which opened to the public in October 2014, traces the history of the Austrian capital through 250 funerary objects, including remarkable masks, and casts from the hands of several deceased personalities.

As in Tim Burton's film *Corpse Bride*, we find the world of the living (in yellow) and the kingdom of the dead (in bluish white). The dead greatly outnumber the living: Vienna is currently home to some 1.7 million living souls and 5 million dead ...

Of these, some 4 million lie in the Central Cemetery, in simple tombs, mausoleums or urns. The number of new arrivals is far from negligible: 43 people a day undertake the one-way journey (we hope). The museum also addresses the fear that ghosts, vampires and assorted zombies inspire in the living ...

The museum contains the notorious "economical coffin", one of the reforms decreed by Emperor Joseph II. While many of his initiatives were strongly opposed, the introduction of a reusable coffin was among the most unpopular. Even the most progressive Viennese considered it a step too far. A fine burial is a human right (or at least a Viennese right). The decree was subsequently annulled.

Other topics covered in the museum include: changing mourning fashions over time, the history of Viennese cemeteries, and the grand funerals that have been celebrated in the city. The films and photos

help you, one hundred years later, to be a spectator at the funeral of Mayor Karl Lueger (1910) or of Emperor Franz Joseph (1916). The Viennese still flock to this kind of ostentatious funeral. An interactive screen allows you to search for notable graves and gives interesting facts about cemeteries and the funeral industry.

As the museum is run by a funeral parlour, advice and information "in case of bereavement" are readily available.

CRYPT OF VIENNESE MAYOR, KARL LUEGER

The petrified "Lord of Vienna"

Central Cemetery, gate 2
Simmeringer Hauptstrasse 234, 1110 Wien
Open daily 8am–6pm
Tram: 6, Zentralfriedhof 2, Tor stop

Strangely, many visitors to the Central Cemetery and its church dedicated to St Charles Borromeo miss the entrance to the church crypt, which houses the spectacular mausoleum of the former Mayor of Vienna, Karl Lueger, one of the city's leading figures at the beginning of the 20th century.

Nowadays a controversial figure because of his many anti-Semitic remarks, Lueger – dubbed "Lord of Vienna" by his devoted followers – ran the City of Vienna from 1897 to 1910. His coffin rests under the church designed by architect Max Hegele, a protégé of Otto Wagner. The Byzantine-style tomb is invariably decorated with flags and standards.

The building and its columbariums are clearly oriented towards the Stephansdom, while its row of columns is turned towards Rome, as can be seen in aerial photographs. The mayor has rested like a pharaoh in

his crypt since October 1910. At the time of his death, in March of the same year, the vault was not yet finished. A funerary plaque (group 34 F, row 43, no. 20) marks his temporary burial site with the following inscription: "From 14 March to 27 October 1910, this grave sheltered the mortal remains of Karl Lueger".

The clocks of the "Lueger Church" have letters instead of figures. In the clockwise direction, numbers 1 to 11 are replaced with the Latin inscription *tempus fugit* (time flies), while a small cross replaces the number 12.

Lueger's body was embalmed by Alexander Kolisko, Viennese professor of pathological anatomy. Six years later, he had the honour of dealing with the corpse of Emperor Franz Joseph. His method used formalin, leaving the body exposed to the air for four full weeks. Medical opinion at the time was that the remains had to slowly petrify, so that Lueger would still be quite recognisable if his coffin was opened a century later.

TOMB OF THE RINGTHEATER FIRE ⑨ VICTIMS

The worst fire in Viennese history

Zentralfriedhof (Central Cemetery)
Gate 2, section 30A
Simmeringer Hauptstrasse 234, 1110 Wien
Tram: 71, Zentralfriedhof 2, Tor stop
Cemetery opening hours:
3 November to February 8am–5pm
March, October to 2 November 7am–6pm
April to September 7am–7pm
May to August, every Thursday 7am–8pm

In Vienna's Central Cemetery, a particularly moving monument by sculptor Rudolf Weyr stands near gate 2, section 30A, in tribute to the Ringtheater fire victims. At the top of the monument, the city of Vienna is represented by its coat of arms, a widow's veil and a funerary crown. Below stands a phoenix, symbol of resurrection. The bird gazes over the tombs of the victims of the fire that ravaged the popular opera house at Schottenring on 8 December 1881.

On that fateful evening, Offenbach's *Tales of Hoffmann* was to be performed and the auditorium was rapidly filling up. While the stage was being set up, a gas lamp failed to light. A workman allowed gas to escape and the lamps exploded, setting fire to a section of the wings. In a moment the curtain was alight and the flames had reached the top rows of boxes. Panic broke out. The doors only opened inwards. Someone finally managed to cut off the gas supply, but then the only light in the theatre came from the flames. The emergency services took away many charred bodies, but it was soon realised that many more were unaccounted for. In all, some 400 men and women lost their lives, among them the elder brother of Mary Vetsera, mistress of Archduke Rudolf of Austria, who was herself found dead eight years later in an apparent suicide pact with her lover.

The bodies of the fire victims that could not be identified were buried together in the Central Cemetery.

Some time after this drama, the director of the Ringtheater killed himself.

However, the fire was the impetus for supporters of worthy causes to form the Wiener Freiwillige Rettungsgesellschaft (Vienna Civil Welfare Society), a direct precursor of Wiener Rettung (Vienna Rescue).

Much of the monument was destroyed in the Second World War, including the wall on which the names of the dead were inscribed.

An office block erected on the Ringtheater site is now a police headquarters.

At No. 35 Weilburgstrasse in Baden, 25 kilometres south of Vienna, stands a statue of the Virgin Mary on a column rescued from the Ringtheater. This is a reminder of the Feast of the Immaculate Conception, celebrated on 8 December, the same day as the catastrophic fire.

JOHANNESKIRCHE

Primeval settlements

Klederinger Strasse (towards city exit from Unterlaaer Platz), 1100 Wien
Open first Sunday of the month during excavations (May to October)
Church and chapel: visits by appointment, information from District Museum
www.bezirksmuseum.at/default/index.php?id=36
Bus: 70A, Johanneskapelle stop

Although the Ruprechtskirche (Church of St Ruprecht) in Vienna's Innere Stadt is said to be the city's oldest church, founded in the 11th century, recent research has revealed that the Johanneskirche (Church of St John of Malta) in the Unterlaa neighbourhood dates from around the same period, though some of its elements are 13th century.

This district, redolent with history, was already populated at the time of the Romans, who had built a temple there. The guided tour, which must be booked in advance, also covers the medieval and modern foundations of the church. Remains found in the neighbouring suburb Am Johannesberg show signs of prehistoric habitation.

Since 1272 these lands had belonged to the Order of the Knights of St John (former name of the Order of Malta), which dedicated the church to St John the Baptist. A hospice, was of the settlement at that time, was demolished along with the castle of Unterlaa around the 15th century. The church underwent other alterations during the Baroque period, and its present plan dates from that time. Destroyed in 1683 during the Turkish siege, it was later rebuilt. The interior is partly 17th century and the spire is topped with a Maltese cross.

Archaeological excavations since the 1960s have brought to light 14th-century tombs, now preserved below the building. The museum has a collection of vestiges dating back to the Neolithic and to the Metal Ages Hallstatt civilisation, as well as the Roman period. The Roman cemetery was on exactly the same site as the present church, as the exhibition demonstrates.

NEARBY

Modelled on the Holy Sepulchre of Jerusalem, the Baroque-style funerary chapel of Unterlaa stands near the church. It was commissioned around 1700 by the Habsburg emperor, who had set himself the task of supporting the Counter-Reformation. To bolster the Roman Catholic faith, places venerated in the Holy Land were copied and symbolically transplanted to Europe. Only about 20 funerary chapels of this type have been preserved throughout Austria, despite the hundred or so built at the time.

Our Lady of Pötsch

The chapel also contains a copy of the famous weeping Madonna of Pötsch, the original of which is in the Stephansdom. The image, dating from the 17th century according to expert opinion, could be one of the very first copies made of this miraculous icon, which was supposed to shed tears, during its journey from Pötsch (Pócs in eastern Hungary) to Vienna in 1697.

FRIEDHOF DER NAMENLOSEN

Memories of the despairing

Alberner Hafen, 1110 Wien
Open daily 7am–6pm

The original Cemetery of the Nameless is no more. The overgrown terrain, completely wild until a few years ago, has now been levelled. The first unidentifiable body, partly eaten by fish, had been buried there in 1840 and the last as recently as 2004. The construction of grain silos in the freight harbour near Albern in 1939 changed the direction of the current: the bodies of drowned people now wash ashore at Freudenau power station.

The "second" cemetery has existed since 1900, but most of the simple metal crosses there carry no name. Whether the bodies were suicides didn't matter: they were buried where the Danube had ejected them. They had no right to a religious ceremony, and Albern didn't even have a parish priest or a church.

While the dam was being erected in the 1930s, the workers themselves decided to build the Resurrection Chapel near the cemetery. The altar stone comes from the ruins of the old Reichsbrücke, first known as the Kronprinz-Rudolf Bridge in homage to Rudolf of Austria, and subsequently as the Suicide Bridge after the crown prince had killed himself at Mayerling. Many who, like him, threw themselves into the Danube in despair were washed up in Albern harbour.

Since the 1920s, a celebration of the nameless dead takes place every year after All Saints' Day (1 November). Fishermen decorate a raft with flowers and candles, and a small tombstone bearing the inscription "To the victims of the Danube" in German, Czech and Hungarian is dropped into the water to the strains of an ancient song of farewell.

If you feel like a drink to lighten the morbid atmosphere, one of the last typical Viennese hostelries is a few steps away: Zum Friedhof der Namenlosen, No. 54 Albern (closed Thursday).

The Viennese band L'Âme Immortelle (Immortal Soul) dedicated a track entitled *Namenious (*Nameless*)* – on a 2008 studio album of the same name – to the memory of the 600 bodies washed up by the Danube and buried in the cemetery at Albern. The CD insert features a photo of intertwined wrought-iron funerary crosses.

JOHANNESKAPELLE

One of Austria's most remarkable circular buildings

On the main road, 2404 Petronell-Carnuntum
Viewable only from the outside
Bus: 274, Petronell stop

Dating back to the 12th century, the Romanesque Chapel of John the Baptist, which can now be visited at the village of Petronell-Carnuntum, is one of the oldest and most remarkable circular buildings in all Austria. A building about 50 years older, probably the first church in Petronell, previously stood on the site. The chapel is the private property of the Abensperg-Traun family, which has used it as a family vault since the 18th century.

The dedication of the church to St John the Baptist and its use as a baptistery – as well as its characteristic architecture – testify to its connection with the Templars. The building also served as a bastion against frequent attacks: the walls, several metres thick, conceal long secret passages.

The chapel's portal suffered serious damage during the wars against the Turks and then the French, and was only restored in the 1950s.

Templars in Austria, on the road to Jerusalem

Documents from 1298 to 1303, together with the Babenberg-era land registers, show that the Order of the Templars was present on Austrian territory, in Vienna, Fischamend, Rauchenwarth and Schwechat. Their commanderies were also found in Prague, Brno and Čejkovice (South Moravia). The ossuary of St Othmar of Mödling, the round church of Petronell and several fortified churches and farmyards between Brno and Vienna are thought to have belonged to the Templars. These assets were strategically located on the road to Jerusalem, and therefore of great economic importance. The main pilgrimage route of the Crusaders was along the Danube and thus crossed much of present-day Austria. After the Brno commandery, the next major assembly point was Hainburg, at the confluence of the Morava and the Danube. The cross on the Braunsberg limestone massif by the shore marked the way.

Outside the Centre East

COLUMN OF REMEMBRANCE ①

Vantage point over military manoeuvres

Bergstrasse, 2102 Bisamberg
Bus: 232, Langenzersdorf stop

Not far from Vienna, Bisamberg is a natural paradise abounding with rare species, including a colony of squirrels. On the plateau named after Elisabeth (361 metres above sea level) there are information panels on local flora and fauna.

The viewpoint is marked with a neo-Gothic column dedicated to the assassinated Empress Elisabeth. Designed by Viennese architect Maximilian Kropf, the monument was erected in her memory in 1898 at the initiative of a women's committee at Korneuburg.

In 1856, Franz Joseph participated in military manoeuvres north of Bisamberg. It is said that Elisabeth, then 18 years old, watched from here. Two years earlier, as a young bride, she had marvelled at the superb view from this vantage point. Later in life, she must have loved her long walks here, on the outskirts of Vienna – apparently she strode out at such a rapid pace that it was an ordeal for her court ladies. She probably regularly went Bisamberg way.

The memorial, destroyed during the Second World War, was restored in the 1960s.

> Bisamberg has traces of fortifications dating from the 1866 campaign against Prussia.

WEINENDE BRÜCKE OF FLORIDSDORF ELEVATED RAILWAY

②

Memories of Italian prisoners of the First World War

Siemensstrasse station, 1210 Wien
S-Bahn: line S1, Siemensstrasse station

Inaugurated in 1999 at the reopening of the Floridsdorf elevated railway, the Weinende Brücke (Bridge of Tears) was designed by Italian-Austrian sculptor Wander Bertoni. It consists of two viaduct arches surmounted by a semicircular steel arc. At the top of this arc, a liquid symbolising tears flows down.

The ceremony was attended by members of the Italian Embassy – the monument was erected in memory of Italian prisoners of war who died in 1916 when the Floridsdorf railway was built. Even today, the part between Jedlersdorf and Leopoldau stations is commonly known as the Italienerschleife (Italian Loop). The railway bridge over Siemensstrasse forms part of this loop, which was built in only seven months by 6,000 Italian POWs. As the Ministry of War decreed, it was intended to improve the supply chain of goods essential to the war effort.

The material used was broomed concrete, to allow for the men's lack of skill in building work. The 114 arches of the viaduct took about 43,000 cubic metres of concrete, which the prisoners mixed by hand. No one knows how many died during the construction work. Many Italians also succumbed to their catastrophic housing conditions or to diseases such as cholera.

The 4 kilometres of line, passing over viaducts and through embankments, had been out of service since the end of the Second World War and the track had collapsed in places. Since recommissioning in 1999, it is used mainly for goods trains.

RECORDING STUDIO OF ELECTRONICS PIONEER MAX BRAND

The first "Vienna Sound"

Langenzersdorf Museum, Obere Kirchengasse 23, 2103 Langenzersdorf
Open Saturday, Sunday and public holidays 2pm–6pm
www.lemu.at
Bus: 533, Langenzersdorf Hauptplatz stop; 232, Wiener Strasse 48/65 stop

The first floor of Langenzersdorf Museum, mainly devoted to sculptor Anton Hanak, houses the original recording studio of the composer and sound engineer Max Brand (1896–1980). Keyboards, loudspeakers and tape-recorders resemble an early version of the electronic equipment with which the popular Viennese duo Kruder and Dorfmeister conquered clubs around the world in the 1990s.

There is also a photograph of Brand in old age, demonstrating the devices he invented.

Brand, a contemporary of Arnold Schönberg and Kurt Weill, and a native of Lemberg (Lviv, Ukraine), stood at the crossroads of late romanticism, futurism and the birth of the electronic era. In 1937, he left Vienna and the Nazis behind and headed for Rio de Janeiro. His emigration put an end to his promising career as an operatic composer. He moved to New York in 1940, where he pursued his goal of building an electronic music machine for the stage, precursor of Robert Arthur Moog's Moogtonium synthesizer. A luminous organ was also planned but it never saw the light of day. Brand returned to Austria in 1975 and ended his days in Langenzersdorf. Unfortunately, he deleted the majority of his recordings during episodes of mental confusion. He died at the Gugging psychiatric clinic, leaving his music collection to Vienna City Library at the City Hall.

FISCHEREIMUSEUM

Discoveries on the Marchfeld Canal

Einzingergasse 1a, 1210 Wien
Open Sunday 9am–noon, also by appointment for groups
Tel: +43 (0)681 2080 6161
www.fischereimuseum.at

The largest and most impressive exhibit in Vienna's Museum of Fishery stands at the entrance: a fishing boat from the First World War, restored with meticulous attention to detail. The fishermen used a particular technique in which they lowered their nets from their cottages on the shore or the edge of the lake.

Although this privately run museum documents the technical aspects of fishing from past and present, it sees itself primarily as an information centre on ecological balance.

Experienced guides take you over the display area of around 200 square metres, introducing a variety of species. You'll see rare fish from the Danube and learn that all the region's amphibians are protected. Not only fish, but frogs, turtles and a large number of reptiles, as well as their river habitats, are explained in a clear and well-documented way.

The aim of this museum is to preserve the traditions of local fisheries and educate visitors in ecology and biology. Nor is the history of Viennese fishery forgotten.

On request, the museum organises walks with guides from the company that manages the Marchfeld Canal. They share a wealth of stimulating and useful information accumulated during their patrols around the conservation pond (a reconstituted marshy habitat). This walk along the lush edges of the canal, which was dug out in the 1990s, is recommended whatever the season.

FLORIDSDORFER SPITZ

Operation Radetzky

Am Spitz, 1210 Wien

The pretty district offices of Floridsdorf, dating from 1901–03, are located in the central area known as the Spitz (Point), at the beginning of Brünner Strasse. On the wall of the building is a rather laconic plaque commemorating "Operation Radetzky", which took place here shortly before the Armistice and cost the lives of three members of the Austrian resistance fighting against the fascist regime.

Four weeks before the end of the war, on 8 April 1945, an SS detachment pulled the three men from their car and publicly hanged them from lampposts at Floridsdorfer Spitz. The unfortunate victims had placards hung around their necks saying: "I collaborated with the Bolsheviks." Their names were Karl Biedermann, Alfred Huth and Rudolf Raschke.

The head of operations, Viennese Major Carl Szokoll, had planned with the Red Army to ensure the rapid surrender of the city to incoming Soviet troops and thus avoid further destruction. Raschke was in charge of a commando squad attacking the Stubenring on the Ringstrasse; Biedermann had to hold several positions in the city centre; and Huth

had to capture the radio transmitter at Mount Bisamberg. But a telephone call between Biedermann and Szokoll was intercepted. The conspirators were arrested and only Szokoll, warned in time, managed to escape.

The execution of these "traitors to the fatherland" was carried out in just 20 minutes. The last words of Alfred Huth, aged just 26, are said to have been: "Long live Austria!" Their bodies were left hanging until the next day. A witness, who was 15 years old at the time, remembers that nobody paid any attention to the executed men.

Nowadays, 8 April is commemorated each year and a wreath is laid at Floridsdorf Spitz in honour of the resistance fighters. Major Szokoll, who had already taken part in the 1944 failed attack on Hitler, died in 2004.

BREITENLEE PRIORY CEMETERY ⑥

A uniquely peaceful atmosphere

Bei Breitenleer Strasse 247, 1220 Wien
Only open during Mass at St Anne's Church
www.pfarrebreitenlee.at/joomla/index.php

Next to St Anne's Church in Breitenlee is a picturesque cemetery filled with ancient wrought-iron crosses and commemorative plaques. Although close to a busy road, it breathes peace and tranquillity. Between 1807 and 1917, 130 monks from the Schottenstift (Scottish Abbey, a Roman Catholic Benedictine monastery) were buried here. Hermann Schubert, the young half-brother of Franz Schubert and a Benedictine priest, is also laid to rest in this cemetery.

Those who know Vienna's Innere Stadt will be familiar with the look of the Breitenlee church. With its simple Baroque forms, it is almost a miniature version of the Schottenkirche in Freyung Square. In 1696, the Schottenstift abbot, Sebastian Faber, had a farm (to the left of the

cemetery), restaurant and church built. The church was completed in 1699, the final step in restoring the village, which had been destroyed during the Turkish siege.

The history of Breitenlee village is closely linked to the history of the Scots in Vienna. Contemporary registers show that the priory owned properties in the region as early as the 12th century. Breitenlee is the oldest site of this Benedictine Order founded in 1155 by Irish and Scottish monks. The Schottenstift monks are still the patrons of Breitenlee parish.

MUSEUM DER SCHLACHT BEI WAGRAM 1809

In the general's headquarters

Erzherzog-Carl-Strasse 1, 2232 Deutsch-Wagram
Open early April to late November, Sunday and public holidays 10am–4pm
www.wagram1809.at/index.htm
U-Bahn: Deutsch-Wagram; Bus: 494 / 495, Theodor-Körner-Gasse stop

The 18th-century house of Archduke Karl has two other names: Napoleon Museum and Museum of the Battle of Wagram 1809 ... and for good reason.

There are over 1,000 exhibits, including memorabilia from the battle, paintings and engravings, various weapons and pieces of equipment used by the troops, uniforms of different ranks from the two armies, and dioramas explaining the nature of this conflict. There is also a horse's skull, booty from fallen soldiers, and the table at which sat Napoleon, Emperor of the French.

It was on this site that the famous Battle of Wagram took place on 5 and 6 July 1809. The house itself had been converted into a residence for the Austrian Archduke Karl and his closest military staff. Karl, the son of Leopold II, was a grandson of Maria Theresa and a nephew of Marie-Antoinette. He began his military career very young, and was married to Henriette von Nassau-Weilburg, who was responsible for Vienna's first Christmas tree.

The battle against Napoleon took place on land near the Marchfeld plains to the north-east of the city. Few battles are as famous as that of Wagram, where Napoleon crushed the ill-equipped Austrian troops. Only two months before, Karl, who bore the title *generalissimo*, had inflicted

the first major defeat on Napoleon during the Battle of Aspern-Essling. This success was not soon to be repeated, but nevertheless temporarily tainted the "invincible" reputation of the French.

Other halls in the museum illustrate the development of the town of Deutsch-Wagram. There is also a former cobbler's workshop and a kitchen with an open fireplace.

The Battle of Wagram is immortalised in Paris on the Arc de Triomphe as well as the eponymous Parisian avenue.

In late April 2017, during the construction of a highway at Deutsch-Wagram, archaeologists discovered a common grave with the remains of soldiers from both armies.

MISTMUSEUM

Visit the "manure heap"

Rautenweg 83, 1220 Wien
Tours May to October, Friday at 2pm and Saturday at 10am (only in good weather)

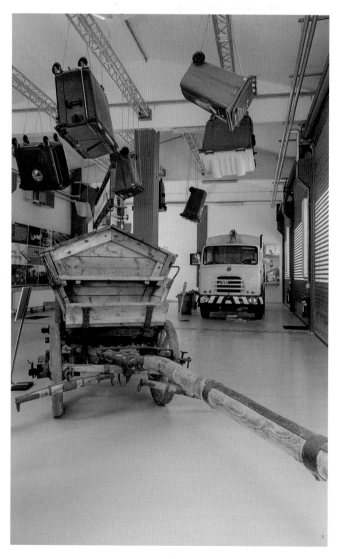

he waste depot of Municipal Department 48 (MA 48) Rautenweg is perhaps the most unusual but little-known museum in Vienna. The best way of getting there is on board the little train of the "Tatzelwurm" ("Crayfish"), which transports visitors around the mountain of rubbish, always followed by a troupe of goats that has lived here since the 1990s. And they aren't alone: the dump attracts ducks, crows, roe deer and rabbits, as well as dozens of species of insect and a very special kind of flora.

In addition to the outside trip, the Refuse Museum has three indoor exhibition rooms where you can learn all about the waste economy of the metropolis. How was rubbish disposed of in the past? How were the roads cleaned? Vehicles and documentaries from 1920s Vienna retrace the evolution of the city's relationship with its rubbish, while audio installations enlighten you on biogas, recycling metals and residual waste.

Certain sections are particularly important, such as the one dealing with ecological reprocessing: we learn everything about the chain from collection to storage of ash, via heat treatment. All this takes place on the Rautenweg site, with a view of the "Rinter Tent", the waste treatment plant opened in 1980–81 and operated by Rinter AG. The company then went bankrupt.

The "manure heap," as it is known in Vienna, leaves no residues except the ash and soot of the incineration centre. It produces ecological electricity and water for Vienna's heating systems.

BLUMENGÄRTEN HIRSCHSTETTEN ⑨

Where Vienna's flowers come from

Quadenstrasse 15, 1220 Wien
Open April to October, Tuesday and Sunday 10am–6pm; June to August also
on Saturday 10am–8pm; October to March (palm grove only), Tuesday and
Friday 10am–3pm, Sunday 10am–6pm
Bus: 22A, Blumengärten Hirschstetten stop

Hirschstetten Flower Gardens, which have for decades cultivated the plants for Vienna's parks, offer a great opportunity to be in contact with nature.

Younger visitors will enjoy the playground and watching the frogs, turtles and squirrels, and farm animals such as sheep and chickens. For the older visitors, several themed gardens offer ideas and information on gardening and how to plant a small balcony. "Ploughman's lunches" are available and there are many places to relax. This enchanting setting, with its cascades of white, pink and blue roses, is a popular venue for weddings.

The 700-square-metre greenhouse has plants and animals from three different climatic zones: they include orchids and cacti, bats and American corn snakes.

The historic farmhouse, dating from 1880, has been converted into an open-air ecomuseum: it has a press, a barn and a vegetable garden and runs courses and guided tours. You'll also find Mexican and Indian gardens, as well as a prehistoric garden with its frog pond and a Provence garden with the essence of lavender that encapsulates summer.

In the last weeks of the year, Hirschstetten holds a Christmas market.

"NEW BRAZIL"

Fine sand just like in South America

An der Unteren Alten Donau 61, 1220 Wien
Neu Brasilien restaurant: open Monday to Sunday 11am–11pm

In 1904 Florian Berndl, a pioneer of the workers' garden movement, rented out some small vegetable-growing plots along the river in an area he called "Neu Brasil". Here, the fine white sand bordering the Danube was like the paradisiacal beaches of South America, or so he claimed.

On the site of the present-day restaurant, Berndl erected a little club-house – a hut surrounded by a few benches. This became the social centre of the colony of gardens he had founded.

This disciple of fresh air and pure water – a sort of early hippie who subscribed to the naturopathy and hydrotherapy theories of 19th-century Bavarian priest Sebastian Kneipp – discovered Gänsehäufel (Goose Island), a bathing spot still popular with the Viennese.

Regulating the waters of the Danube in the early 1870s had separated the main branch of the "old Danube" from its new course, forming the islet in question. Berndl was the first to recognise the potential of the fine sandbanks, gently sloping down to the water, for local residents keen to take the regenerating "baths of water and sun".

The City of Vienna authorities heard of this and revoked their contract with him. In 1907 they opened the public beach that still exists today, but we owe the concept of "New Brazil" to Florian Berndl.

MUSEUMS OF THE BATTLE OF ASPERN-ESSLING 1809

"War and Peace"

Museum Aspern, Asperner Heldenplatz 9, 1220 Wien
Museum Esslinger Schüttkasten, Esslinger Hauptstrasse 81–87, 1220 Wien
Opening hours of both museums: April to October, every Sunday 10am–noon

The museum commemorating the Austrian victory at Aspern on 21 May 1809 provides an overview of the military strategies of the Napoleonic troops and the Austrian armies led by Archduke Karl. Since 1979 the Aspern Museum has been housed in an ancient mausoleum near the village church, just behind the statue known as Der Löwe von Aspern (The Lion of Aspern) by German-Austrian sculptor Anton Fernkorn, symbolising the courage of Austrian soldiers who fell during the battle.

One room contains handwritten documents such as battle orders and letters, as well as objects found on the battle site, fragments of uniforms, buttons, medals and cannonballs. A flag dating from 1809 is on display. The museum also contains weapons of the time, portraits of military leaders and generals of the two opposing camps, and a lovely miniature of Napoleon's son the Duke of Reichstadt, who died aged just 21 in 1832.

The arm of the Danube at Essling played an important role on the second day of the battle, 22 May 1809, as Napoleon attempted a forced crossing. The French and their allies were driven back by the Austrians – the first time Napoleon had been personally defeated in over a decade. However, Archduke Karl failed to secure a decisive victory as Napoleon was able to successfully withdraw most of his troops. This is why the name "Essling" appears among the list of Napoleon's victories on the Arc de Triomphe in Paris. Aspern isn't mentioned. In the well-preserved building that houses the Esslinger Schuttkasten branch of the museum, you can see the largest diorama in Central Europe and follow the course of the battle "as if you were there". Barns are burning, dogs are barking, soldiers are dying … More than 8,500 figures fill the wooded landscape, painstakingly reconstituted over some 12 square metres. A variety of acoustic and optical effects chronicle the military engagements of these two days in May 1809.

The war between Austria and France continued at Wagram on 5 and 6 July of the same year. Napoleon triumphed by defeating the armies of Archduke Karl, who was removed from his post as supreme military commander (*generalissimo*) by his brother the Emperor of Austria, Franz I.

FATTY GEORGE JAZZMUSEUM

Jazz in the men's room

Esslinger Hauptstrasse 96, 1220 Wien
Open during events or by appointment
www.kulturfleckerl.at/
Contact Frau Hanappi; Tel: 0699 1806 4640

The Vienna Jazz Museum is imaginatively housed in Wilhelm-Beetz's Art Nouveau public toilets. Classified as a historic monument, they were restored and converted into a museum in 2005 in honour of Austrian jazz musician Fatty George (1927–82), who grew up in the 22nd district of Donaustadt, where his mother ran a restaurant.

In the Essling museum, close to Bill-Grah-Park (named after a German jazzman who played mostly in Austria), where the world's first jazz sculpture stands, several personal effects are on display, including some belonging to Fatty George: documents, photos, records, cartoons, posters. Other national jazz legends such as Joe Zawinul also get a mention. Concerts are held there as often as possible.

Fatty George's real name was Franz Georg Pressler ("Fatty" was the nickname given him by the Americans based in Vienna during the Occupation). He learned the saxophone and clarinet, and Joe Zawinul sometimes played in his band. In the 1960s and again in the 80s he ran "Fatty's Saloon" in Vienna, inviting international greats such as Lionel Hampton and Ella Fitzgerald. Fatty George was one of the main promoters of mainstream jazz in Austria.

FRENCH VESTIGES FROM THE BATTLE OF ASPERN-ESSLING ⑬

Open-air museum of a Napoleonic struggle

Lobau, 1220 Wien
Approximately 4 hours to visit all the sites (11 km)

A visit to the Lobau floodplain, part of the Danube-Auen National Park, takes in several sites of the Battle of Aspern-Essling (May 1809), when Napoleon attempted a forced crossing of the Danube near Vienna, but the French and their allies were driven back by the Austrians under Archduke Karl. All the walks are clearly indicated, with signs to site-marker stones often placed a little way off the road.

From the house on the riverbank at Grossenzersdorf, the road leads to former islands where the remains of fortifications can still be seen. Crossing a small bridge, you pass the store where the French kept their gunpowder ready for the battle. A little further on is the "French cemetery", where only one commemorative stone still remains. Yet some 2,000–3,000 French soldiers were buried here in a mass grave after a two-day battle in which 10,000 men were killed and 30,000 wounded, with Austrian losses even higher than the French. After the French withdrawal, Lobau was turned into a military camp with field hospitals, bakeries, foundries, and so on.

Near the cemetery is the forest house from where you can continue through the fields. Along Napoleonstrasse, you reach Panozza, a lake where two stones commemorate the battle. The one marked "Strasse"

indicates the end of the route the French took through Lobau, which has not changed since. The "French ford" is the place where the troops crossed the Danube 42 days after the battle. The Austrians could not prevent them, and were decisively beaten at Wagram in July.

Through more woods and meadows, and past flowing streams, you arrive back at Grossenzersdorf.

A highly recommended walk for all seasons.

DONAU-ODER-KANAL

Swimming in clear water

Via Grossenzersdorf, follow Lobaustrasse to the end (Uferhaus restaurant), second canal 10-minute walk south, third canal 5-minute walk west
Via Lobaugrundstrasse (OMV gas / oil storage facility) and the high-water dam of the first and second canals
Bus: 26A, Grossenzersdorf Busbahnhof stop / 92B, Zentraltanklager stop

If you want to escape the hustle and bustle of Donauinsel (Danube Island) or the Alte Donau (Old Danube) branch of the river on hot summer days, head to the natural beaches on the border between Vienna and Lower Austria. The fact that this heavenly place is a relic of the Second World War no longer bothers anyone today.

The canal was originally planned as a navigable waterway on which barges could transport their cargo to the North Sea and the Baltic. Although such a project already existed at the time of the Austro-Hungarian monarchy, it was resurrected after the EU enlargement before being abandoned again. The waterway is again part of plans for a European Danube–Oder–Elbe Canal project that would also connect the Elbe River.

As the land is now part of the Danube-Auen National Park, only a few zones of the Lobau floodplain allow bathing.

The Danube-Oder is undoubtedly one of the most beautiful of canals. It has four sections, two of which are perfect for swimming. At the northern end of Danube-Oder I is a beautiful lawn, while Danube-Oder III is mainly surrounded by small gardens. The south section is freely accessible and ideal for sunbathing.

In summer, the crystal-clear waters of the canal invite you in, and the many shallow places allow families with young children to swim in safety. The water quality is constantly monitored.

Naturists will find an island of peace and tranquillity in Dechantlacke, in the depths of the alluvial forest. At Stadler Furt (ford), the shoreline bordered by a vast meadow tempts you to take a break.

In winter, long walks amid frost-covered forests or along the frozen Danube are particularly enjoyable.

ALPHABETICAL INDEX

ALPHABETICAL INDEX

ALPHABETICAL INDEX

ACKNOWLEDGEMENTS:
The authors thank all the institutions that made them so welcome while they were researching this guide.

PHOTOGRAPHY CREDITS:
All photos © **Karl Bach**

with the exception of:
Bezirksmuseum Döbling: 283, 297
Dominikanerinnenkloster Lienz: 25
Langenzersdorf Museum: 453
Naturhistorisches Museum: 187
Parlament Wien: 183
Stift Klosterneuburg: 269, 271
Wien Museum: 22, 49, 73, 77, 89, 95, 105, 119, 129, 133, 139, 153, 163, 171, 173, 179, 181, 199 (beide), 211, 239, 245, 247, 259, 261, 273, 279, 280, 281, 287, 295, 299, 303, 309, 313, 319, 321, 323, 331, 333, 339, 347, 353, 357, 359, 363, 371, 381, 388f, 395, 399, 423, 425, 427, 429, 439, 447, 455, 465

Cover: Rabenhof-Theater, 1030 Wien

Maps: **Cyrille Suss** - Layout Design: **Coralie Cintrat** - Layout: **Stéphanie Benoit** - Translation: **Caroline Lawrence** - Proofreading: **Jana Gough and Eleni Salemi** - Edition: **Lorraine du Chazaud**

© JONGLEZ 2018
Registration of copyright: March 2018 – Edition: 01
ISBN: 978-2-36195-172-6
Printed in Bulgaria by Dedrax